# Inventing HIGH and LOW

# Inventing HIGH and LOW

Literature, Mass Culture,

and Uneven Modernity

in Spain

## STEPHANIE SIEBURTH

Duke University Press  Durham and London 1994

*A publication grant from the Program for Cultural Cooperation Between Spain's Ministry of Culture and United States Universities is gratefully acknowledged.*

Designed by Cherie Holma Westmoreland
Typeset in Trump Mediaeval with Gill Sans
display by Keystone Typesetting, Inc.
Library of Congress Cataloging-in-Publication
Data appear on the last printed page of this book.

171903

In memory of my father, Guenter Sieburth,

who taught me the love of ideas.

# Contents

• • • Yo he preferido hablar

de cosas imposibles,

porque de lo posible

se sabe demasiado.


I prefer to speak of

impossible things,

because we already

know too much about

the possible.


—Silvio Rodríguez,

"Resumen de noticias,"

from the album

*Al final de este viaje*

# Acknowledgments

• • • This book owes its existence to many kinds of support. I first want to offer my warmest thanks to my department chair, Jean-Jacques Thomas, who enabled me to take the leave time necessary to complete the project, and who has given me constant support in many other ways. The National Endowment for the Humanities Fellowship for University Teachers funded a much-needed, uninterrupted year of research; at Duke, yearly grants from the University Research Council and the generosity of Dean Malcolm Gillis funded research assistance and other expenses related to this study. My research assistants have been many over the years, and their meticulous work has made my task immeasurably easier. Juan Poblete deserves special mention, for he has worked on this and other projects as assiduously as if they were his own; this book could not exist without him. I also want to thank Clark Goodman, Santiago Colás, and Ruth Hoff for graciously bearing the brunt of the legwork involved. Thanks are also in order to the undergraduate and graduate students who attended my courses on Hispanic literature and mass culture, and whose input helped me develop the ideas presented here. Parts of chapters 1, 3, and 5 appeared in *A Sesquicentennial Tribute to Galdós*, ed. Linda Willem (Newark, Del.: Juan de la Cuesta, 1993); *Journal of Interdisciplinary Literary Studies* 2 (1990); and *Revista hispánica moderna* 43 (1990); I am grateful to the editors and presses for permission to reprint. I wish to thank Paul Simon Music for permission to use the lyric "I Am a Rock," by Paul Simon, as an opening quote in chapter 4: copyright © 1965/copyright renewed by Paul Simon.

I am deeply indebted to the many scholars who read parts of this book at various stages and gave me invaluable feedback: Gustavo Pérez Firmat, Patrick Hub, Debra Castillo, John Kronik, Julio Ramos, Catherine Jagoe, Helen Solterer, and Renée Sieburth. Noël Valis not only read most of this study and made rigorous and suggestive comments, but generously offered bibliographical information that was crucial to the project. And Harriet Turner graciously used precious vacation time to help me make Galdós's language come alive in English. Many thanks also to Reynolds Smith for his patience and faith in this project, and to his readers for their helpful suggestions for revision and for the thoroughness of their reports.

In the most immediate of ways, this book could not have been written without the help of Amy Saunders, Laura Lowenbergh, Ray Collins, John Papajohn, and Margie Brache, who assured the well-being necessary for its emergence. I can never thank Renée Sieburth enough for giving me a space to write during hot summers, and for her constant encouragement and faith in this project, which she has read in many versions. I am especially grateful to my friends, who enabled me to grow, thrive, and enjoy myself while this book was being written. All my friends in many places gave me crucial support, but a few in particular have left traces of their magic on this book. Jodie Waisberg, despite a distance of many miles, is never far away; she has shared innumerable joys, sorrows, succulent meals, and laughs while this book was being written. Linda Chapman's deep solidarity and creative spark have been constant sources of energy and inspiration. I have been lucky enough to indulge in wonderful marathon sessions on literature and life with Harriet Turner, always coming away renewed. Roland Greene shared countless memorable dinners and conversations in Boston; I will always be grateful for his friendship and generosity, both in person and over the phone lines. Regina Schwartz has shared my quest to make sense of life ever since I arrived in Durham and has given me much-needed support in both difficult and joyful circumstances. And Helen Solterer has helped me to bring the unexpected into being through talk, music, and laughter.

# Note on the Translations

• • • Goytisolo's and Martín Gaite's texts are available in excellent translations by Helen Lane; I thank Viking Press and Columbia University Press for the use of quoted materials. I indicate with an asterisk places where I have modified her translation to render the Spanish more literally. Page numbers given in parentheses for *Reivindicación* and *El cuarto* refer to the English translation, unless the Spanish text is directly quoted. Translations of the Galdós novels were last done in the 1950s and sound stilted today; Harriet Turner kindly helped me produce new translations of Galdós's prose and of occasional quotations from other authors in the Galdós chapters. The reader should thus assume that all translations other than those of *Reivindicación* and *El cuarto de atrás* are my own and attribute all shortcomings to me alone.

I have given only the English version of short quotations contained in the body of a paragraph, except in the few cases where the wording of the Spanish was exceptionally important. In the case of longer, indented quotations, I have given the Spanish first, with the English following.

# Introduction

## The High/Low Opposition and the Spanish Novel

• • • At the end of the first part of Cervantes's *Don Quijote,* the self-declared knight-errant is imprisoned in a cage and taken back to his village. He is the first of many novelistic characters to enact the possibilities inherent in the especially fervent consumption of mass cultural texts—in his case, chivalric romances, the first printed fictions to achieve great popularity. He is also the first of many characters to be punished for his behavior. During his journey in the cage, Don Quijote carries on a debate on the novels of chivalry with the canon of Toledo.[1] The canon, in keeping with the neo-Aristotelian literary theory of his time, believes that literary texts should be harmoniously structured, with parts proportional to the whole and a logically unfolding plot. He states that texts lacking verisimilitude, like the novels of chivalry, cannot possibly please or impress their audience. And he suggests that Don Quijote read biblical or historical texts rather than the extravagant fictions that have addled his brain.

As Don Quijote responds in defense of his chivalric heroes, he

---

1. The following account is drawn from Alban Forcione's *Cervantes, Aristotle and the* Persiles, ch. 3.

ingeniously blurs the line between history and fiction, lumping El Cid and Charlemagne in with the fictional Amadís of Gaul. Historical figures like the Cid have become the heroes of legends, and we will never know exactly at what point they cross the line between history and fiction. Don Quijote goes on to defend the intense pleasure his fictions can bring, spinning off a sensuous episode about a knight who dares to throw himself fully armed into a lake of boiling pitch, only to land in a beautiful meadow and to be fed, bathed, and anointed by young maidens in a palace made of gold and precious stones. The canon is spellbound by the tale, despite its utter implausibility. Finally, Don Quijote defends his novels on the grounds that they are widely appreciated, by old and young, rich and poor alike; the canon, of course, prefers books appealing only to an intellectual elite.

Almost four centuries later, Neil Postman and Camille Paglia would have dinner and debate the relative merits of books and television.[2] The same oppositions would recur: coherent plot development vs. quick changes of program or scene; the intellect vs. the senses; minority vs. mass appeal. And the same dangers: confusing history with fiction, falling prey to the seductions of the image, losing sight of the sacred. The tradition of apocalyptic prophesies of the end of "high culture" because of the spread of "lowbrow" forms—echoed in Postman's argument—goes all the way back to the Greeks, though the debate takes on a special intensity beginning in the nineteenth century.[3] After two thousand years of repetition, it seems it is time to question the terms in which the debate repeatedly cloaks itself, to examine the kinds of social and cultural tensions that make each new generation reinvent the high/low opposition, and to try to envisage what it would take to move beyond it.

While some form of the high/low debate has existed for thousands of years, we owe to the nineteenth century most of the terms of subsequent debates on culture, including those of the present day. The word *culture* itself took on important new meanings in the late eighteenth century and the first half of the nineteenth. Raymond Williams has traced the changes of meanings in words such as *industry*, *class*, *art*, and *culture* over this period; simply to recognize that

2. "She Wants Her TV! He Wants His Book!" *Harper's* Mar. 1991: 44–55.
3. See Brantlinger 24–25.

these particular words changed in meaning at the same time already alerts us to the way the term *culture* in its current sense evolved as a response to, and as an attempt to intervene in, an acute transformation in economic and social relations.[4] Culture had previously been a synonym for "cultivation"; it denoted a *process,* applicable to plants, animals, or human faculties. But in the early nineteenth century it began to refer to a thing in itself, an absolute. Culture is thought of by Coleridge and others as a kind of intellectual perfection, an ultimate standard for valuation. It is contrasted to "civilization," understood as an increase in material prosperity which is potentially corrupting. And culture must act as a counterweight to the deleterious effects on thinking of the mechanical occupations of workers in the new industrial system:

In such an environment, evidently, cultivation could not be taken for granted as a process, but must be stated as an absolute. . . . Cultivation was isolated precisely because it had to be abstracted from one way of life, by way of preservation, and then transmitted and extended to another and (in the view of Coleridge and Wordsworth) inferior way. Against materialism, the amassing of fortunes, and the proposition of utility as the source of value, it offered a different and a superior order. ("Idea" 39–40)

Where the concept of a perfect ideal had previously been associated with religion, it is spoken of increasingly in terms of the new idea of "culture" as the nineteenth century wears on ("Idea" 41).[5] Williams, then, reads the idea of culture as "the response of certain men, attached to certain values, in the face of change and the consequences of change"; it is a response to the impact of the Industrial Revolution ("Idea" 34).

Williams is thus hypothesizing that the term *culture* ceases to refer to a process and begins to refer to a state in reaction to the threat

4. The term *industry,* from being a human attribute (diligence) becomes a thing, an institution; the adjective *industrial* appears in the early nineteenth century. *Class* replaces *rank;* it is a more indefinite term and records a change in the attitude towards social divisions (Williams, *Culture and Society* xiii–xv).

5. We might note here the etymological link between *culture* and *cult,* brought out in the Spanish *Diccionario de Autoridades* of 1726, where "cultura" still means a process of cultivation rather than an achieved state. Its third meaning is given as follows: "Vale también lo mismo que Culto en el sentido de reverencia o adoración" (699) ("It also means the same thing as 'Cult' in its sense of reverence or adoration").

posed to an older way of life by industrialization. This would lead us to expect that the change in meaning would occur later in Spain, where industrialization began later and was not as pervasive as elsewhere in Europe, and this is in fact the case. The *Diccionario de Autoridades* of 1726 gives three meanings of *cultura:* (1) the cultivation of the land; (2) the process of cultivating the spirit; and (3) a synonym of "cult" in the sense of reverence or adoration.[6] In the Royal Academy's dictionary of 1783, a fourth meaning is added: of elegance or refinement of style or speech; this meaning will generalize to refinement of manners, or civilized behavior, in a dictionary from 1872.[7] Also in 1872, the cultivation of the land drops out of the list of meanings of culture. But no definition of culture as an intellectual state has yet appeared. The first listing I could find was in a dictionary published in 1882 in Buenos Aires; the definition reads: "Result or effect of cultivating human knowledge and of refining by exercise the intellectual faculties of man."[8] Madrid dictionaries of 1882 and 1887–89 do not include this definition. The first dictionary I could find from Spain with the new meaning dates from 1890–95 and is published in Barcelona.[9] Soon afterwards, the meaning of culture as the *process* of cultivating the spirit drops out. The definition of culture as an intellectual state in the Buenos Aires dictionary has remained unchanged to this day, and can be found in the Spanish Royal Academy's dictionary of 1992. Given the habitual lag time between the appearance of a new meaning in usage and its recognition in a dictionary, one can probably assume that the new meaning of culture entered current usage sometime in the 1870s.

The word *art* was also changing in meaning. Where previously it had been used to speak of any kind of human skill, now it came to refer to an institution—the "imaginative" or "creative" arts. "The arts" were grouped together as distinct from other human activities (Williams, *Culture and Society* xv–xvi). And artists came to be seen as qualitatively different from the rest of society, as having access to a privileged truth—that of culture. The artist's place in society was

6. *Diccionario de Autoridades* 699.

7. "Finura, urbanidad, civilización," *Diccionario enciclopédico* 699.

8. The Spanish text reads: "Resultado o efecto de cultivar los conocimientos humanos y de afinarse por medio del ejercicio las facultades intelectuales del hombre" (*Diccionario filológico* 1648).

9. *Diccionario de la lengua castellana* (1890–95) 1034.

also undergoing changes in the shift from patronage to the market, and, for the writer, in the growth of a new middle-class reading public. This new readership would develop in the eighteenth century in England, but not until well into the nineteenth century in Spain; Galdós's novels are still reacting to this change. The English Romantic writers, beginning to be subject to market forces, felt the need to proclaim their autonomy and exemption from the requirement of pleasing an uncultivated public. They set their standards higher—in an ideal reader with "culture." Galdós, in 1870, would begin his literary career with similar polemicizing against serial literature and its readers.[10]

Williams also notes the ways in which the relationship of culture to class was a source of uncertainty in the early nineteenth century, both with regard to the need for a class of people to maintain and extend culture, and with regard to what sort of relationship to culture, if any, the newly organized working class ought to have. Williams concludes:

In a society characterized by rapidly-changing class-relations, in which change could by no means be separated from violence, and complicated further by the expansion of new economic techniques and of ways of thinking which these techniques engendered, the idea of "a spiritual centre," an agreed Culture towards which the processes of education and cultivation might be directed, was seen by minds of the character of Coleridge and Newman as vital. The Idea of Culture, with its elements of continuity and of the search for perfection, received the necessary stress. ("Idea" 56)

The very term *culture*, then, is problematic in a study devoted to questioning the high/low division, since it was developed specifically to preserve a condition conceived of as "high" from dilution and corruption by new forces seen as "lower." The idea of veneration attached to the word *cult* remains present in this idea of culture. Williams notes that by the present day, the term is used in three ways, and my own discourse will undoubtedly vacillate between them. The narrowest is "the general body of the arts"; broader is "the intellectual side of civilization," which includes philosophical, religious, and scientific thought as well as the arts. The broadest mean-

---

10. See his "Observaciones sobre la novela española contemporánea" (1870) in Bonet 105–20.

ing, used in sociology and cultural anthropology, is that of "a whole way of life" ("Idea" 29). My own use of the term will probably be closest to the second meaning, but will include all kinds of fictional and nonfictional production, directed at any kind of audience. My reader should be forewarned, however, that the "high" connotation of the term *culture* may easily creep back into my own usage.

Terms such as high, folk, popular, mass, and the like are recognized in current scholarship as misleading and dubious at best; naturally, they came into being as modifiers for the term *culture* once the latter concept had ceased to refer to a process.[11] The period of the Industrial Revolution was also the time when the link was made between technological progress and cultural decline; this connection has been so often repeated that it was rapidly naturalized and is rarely questioned even today. Morag Shiach argues that the idea of "popular" or "folk" culture, as well as the concept of "mass" culture, must be seen as responses to developments in communications technologies, to increased literacy, and to changes in class and gender relations.[12] The new availability of serialized fiction was assumed to lead to corruption, and the development of this kind of mass cultural product was often seen as a metaphor for the development of an organized working class. Mass culture therefore meant, in the eyes of the dominant class, a threat to social control. In response, bourgeois discourses from the most conservative to the radical associated mass culture with corruption, triviality, and decay. The assumption, firmly entrenched until our own day, that culture is in rapid decline triggered a search in the nineteenth century for examples of cultural authenticity. This led to the invention of imaginary categories like the illiterate "folk," supposedly untouched by modern civilization or social transformation. (As Shiach notes, the actual producers of "folk culture" did not fit the description, but the bourgeois collectors of folk songs, poetry, or crafts did not care.) The other "authentic" sphere was, of course, that of "high" culture, enshrined in the university to preserve it in all its purity. Cultural critics of the nineteenth century evidently had a stake in sealing off the spheres of the "au-

11. Williams locates the first English use of the term *masses* in 1837 ("Idea" 51). The term *mass culture* was coined around the time of World War II; but the masses were an obsessive topic of debate in the nineteenth century, and theories of mass psychology developed in the 1870s. See Naremore and Brantlinger 12–13.

12. See especially his introduction 1–18.

thentic" from the contamination of mass culture; therefore, they refused to theorize the connections between different cultural spheres or the effects of historical change on different arenas of culture (Shiach 10–11).

Anxiety about changes in the role of women also played into critical discourse about culture. Women had taken on prominence as writers and critics by the 1840s in England and the 1850s in Spain. Women began to achieve prominence as writers of poetry, novels, and newspaper articles in the 1840s. In the 1850s and 1860s their numbers grew, and journals aimed at women appeared, often directed by women as well. Angela Grassi, who was a prolific poet in the 1840s, directed the journal *El Correo de la Moda* from 1867 until her death in 1883. María del Pilar Sinués de Marco founded the journal *El ángel del hogar*, directing it from 1864 to 1869. She was the author of a bestselling novel by the same title and over a hundred other didactic and fictional works. Faustina Sáez de Melgar edited numerous journals for women from the 1860s to the 1890s. These and other women writers also contributed to political and literary journals aimed at a male audience, writing for such periodicals as *El Imparcial, La Epoca,* and *Revista de España*.[13] Common male responses to women writers were to satirize them or to accuse them of immorality (Kirkpatrick 87–89). It was also feared that the housewife would be distracted from her family duty by reading the cheap romantic fictions the newspaper brought; hence, these were denounced as corrupting influences despite the fact that their content was often moralistic and reinforcing of domesticity. The metaphors applied to mass culture by cultural critics are feminine, while "folk" and "high" culture are associated with masculinity; the association of mass culture with women, begun in the nineteenth century, continued in the discourse of cultural critics until very recently (Jagoe, "Disinheriting"; Huyssen).

Shiach's book demonstrates the continuity of the terms of the debate on culture from their initial crystallization in the early nineteenth century until the present day: "What we have inherited is not

13. See Jagoe, *Gender*, ch. 1; Andreu, "Arte y consumo"; Kirkpatrick; and Charnon-Deutsch, "On Desire." Alicia Andreu traces the commercialization of literature in Spain, linking it to women writers and readers (*Galdós y la literatura popular*, chs. 2–4). The most complete information on women authors of the nineteenth century and where they published is found in Simón Palmer.

just the cultural 'problems' of the nineteenth century, but also distinctive ways of theorizing them" (72). The nineteenth-century story we are accustomed to taking for granted is one of cultural decline, the dangerous proliferation of mass culture, the eclipse of "authentic" regional cultures (71). Shiach argues persuasively that these powerful assumptions about culture, second nature to us by now, straitjacket our ability to speak fruitfully about culture. They make it difficult for us to analyze cultural relations at given historical moments, and they obfuscate the relations between cultural production and social power. Lawrence Levine is similarly insistent about the impoverishment of theories about culture that rely on hierarchy, denouncing "[t]his world of adjectival boxes, of such crude labels as 'highbrow,' 'middlebrow,' 'lowbrow,' of continual defensiveness and endless emendations; this world in which things could not be truly compared because they were so rarely laid out horizontally, next to one another, but were always positioned above or below each other on an infinite vertical scale" (3). Shiach responds to the problem by analyzing discourses on "popular" or "mass" culture from the eighteenth century's fascination with "peasant poets" to contemporary views on television. By pointing out the assumptions and blind alleys repeated over centuries in debates about very different kinds of texts, he hopes to free cultural criticism from them so that we may invent new ways of thinking about how different sorts of texts relate to one another. Lawrence Levine and other cultural historians such as Paul DiMaggio are examining how the institutions which today serve to separate out "high" culture from the masses were initially established.[14] They note the heterogeneity of American audiences and of the spectacles they witnessed before the late nineteenth century. And they trace the social changes that led, for example, to the defensive creation in late nineteenth-century Boston of institutions of elite culture like the modern museum and the symphony orchestra. They hope to free us up by demonstrating that the cultural categories which we have been taught to believe were "permanent and immutable" (Lawrence Levine 6) emerged only recently, that previously, museum, theater, and concert audiences experienced what we might today consider a hodgepodge of "high" and "low."[15]

14. See Lawrence Levine and DiMaggio.

15. Levine became intrigued with the topic when he noted the omnipresence of humorous allusions to Shakespeare in nineteenth-century black minstrel shows. Di-

In literary studies, the canon controversy has led to an erosion of the sacred, isolating walls that protected the "great books," even as it has led to a defensive reaction which attempts to fortify them. In the new discipline of "cultural studies," it is considered permissible, even "hot," to study mass culture and its consumers, from punk rockers to readers of romance novels.[16] We have thus progressed very far from the nineteenth-century critics who inveighed against mass cultural fictions without reading them or consulting those who did, and we have gotten past the dead end of the apocalyptic criticism of Horkheimer and Adorno, who could similarly be accused of not understanding some of the forms they anathematized in the 1940s. But studies of the relationships *among* different kinds of cultural production that do not resort to the limiting and falsifying categories of "high" and "low" are still in their infancy.

It is clear that the high/low opposition and the more specific categorization of artistic products as folk, popular, or mass do not stand up to intellectual scrutiny. Dickens began as a serial writer of immense popularity, yet now he is considered "classic"; Umberto Eco's *The Name of the Rose*, with its untranslated Latin quotations, became a bestseller in this country through astute marketing; Jane Austen's novels obey formulas as rigorous as those governing the situation comedy. Yet the determination to separate out and enshrine some works as "high" has persisted among otherwise brilliant intellects since the Industrial Revolution. Generalizations are routinely made about cultural products with no consideration of time period, political context, actual readership, format, or circuits of production. Why, if the high/low opposition is so logically untenable and so detrimental to fruitful thinking about artistic texts, is it so remarkably persistent?

Peter Stallybrass and Allon White offer an answer in their book *The Politics and Poetics of Transgression*. Noting that the idea of the "classic author" originally came from ancient taxation categories which opposed the rich *classici* to the common people (the *proletarius*), Stallybrass and White argue that

---

Maggio notes the mixture of "fine art and sideshow oddities" in the Boston Museum in the 1840s; musicians mixed serious music with light and did not hesitate to transcribe classical themes for mouth harmonica (378–79).

16. To give but a very few examples, see Hebdige, Marcus, and Radway.

[t]he ranking of literary genres or authors in a hierarchy analogous to social classes is a particularly clear example of a much broader and more complex cultural process whereby the human body, psychic forms, geographical space and the social formation are all constructed within interrelating and dependent hierarchies of high and low. . . . The high/low opposition in each of our four symbolic domains . . . is a fundamental basis to mechanisms of ordering and sense-making in European cultures. . . . Cultures "think themselves" in the most immediate and affective ways through the combined symbolisms of these four hierarchies. (2–3)

Regarding the nineteenth century, where our current cultural schemas began, Stallybrass and White demonstrate that the bourgeoisie had been defining itself as a class by the repression of functions associated with the lower body; but the "low" got its vengeance by becoming central to bourgeois fantasy life. The bourgeoisie becomes obsessed with the "low" half of the city—the slums—and with figures like the prostitute who both embody forbidden sexuality and threaten to contaminate the "high." In this context, we can read the nineteenth-century cultural critics' discourse on mass culture (which they often link through metaphor to the working class, prostitution, and grotesque excess) as yet one more form of displacing the lower body onto another symbolic domain.

Stallybrass and White's analysis, then, shows that the high/low opposition is a longstanding way of making sense of the world in Western culture. It also makes clear that a fear of various kinds of *mixtures* underlies the construction of "clean" high/low distinctions. The theoretical equality of all people before the law, enshrined with the French Revolution, and the subsequent organization of the lower classes put into question the bourgeoisie's recently won dominance. The first major women's movement in Europe threatened to alter gender relations, provoking anxiety among some males. The desire to keep certain social classes apart, and to keep the two sexes and the gender roles conventionally assigned to them comfortably distinct, lurks behind the discourse distinguishing high from low culture. Gender is not a variable in Stallybrass and White's analysis of the high/low division, but the view of the female body as contaminating is present already in the teachings of medieval church fathers. And nineteenth-century science defined man by the functions of the upper body (reason) and woman by the reproductive organs, which were thought to determine every aspect of her behavior. The man/ woman opposition, then, is another important "symbolic domain" into which the high/low opposition is frequently transcoded. In chapter 4, I will examine the key role played by the man/woman opposition in the attempted separation of highbrow literature from mass culture.

If we are to be able to discuss literary and artistic texts without falling into the high/low division, we must have a firm understanding of the class and gender factors that produced such an impassioned stake in making these divisions. We must also be able to visualize an interaction between different kinds of cultural products that acknowledges the value of each, as well as the continuity among them. Yet it is still more frequent for critics who discuss both mass and high culture—unless they are talking about postmodernism—to focus on periods of maximum contrast between the two, interpreting the difficulty of modernist texts, for example, as a reaction against, and flight from, the flood of bestsellers on the market by the early twentieth century.[17]

My own impulse has always been to question such divisions. As a child, I mediated between my European-born, intellectual parents, who listened only to classical music, and my friends, who listened only to folk, rock, jazz, or country. For me, music of all types was as necessary as breathing, and I could never understand why listening to one type should mean excluding another. It is perhaps for these reasons that novels which directly confront their own relationship with mass culture have always fascinated me. These novels were also "in-between," hybrids of high and low. I will call these texts "mass cultural novels."

Mass cultural novels have been particularly numerous in Spain (and in Latin America as well). One reason for this is undoubtedly the force of the model set by *Don Quijote* in its response to the increased dissemination of fiction by the printing press. But there are other reasons for the prevalence of such novels in the Hispanic world. I believe that they arise from the ambivalence of Hispanic writers about the spread of consumerism and of mass cultural fictions in societies where political freedom has not accompanied such changes. Writers

17. See, for example, Jameson, "Reification."

are caught between old, authoritarian structures which they cannot condone, and a tardy modernity which imitates foreign models and seems dangerously complacent. The kinds of dreams nursed by the protagonists who devour mass culture seem to flourish in unevenly modern countries, which see themselves as inferior to America or Europe and compensate with delusions of grandeur. I will develop these ideas further in the conclusion, after some of the economic and cultural peculiarities of Spain have been brought out in the chapters. We find in Spain, then, a large number of novels by prominent writers featuring protagonists who avidly consume popular texts and try to live their patterns out in "real life." Nineteenth-century characters created by Galdós and Clarín read serial novels and try to put them into practice. In the 1920s, Gómez de la Serna and Zamacois create characters starstruck by film or addicted to romance novels sold in kiosks on the streets. By the 1970s, the protagonists of novels by Marsé, Moix, Goytisolo, and Martín Gaite grow up with dreams derived from radio songs and movies.

The 1850s, 1860s, and early 1870s witnessed major technological, social, and cultural changes in Spain. A century later, during the late 1950s and the 1960s, an economic boom based on tourism would again radically alter the material standard of living and the kinds of cultural products consumed. In each case, these periods of change were followed by a spate of mass cultural novels, in which the most prominent writers of the day represented and interpreted such changes. Novels of the late nineteenth century react to industrialization, the rise of a newly literate lower middle class, the organization of the working class, greater participation by women in the workforce and in the writing of fiction, and the popularity of the serial novel in the previous decades. In the 1970s and 1980s, novels respond to the transformation of most of Spain from a state of underdevelopment to a consumer society during the 1960s, and to the role of television and advertising in those changes. In both periods, the first mass cultural novels to react to the preceding changes suggest that the new forms of mass culture that have recently developed mean the end of culture. In the writers' metaphors, the high has become *contaminated* by the low, and Spain is a *prostitute* who has sold out lofty ideas for love of material comforts. These novels are *La desheredada* (*The Disinherited Woman*, 1881), by Spain's most prominent realist novelist, Benito Pérez Galdós, and *Reivindicación del conde don Julián* (*Vindication of Count Julian*, 1970), by Juan Goytisolo, a celebrated *enfant terrible* who spent most of his novelistic career in self-imposed exile from Franco's Spain. Later novels of each period begin to suggest that "highbrow" literature has always in fact depended on devices and formulas which also appear in mass culture. These novels present the possibility that the fusion of the "highbrow" literary tradition with popular forms might be productive rather than disastrous. Galdós's *Tormento* (*Torment*, 1884) is a hybrid text which fuses realism with romance (in the form of the serial novel) to criticize existing political conditions in Spain and to suggest a different, utopian way of life. Carmen Martín Gaite's *El cuarto de atrás* (*The Back Room*, 1978), written after Franco's death, portrays the radio songs and sentimental novels of the 1930s and 1940s as repositories of dreams of freedom and as sources of energy to resist the repressive conformity imposed during the Franco era.[18] Mass culture in this novel plays a key role in preserving the essence of the pre-Franco democratic era that Franco had tried to obliterate; with the death of the dictator, all the dreams and memories triggered by popular texts will permit the recovery of such a democratic system. In both *El cuarto* and *Tormento*, the fusion of mass cultural formulas with more "highbrow" styles of writing is inseparable from the political ideal of abolishing the Old Regime, or dictatorship, and achieving democratic freedom; here, mixtures are shown as healthy. For my purposes in studying recurrent responses to cultural change, it will be most fruitful to look not at the continuities between the novels produced within a few years of one another but at the relationships between the "apocalyptic" novels that lead off each period (*La desheredada* and *Reivindicación*) and between the more "utopian" novels appearing later in each period (*Tormento* and *El cuarto*), which are more sanguine about literature's overlap with mass culture.

What can the study of novels provide that is not found in the theoretical discourse on the high/low opposition? First, to create a rounded character incited by forms of mass culture, the novels must necessarily present some of the factors which led the character to consume large amounts of such fiction. This will amount to a fic-

---

18. Such popular texts include songs by Conchita Piquer and Machín and romance novels by Elisabeth Mulder, Pérez y Pérez, and Carmen de Icaza.

tional theory about what sorts of political, psychological, and social circumstances draw a person to mass culture and give him or her a strong investment in it. The narrators of *La desheredada* and *Reivindicación* are at times overtly didactic as they try to show the dangers of succumbing to such temptation. (I will argue, however, that other levels of the texts undermine the narrators' moralizing message.) *Tormento* and *El cuarto* present repressive situations in which mass culture may provide a means of survival, so the theories they proffer about why readers seek out such fictions are not so weighted against mass culture. But all four novels provide a specific context that "explains" the consumption of mass culture. They can thus complement nonfictional theories on the subject. Secondly, the narrator's discourse is often laden with metaphors which reveal his or her preoccupations with class relations, gender roles, or family relationships and explain why he or she has created such a plot in the first place. And the intertextual relations established in these novels, between the mass cultural text that the protagonist reads and the narrator's text that we read, often show up similarities between the two kinds of text, whereas the narrator might have tried to present his text as the antithesis of the mass cultural text read by the character. Thus, if one level of the text strongly condemns mass cultural fictions and their readers, other levels may negate or question that condemnation. The ambiguity, heteroglossia, and multileveledness of the novel form, then, give it a privileged way to examine the contradictory relations between literature and mass culture, and the political effects—often a mixture of progressive and reactionary—of consuming mass cultural fictions.[19]

This book attempts to mediate between the unique circumstances of Spain in the late nineteenth and twentieth centuries and general trends common to all of Western culture in the last two centuries. It also mediates between a kind of analysis specific to literature and conclusions about the high/low division which are applicable in a wide variety of disciplines. My chosen novels are significant in their specificity, serving as arguments about the impact mass culture has,

19. The term *heteroglossia* is drawn from Mikhail Bakhtin's work on the novel. It refers to the novel's incorporation of the most varied kinds of discourses—romance novels, political speeches, journalistic style, poetry—into its fabric, where they are made to dialogue with one another. See "Discourse in the Novel" in *The Dialogic Imagination.*

both in a particular social and political context and on particular readers. As such, they provide models for criticism, showing us how theories about mass culture and its effects must be grounded in a very specific political, cultural, and economic matrix. However, the strategies used to treat mass culture in these works—and the chains of metaphors associated with it—are found across Europe and in the Americas. The mass cultural novels, then, are gold mines for cultural analysis, both in their uniqueness and in those aspects that transcend national boundaries.[20]

The first text I will examine is Galdós's *La desheredada* (*The Disinherited Woman*, 1881), set in a Madrid in the throes of modernization and political change. Its protagonist, Isidora, believes she is the illegitimate child of nobility, though she has been raised by humble parents; this is, of course, a repeated story in serialized fiction. The plot of this novel poses the question of how to tell who is noble, and how to define nobility, in a society where all are supposedly equal and where the penniless are willing to undergo immense sacrifices to dress up and appear like the titled aristocracy. Isidora's striking beauty and taste further complicate the question. On the level of narration, the text is posing the parallel question of how art can maintain its distinction (its "nobility") in a world of cheap reproductions and new access to culture by sectors not equipped with the education and "cultural capital" of the elite.[21] The narrator explores the problem of art by dwelling on the paintings, music, and texts consumed and produced by the characters, and by modeling his own text both on the typical plots of serial novels and on the "highbrow" Spanish literary tradition. The narrator's enterprise thus parallels his protagonist's quest to establish her noble lineage and deny her humble birth: he wants to deny his ties to the market and to mechanical reproduction and establish his artistic legitimacy by making use of prestigious narrative models from the Spanish Golden Age.

Over the course of the novel, the mass cultural texts which tell stories of disinherited children, and which Isidora reads as confirmation of her claim, become laden with associations frequent in the

20. For readers unfamiliar with these novels, I have included plot summaries in the appendix.

21. The term *cultural capital* is drawn from Pierre Bourdieu's *Distinction*, which insists upon the determining function of education, social class, and home background in the acquisition of culture and taste.

nineteenth century. Being mass produced in large numbers with no "original," they are linked to sexual promiscuity, illegitimate children, and monstrous birth. They are associated with madness; Spain, likened to a madhouse, is shown as inundated with massive quantities of texts, both bureaucratic and fictional, which lack all reference to reality; many of these texts are written by madmen. Mass culture, with its cheap reproductions of hand-done, original works of art, is associated with falsification and social climbing; it is contrasted with an oral, folk culture in which the common people knew their place and provided local color. Mass culture is like a tinderbox that inflames passions which the nineteenth-century bourgeoisie would prefer to forget: female sexual desire, incarnated here in Isidora, and working-class rebellion in the case of men. Isidora's brother, Mariano, works at a printing press which once put out a "red" newspaper; he becomes intoxicated by the socialist ideas of his employer and then throws bombs for the anarchists. Finally, mass-produced fiction is linked to a fear of engulfment by the large crowds of the modern city—crowds where strangers may touch each other in sensual or contaminating ways. The figure who concentrates that fear is of course the prostitute; prostitution appears in this novel as a potential consequence of daring to dream the dreams of the mass cultural text.

My reading of La desheredada sets up many of the premises on which the remaining readings depend. For this reason, I will devote two chapters to this novel. The first will explore midcentury modernization in Spain and its consequences for class and cultural relationships, as well as the difficulty experienced by the novel's narrator in representing this confusing new world. The second will explore the narrator's dream of retaining an uncontaminated sphere of artistic distinction and the reasons why his enterprise is doomed to failure.

Tormento (Torment, 1884) explores the question of how different kinds of literature relate to the political and social conditions in which they appear. The narrator writes his text in 1884, during the stagnation of Spain's Restoration period, but sets the action just before the bourgeois revolution of 1868 that dethroned Isabel II. The last decades of Isabel's reign were the heyday of the serial novel in Spain; by 1884 the exotic and melodramatic plots of the serials were on the wane, and realism was becoming the generic dominant. Tormento's narrator presents himself in competition with one of his characters, José Ido del Sagrario, who in 1867 is writing a serial novel about the two orphaned young women who live next door to him. The narrator will write about them as well, revealing the dark underside of their behavior and of the society in which they live, the aspects which Ido's serial novel glosses over. In the process, many of the complexities of the relationship of romance to realism, and of literature to politics, become apparent. The realist narrator, though he claims to represent what José Ido would never dare include in his serial novels, also makes clear that his text is saturated with borrowings from the serial novel—from suspenseful chapter endings to techniques of characterization and melodramatic episodes. *Tormento* also questions the way in which a literary genre relates to its social matrix; both the serial novel and the realist novel are shown as at once complicitous with and critical of the political regimes in which they appear. The hybrid mixture of realism and romance in *Tormento* creates an ending to the novel which partakes of both genres and which tries to point towards an alternative to the repression which governs Spanish society both in 1867 and in 1884. Where *La desheredada* had tried to defend the nobility of "high" art and separate it from mass culture, *Tormento* admits both realism's continuities with the serial novel and its stake in the status quo. But despite its hard-hitting critique of the norms of Isabelline Spain and of the generic conventions of fiction, *Tormento* is unable to question fully the ideal of womanhood propagated in the mass culture of the day—that is, the "angel in the house." Amparo, one of the orphaned sisters, has all the characteristics of that angel except virginity—she has had an affair with a priest, and is now thoroughly repentant. The narrator questions the social norms that would insist on punishing her for a sexual slip motivated by poverty and weakness; but he defends Amparo precisely because in all other respects she is the domestic angel. Where male characters are affirmed in their questioning of the claustrophobic puritanism of Spanish society, female ones are characterized positively insofar as they desire nothing more than that stifling family structure. Agustín Caballero, the rich businessman who has made his fortune in America, decides Spanish society is entirely hypocritical in its prudery, and he takes Amparo to France as his lover; the narrator affirms Caballero's discourse as he questions conventional institutions like marriage and dares to break out of the expected mold. Yet when Amparo's sister refuses to be victimized by the respectable bourgeoisie and takes up a bohemian lifestyle, she is roundly condemned. Amparo herself is considered charming for desiring nothing more than a quiet family life inside the home. In this way, while the text seems to affirm the value of mixing fictional genres and links that mixture to political freedom and revolution, it maintains a stake in a neat division between the genders and in the perpetuation of the extant ideal of womanhood.

Goytisolo's *Reivindicación del conde don Julián* (*Vindication of Count Julian*, 1970) takes up the apocalyptic refrain once again. In it, we witness the daily routine of a schizophrenic and bisexual narrator who lives in Tangiers within sight of Spain. He imagines a new invasion of Spain by the Moors that would end Francoism and centuries of sexual repression. He mentally rehearses the invasion as he walks through the city, idealizing its underdevelopment and its latent savagery and sensuality. The narrator is a writer, and his fragile ego shores itself up against a host of threatening elements by insisting on the high/low opposition in culture and on the opposition between the sexes. Some of his predicament can be generalized. By the late twentieth century, man's sense of individuality is threatened: by a mechanization which reduces his power and ability to control his own life; by the huge crowds in the city in which he gets lost; and by the access of women to spheres previously available only to men—including literature. Our narrator reacts to such pressures by fleeing to "higher" aesthetic ground, creating a circular, self-contained, Joycean text laden with allusions to the whole Spanish literary tradition as well as to the discourses of modern mass culture. His text belittles both canonical Spanish literature (shown as buttressing Francoism) and mass culture by portraying them as feminine, grotesque, corrupt. He constructs a counter-canon of Spanish authors who are renegades, exiles, homosexuals—and, of course, all male. At the same time, he attempts to construct Morocco as an idealized, primitive world in which men are hypermasculine and women are muzzled, and in which poverty means being pure, uncontaminated by capitalist consumerism. But Tangiers has been invaded by American tourists and by mass culture—American radio songs, Spanish television; the impulse to construct a "pure" space fails, just as it did for the narrator of *La desheredada.*

Spain is seen in *Reivindicación* as having been thrice denatured—first by puritanical Catholicism; then by Francoism; and finally by mass culture. The latter has devoured and co-opted everything anti-thetical to it, including Catholicism and the initially austere doctrines of Francoism. Mass culture, as in *La desheredada*, is linked in *Reivindicación* to the chaos of the modern city, to the crowd, to social climbing, to prostitution. Spain's transformation into a consumer society, via the tourist industry, is described graphically as a voluntary prostitution. In order to get money for sports cars and summer homes, Spain throws out its traditional chastity and austerity and allows itself—as a giant Vagina—to be penetrated by groups of tourists. Their guide spouts stereotypes about Spain mixed with advertising for souvenirs. The Vagina is described by the narrator in these terms:

la masa de horror, de ponzoña y de asco entre paredes de tejido muscular ornadas de una fauna submarina dúctil e inquietante . . . horrible mundo, rezumante y viscoso, de . . . secreciones, membranas y vasos, proteico reino de lo blando e informe, . . . de la obscena ebullición de lo inorgánico. (169–71)

these hideous, poisonous, nauseating surfaces, hemmed in by walls of muscle tissue covered with disturbing, sinuous submarine fauna . . . a hideous, oozing, viscous world of . . . secretions, membranes and sacs, the proteiform realm of the flaccid and formless, . . . of the obscene bubbling of the inorganic. (143–44)

The Vagina—and the mass cultural discourses associated with it—have become the devouring female, redolent of excess flesh, oozing organs, terrifying sexuality. The narrator's Joycean discourse, by contrast, is likened to a graceful, violent phallus which rapes Spain triumphantly. The narrator constructs his difficult, symmetrical, modernist text as a fortress against woman and mass culture; but since both are central to his psychological makeup, his fortress is no protection. In this chapter, I will link the theory of Stallybrass and White to nineteenth-century theories of women, the masses, and mass culture. I will show how this late twentieth-century text rehashes the previous century's repression of the lower body and female sexuality and how it tries to compensate for the intense fears resulting from this repression through insistence on a high, male culture which serves as protection and orientation in an unsafe world.

Carmen Martín Gaite's *El cuarto de atrás* (*The Back Room*, 1978) offers two important novelties with respect to the other novels studied: it is a mass cultural novel written by a woman; and it is written during a period of democratization and hope. One must ask how the change of gender relates to the virtual dissolution of the high/low division in this novel; mass cultural texts and more prestigious kinds of literature exist on a continuum, and their contents flow back and forth without resistance. And the text also questions the association of mass culture with authoritarianism common to the other three novels, which were written in periods of limited political freedom.

*El cuarto* is the story of a middle-aged writer (based on the author herself) who strives to recapture the feelings of her childhood in the 1930s and 1940s in all their original nuances. She is able to achieve this through the vehicle of the mass culture of her youth—the radio songs, romance novels, and movies which are suffused with the sensations and memories of childhood. As the mature narrator tells her memories to a mysterious male visitor, she realizes how deeply her present dreams, desires, and modes of narration have been influenced by the mass culture of her youth.

This novel presents a rich panoply of roles which mass cultural texts can play. These roles could not be explored fully in the male-authored, apocalyptic texts, where the interaction of mass cultural texts and their consumers was coded from the start as negative, feminized, and corrupt. The complexity of the role of mass cultural texts in those novels became apparent only against the grain of the overt narratorial message. And the apocalyptic narrator tended to make the mass cultural text an empty sack to be filled with his own projected fears about modern life. In *El cuarto,* where there is no longer a stake in the high/low division, the extraordinary variety of mass cultural texts and of their functions can unfold. First, Martín Gaite's narrator differentiates texts not by "quality," but by the political ideas they reinforce. Some romance novels presented independent women who went out alone at night; others, popular once Franco came to power, idealized the domestic woman who was tireless in her activity on behalf of others. Some postwar radio songs preached patience and honorable poverty; others laid bare the deep suffering and bitterness that could not be directly expressed during those years. For the narrator as a child, mass culture offered a refuge, a space of escape from repression, cold, and fear; during her adolescence, it fed her dreams of rebellion against the narrowminded mediocrity of the postwar period. During the long years of the Franco regime, mass cultural texts served as repositories of hopes and dreams of a better life; in the present moment of narration, now that the dictator is dead, those dreams can be recovered and put into action.

Mass culture is also presented here as a key to writing the history of everyday life. It is a means of recalling the past as a lived experience rather than as a collection of dry dates and facts. The history of the songs, films, and fashions of the postwar period mediates between the history of the few, which records the actions of rulers and politicians, and the individual biographies which fill the stores after Franco's death and bore the narrator to tears. Mass culture enables the narrator to convey an experience shared by many people without losing sight of the feelings and anecdotal details which give that experience its life.

The mixture of high and low in this text is, in a sense, an inversion of what we find in *La desheredada.* The Galdosian narrator had tried to emphasize his links to the tradition of "high culture" and play down his debt to the serial novel. Martín Gaite's narrator also writes a text which draws on many canonized authors; but she openly structures the novel using the conventions of her childhood romances, while the classics are used much more subtly. And mixture in this text is seen as healthy, as a way to overturn and undo the rigid hierarchies of the Franco regime and the misunderstandings between the sexes. Martín Gaite's text thus takes us some distance beyond the assumptions about culture which we have inherited from the nineteenth century, and in which Goytisolo's text was still mired.

*El cuarto de atrás* also breaks down the association of mass culture with materialism prominent in our apocalyptic texts. In Martín Gaite's version, mass culture functions most powerfully precisely under conditions of extreme deprivation, where it is not a catalyst for consumerism but a substitute for it. In situations of limited opportunity, such as the long and harsh postwar period in Spain, mass culture stimulates dreams, resistance, and artistic creativity—precisely the opposite of its role in our apocalyptic novels, which had looked at mass culture in the context of modernization and nascent consumerism.

Martín Gaite's text is open about its hybrid nature, much like *Tormento.* In both texts, the high/low mixture is linked to a liberation from repressive political systems. But Martín Gaite's text breaks with the apocalyptic texts in much more striking ways than *Tormento*. In the final chapter of the book, I put Galdós's and Goytisolo's texts in dialogue with *El cuarto*. This provokes meditations on several questions. How does mass culture relate to escape, and how does escape relate to politics? Such questions are central to both *Tormento* and *El cuarto*. These novels oblige us to question the facile stigmatizing of "escapism" and the confident connection often made in mass cultural theory between escapism and political passivity. What conditions are required for the creation of original art? *La desheredada* and *El cuarto* offer opposite answers to this question. Goytisolo's and Martín Gaite's novels each thematize the relationship between mass culture and sexual conduct. By juxtaposing *Reivindicación*, whose narrator constantly imagines raping women, with *El cuarto*, whose narrator is sexually repressed, we can see much more than the evident contrasts between the texts. The anxieties of each narrator about sex are linked to the stereotypical images of gender roles propagated in the mass culture of the postwar period. And writing fulfills a similar function for both narrators, helping them to constitute imaginary worlds which alleviate the many kinds of fears that originated in their childhood, but which continue to haunt them as adults.

My readings of the twentieth-century texts continually look back to those of the Galdosian novels to point up features common to the two periods as well as new developments. The conclusion, grounding itself in the political, economic, and cultural circumstances brought out in the chapters, attempts to specify the conditions of possibility of such rich and multilayered mass cultural novels. It describes the contradictory, uneven, and discontinuous modernization of Spain that stretches over the entire period from *La desheredada* to *El cuarto*. It then describes the dilemmas which our writers faced as they tried to find a role for themselves in a society where old and new existed in tension, and where modernization was not accompanied by political freedom.

I have chosen to focus on novels of the Restoration and of the 1970s because of the sweeping changes in material and cultural conditions that preceded these two periods. These two time periods also seem especially appropriate because some of the most prominent novelists of each period devoted long and complex novels to the question of mass culture. In the 1880s, Leopoldo Alas devoted his *tour de force, La Regenta* (1884–85), to the problematic relationship of high and low culture in the late nineteenth century. His novella, *Doña Berta* (1892), traces the effects of romantic novels and impressionist painting on a woman otherwise isolated from civilization. Other fictions which foreground the effects of popular fiction and of reading in general abound, from Palacio Valdés's *Marta y María* (*Martha and Mary,* 1883) to Pardo Bazán's *El cisne de Vilamorta* (*The Swan of Vilamorta,* 1884) and Galdós's reworking of crime fiction in *La incógnita* (*The Mystery,* 1888) and *Realidad* (*Reality,* 1889). In the 1970s and 1980s, prominent novelists again focused on the role of mass culture. Juan Marsé's novels and stories all emphasize mass culture to some degree; I would especially mention his novel *Si te dicen que caí* (*If They Tell You I Fell,* 1973) and his later stories "Historia de detectives" ("A Story of Detectives") and "El fantasma del cine Roxy" ("The Ghost of the Roxy Cinema"), collected in the volume *Teniente Bravo* (1987). Also worthy of special mention is Terenci Moix's *El día que murió Marilyn* (*The Day Marilyn Died*), originally published in Catalan in 1970.

In the present day, Spain continues to undergo rapid transformation. And novels which incorporate forms of mass culture continue to appear. But the high/low division is not at issue, nor is politics foregrounded. Many novels play with the conventions of detective fiction; one need only think of the novels of Eduardo Mendoza.[22] Antonio Muñoz Molina, in *El invierno en Lisboa* (*Winter in Lisbon*) (1987), nostalgically recreates the atmosphere of the Bogart-Bacall films based on Chandler or Hammett novels. Carmen Rico Godoy parodies the ubiquitous "how-to" books in her novel, *Cómo ser una mujer y no morir en el intento* (*How to be a Woman and not Die in the Attempt,* 1989). But literary characters who dream of something better through mass culture do not abound as they did in the 1970s. Martín Gaite's novel can thus be seen as pivotal, making a transition between two ways of writing about mass culture. On the one hand, it looks forward, working to neutralize the high/low division, vindicating mass culture just as it valorizes other phenomena treated as marginal or nonexistent under Franco. On the other hand, the novel still

22. See, for example, his *La verdad sobre el caso Savolta* (*The Truth About the Savolta Case,* 1975) and *El misterio de la cripta embrujada* (*The Mystery of the Enchanted Crypt,* 1979).

has a clear political purpose, a sense of itself as an intervention in Spain's transition to democracy. The younger generation of novelists does not feel the need either to attack or to defend mass culture, nor to link literature clearly to politics. It remains to be seen whether such recreational literature will continue in the new Spain, as it strives yet again to catch up with Europe. I will limit my study to consideration of the last years of the Franco regime and the early years of Spain's transition to democracy, which have ample common ground with the novels of the late nineteenth century.

The novels I have chosen to explore the high/low division, then, are representative of a larger trend in the Spanish literature of these two periods. These four novels have always held a particular fascination for me, because they so explicitly foreground both the tensions and the areas of overlap between genres aspiring to be enshrined as culture and genres conventionally relegated to the "low" sphere of mass culture. Only as I worked on these novels did I discover the tight thematic and structural connections between the two apocalyptic novels and the two more utopian ones. These connections seem to me all the more significant because Goytisolo and Martín Gaite had not necessarily read *La desheredada* or *Tormento*. The similarities cannot, therefore, simply be put down to the "influence" of a specific text. Rather, they stem from the persistence of nineteenth-century assumptions about culture in the Franco era and from the similarities between the social transformations of the mid–nineteenth century and those of the 1960s, in which Goytisolo's and Martín Gaite's novels are rooted.[23]

This book has several aims. For scholars of mass culture, it seeks to uncover the deep cultural and psychological motivations which underlie the persistent division between high and low. When mass culture critics simply demonstrate that this division does not hold

---

23. A direct intertextual link *can* be made between *Reivindicación* and Alas's *La Regenta*. Goytisolo reworks many episodes of Alas's text. But Alas's novel takes place in the provinces and does not confront the problems of the large modern city. The similarities with Alas, then, are of plot and theme; especially salient is the critique in both novels of the Church's repression of sexuality. The parallel between *Reivindicación* and *La desheredada* is rather one of form and structure; both are examples of the heterogenous, almost monstrous form of novels that attempt to represent unevenly modern cities and the new mass culture that threatens to displace the classics.

water in logical terms, they have only addressed the surface of the problem. The high/low opposition buttresses our self-definition as Westerners; until we understand the ways in which our identity has depended on it, we cannot be successful in the attempt to move beyond it. Accordingly, the readings of the two "apocalyptic" novels serve as analyses of the ways in which the high/low division serves as a tactic of self-protection and legitimation. The other two novels, which more openly fuse high and low, should serve cultural critics as models of productive ways to talk about culture without falling into the cliché of cultural nostalgia—the belief in a "Golden Age of Culture" immediately preceding the critic's own generation—and without skewing arguments about mass culture in order to buttress established privileges based on class or gender. Finally, scholars of mass culture should find in this book some of the raw materials for a method of cultural analysis. Fictional texts cannot be considered outside of a specific historical and geographical context; the same movie may be received in very diverse ways at different periods, or at the same time in different countries. Relationships among different kinds of texts cannot be divorced either from gender relations or from those of class. And formal characteristics of cultural products must be linked to their social matrix.

For Hispanists, this book makes yet a few more claims. Given the prominence and number of novels focused on the high/low opposition in Spain, very little work has been done from this vantage point; more has been done on high/low relations in Latin American culture.[24] The consideration in this study of the relationship between politics, economics, gender, and novelistic form could provide a fruitful model for further studies of Hispanic culture. Secondly, very few studies have linked late nineteenth-century Spanish fiction to that of postwar Spain. Specialization has meant that critics of the postwar period rarely consider this connection; in my view, it is impossible to achieve an adequate understanding of postwar fiction without looking at the persistence of many nineteenth-century cul-

---

24. On the high/low opposition in Latin American culture, see Minc, Solotorevsky, Monsiváis, and Franco. Much attention has been given to the high/low question with regard to the novels of Manuel Puig and Mario Vargas Llosa. To name but a few studies, see Kerr, Lindstrom, and Alonso.

tural assumptions and economic relations during the postwar period. Last, on the level of exegesis, I have hoped to provide new and provocative readings of each of the four novels by focusing on the high/low opposition and its relationship to political repression, technological change, gender relations, and economic opportunity.

# Chapter One

Modernity and Narration in Galdós's *La desheredada*

• • • The Spanish novel of the 1880s is in many respects a confrontation with modernity, a meditation on the significance of the vast transformations that have taken place in the previous decades. These include the rapid industrialization of the modern city, the increased access of the masses to political equality, and the spread of mass-produced cultural artifacts such as the newspaper serial, the lithograph, and photography. These cultural newcomers competed with the art and literature which considered themselves "serious," irreversibly modifying relationships among different kinds of cultural production and between each text and its audience. Pérez Galdós's *La desheredada* (1881) opens the decade with a thorough, complex, and anguished meditation on these questions. I will focus here on the novel's narrator, who attempts to carve out a place for his art in the new modern context, and who is involved in a search for artistic identity which parallels the search of his protagonist for confirmation of her lineage. This chapter and the one that follows will put forth a metareading of *La desheredada*'s plot and narratorial discourse as a reflection on the role of art in the modern age. In order to understand the text's polemic on art, however, a brief overview of the social, economic, and cultural changes in Madrid will be crucial. The narrator's own myth of modernity is created in response to these changes, and it leads him to search for ways in which art can maintain its distinction under the new conditions.[1] The most salient change in Madrid in the decades preceding *La desheredada* was without doubt the growth of its population. In 1840, it had 160,000 inhabitants. By 1885, the population had more than doubled to reach 400,000. Territorial expansion had not taken place in proportion to this rapid rise in population, so the size of the crowd in the streets was unprecedented (Pla 12ff.). But who were the new immigrants to the capital? Most had come from rural areas of the country in search of work. But the city had not industrialized sufficiently to employ all of them. They lived in crowded conditions in slums on the city fringes; some would become criminals, others prostitutes, for lack of alternatives (Díez de Baldeón 118ff.; Cuevas 168ff.). The evident fascination with crowds in *La desheredada* is inseparable from anxiety about the working class.

Politically, Spain had undergone many changes of regime in the years preceding the writing of *La desheredada*. In 1868, Isabel II was dethroned in an attempt at bourgeois revolution. Two years of rule by a revolutionary junta were followed by the importation of a foreign monarch, Amadeo de Saboya, in 1871; he would abdicate after only two years. A short-lived Republic (1873–74) was put to rest by a military coup, which inaugurated the restoration of the Bourbon dynasty in the person of Alfonso XII, Isabel's son. The first part of *La desheredada* takes place during the reign of Amadeo and ends as the Republic is declared. The question of political equality is in the air. The Restoration, however, will be characterized by a pact between the bourgeoisie and the nobility which puts an end to bourgeois revolution by allowing the financial bourgeoisie more administrative power and freedom, but which maintains many Old Regime structures intact. Peace is achieved by sacrificing true democracy; elections are rigged so that conservatives and liberals alternate in power, a procedure known as the *turno pacífico*.

The intolerable living conditions of the working classes had led to their radicalization and organization, especially after the *International* was established in Spain in 1870.[2] Many proletarian newspapers came into being, taking advantage of the liberal press policies

---

1. A plot summary can be found in the appendix.
2. The *International* was banned, however, in 1871.

of the years 1868–74 (Seoane; Valls). Following a period of enforced clandestinity in the early years of the Restoration, the Socialist party was founded in 1879. The anarchists were able to emerge from clandestinity in 1881, the year *La desheredada* was published; but in the preceding years, they had come out with increasingly radical pronouncements. Individuals influenced by anarchist doctrine and by the international climate of violence across Europe set off bombs and attempted assassinations of public figures. Two attempts were made on the life of King Alfonso XII, in 1878 and 1879. While these actions were not really the result of a coherent policy of the Madrid anarchist federation, they were taken as such by the government and the bourgeoisie (Gutiérrez Sánchez 107). The Spanish bourgeoisie of the 1870s thought and wrote much about the working class, proposing building projects to better its living conditions. They were conscious that simple repression of working class demands would only lend the workers moral authority and attract more of them to their political organizations (Díez de Baldeón 118–19). Yet the bourgeoisie lacked the will to actually put reforms into practice. During the Restoration, the upper classes founded hospices and soup kitchens, which did nothing to change the precarious living conditions of the poor (Díez de Baldeón 134). The bourgeoisie's ambivalence between recognition of untenable conditions and unwillingness to sacrifice its own financial resources informs the discourse of the narrator of *La desheredada*.

Technological progress was also rapid after 1850. Railways were connecting the country beginning in the 1850s; tram cars began to run from the Puerta del Sol to Salamanca's rich new neighborhood in 1871. A telegraph agency was established in 1865, making international events rapidly accessible. New print technology made rapid reproduction possible, and illustrations appeared in the newspapers in the 1860s; advertising would follow in the 1870s. (Photography had entered the country in the 1840s.) Twenty-eight daily papers were sold in Madrid in 1874; by the mid-1880s there were fifty-two (Díaz 370). The means of photographic reproduction were perfected, so that beginning in the 1870s, illustrated magazines proliferated in Spain as well as the rest of Europe; they featured duplications of famous art works.[3]

3. The most famous of these magazines in Spain was *La Ilustración Española y Americana* (Díaz 369).

Despite the lack of new schools and the consequent stagnation in literacy rates relative to other countries, important changes in the Spanish population's access to culture and information had been occurring throughout the century, especially after 1850. The pitifully small circle of erudite noble and bourgeois readers, which formed the public of the literary journals during the eighteenth and early nineteenth centuries, was broadened by the bourgeois newspapers in the years following the death of the absolutist king, Fernando VII, in 1833. The political news required less erudition than the literary journals, so that the newspaper was able to serve as a mediator between the educated few and the literate but less-cultivated middle class (Fontanella, ch. 1).

With the death of Fernando VII came greater freedom of the press, but only a small public was prepared to greet it; a larger public would have to be created by the press itself.[4] An audience for information was increased in several ways. The oral tradition of storytelling, very much alive in Spain, took on a new function in the collective reading of newspapers, both in reading rooms and in town squares. The press took on aspects of the popular broadsheets traditionally sold and recited by blind men, which recounted sensationalist pieces of news. After 1850, illustrations and caricatures in the press narrowed the gap between written text and uneducated reader.

But it was the serial novel which perhaps did most to provide an introduction to reading for the rather impoverished petty bourgeois stratum of society.[5] Members of this nebulous social class were high enough on the social ladder to identify with and aspire to the status that came with bourgeois culture. But they could ill afford the costly purchase of an entire book from a bookstore, and their lack of experience in reading made access to classic, "highbrow" literature difficult at best. Jean-François Botrel has shown how the serial novel addressed the needs of a class in its literary infancy. First, the advertising for new serials stressed simultaneously the low cost of subscription and the beauty and luxurious appearance of the edition, which could be bound once all episodes were collected; the aspiring

4. The following account is drawn from Valls 27–40.

5. For the following account of new readers and the serial novel, see Botrel, "La novela por entregas." Other important studies of the serial and installment novel in Spain include Ferreras, Romero Tobar, and Marco. See also Ouimette.

petty bourgeois who fetishized the appearance of the leather-bound book was thus assured that he would share in the experience of owning one. Next, by offering short, weekly episodes with suspenseful endings, a public was created which had a need to consume reading matter regularly. Finally, several strategies facilitated the new reader's first efforts at comprehension. Illustrations, a residual element of oral culture, regularly summarized key moments in the action. Large print, widely spaced, shows the serials' preoccupation with an audience which had only recently learned to read. All elements of the reading experience were fragmented into easily digested chunks—spaces between words, short sentences, frequent new paragraphs, and the short length of the episode all ensured the novice ample opportunity for "rest stops" during the reading.

The serial novels were at their most popular during the years 1850–70. Although the number of serials published was small relative to the number of total publications in those years, the editions were exceptionally large. Botrel estimates that 800,000 to a million people (a quarter of the literate population) might have read weekly serials in 1868. The readership was predominantly urban, with an increasing proportion of women, who in the cities were relatively well off and forcibly idle. Thus, while the national percentage of literate women in Spain was only 9 percent in 1860, it was 37 percent in Madrid; by 1877, it had grown to 47 percent (15 percent nationally).[6]

Factors such as those outlined above should put us on guard when we read the complaints of the writers of the day against the low cultural level being propagated by the serial novel. Rather, such mass-produced products provided a training ground where those of limited income and recently acquired reading skills could develop a taste for cultural consumption; after 1870, this public would turn its attention more and more to the (highbrow) novels written by Galdós and others. Thus, the distinction which "highbrow" writers might want to make between the readers of their texts and the readers of sensationalist serials would not necessarily hold water.

---

6. Juan Ignacio Ferreras, in his foundational study of Spanish installment novels, specifies three kinds of readers which the editors clearly had in mind: the working class; the petty bourgeoisie; and female readers (27–30). Ferreras does not present data on how many workers might have known how to read; but it seems clear that all three categories represent people relatively new to the habit of reading.

Now that we have surprised Spain in its uneasy moment of transition to modernity, where old and new social structures overlap, where crowds teem in Madrid as never before, where culture is changing its social base and machines flood the market with ever-new, mass-produced objects, we can understand why images of fragmentation, uniformity, and unbridled reproduction recur obsessively in the discourse of *La desheredada*'s narrator.[7] Modernity is associated with the dizzying proliferation of objects, papers, numbers, words, and even people. The fear that these quantities will become uncontrollable is just below the surface of the description, and sometimes is even made explicit. Madrid at Christmas, for example, is an "insane asylum on the loose," where pedestrian traffic *triples*, and fish stores *inundate* the capital with every fish ever created (1062, italics mine).[8] Texts whose referents cannot be found proliferate wildly—"grandiose paper monuments" (1030) are generated by commissions about reform schools which are never built. Endless laws, regulations, and recommendations are signed by that bureaucratic "machine," Manuel Pez, Joaquín Pez's powerful administrator father. The *marquesa*'s daughter writes delirious letters in which illegible scribbles give way to the demented repetition of a single word. Crazy statistics and calculations abound. Dizzying columns of numbers rise and fall in the margins of the map of Spain in the asylum. Isidora's unemployed godfather keeps voluminous tomes of accounts for a family whose finances are nonexistent. Even scarier is that the people who produce paper monuments and statistics are themselves prone to multiply. Don Manuel Pez occupies a high administrative post and gives jobs to his numerous relatives in all of Spain. The Pez family follows the biblical injunction quoted by the narrator: "Be fruitful and multiply and fill the waters in the seas" (1053). The number of "fishes" in the ministries of Spain "was such that it could never be counted" (1054), and it is what exceeds calculation that terrifies the narrator.[9]

7. We should recognize, however, that the narrator is reacting not only to the modernization of Spain which he observes in Madrid but also to the more thorough modernization of Europe, which he receives through the filter of writers like Zola. *La desheredada* is in many respects an encounter with and revision of Zola's naturalism.

8. Page references are to Benito Pérez Galdós, *La desheredada*, in *Novelas*, vol. 1 (Madrid: Aguilar, 1970).

9. In any given instance where the narrator describes multiplication, an ironic and

The tendency of a single figure to multiply into many is analogous to another obsessive tendency in the text, in which a single object falls into fragments, particles, or ruins. If, in modern Spain, the unique is reproduced in many copies, in the old Spain which coexists with it, everything is falling into ruins; thus fragmentation, for the Spaniard, is inescapable. In the squalor of the poor, southern quarter of Madrid, the houses fall to pieces:

Todo es allí vejez, polilla; todo está a punto de desquiciarse y caer. Es una ciudad movediza compuesta de ruinas. (1025)

Everything there is old and moth-eaten; everything is about to crumble and fall. It is a city that wavers, cobbled together from ruins.

In the rich quarter, the situation is much the same. Death and decay pervade the Aransis palace. The _marquesa_ examines for the first time in nine years the room where her daughter met her death. The flowers of nine years earlier are disintegrating into particles, and the daughter's clothes, "invaded" by death, are about to do the same (1044). Efforts to realize wholeness in this novel have a similar fate; Mariano comes home with his new suit in tatters (1069), and Isidora's dreams are "shredded" (_despedazadas_) (1078).

Opposite to this tendency of the _one_ to fragment into the _many_, and equally alarming to the narrator, is the creation of uniformity out of diversity. As the many melt into one undifferentiated mass or into identical units, individuality is threatened. The fear, of course, has a class basis; the idea of equality threatens to engulf distinction. Soon even beggar women will be wearing hats, says the narrator: "With the growth of industry and off-the-rack clothing, Humanity is on its way to being either uniformly elegant or uniformly tacky" (1039). Uniformity is often achieved by machine in the novel. We first see Mariano at work in a rope factory, where thousands of filaments are described as being mercilessly twisted and tortured until they form one, uniform piece of rope. Human beings often act with the regularity of machines in the text. The secretary at the insane asylum writes with such uniform, regular characters that the narrator calls him a "writing machine" (991). The fact that this man will later have a crazed fit and turn out to be mad only indicates the

---

humorous tone is present; it is his insistent, repeated presentation of cases of multiplication that I interpret as stemming from fear.

dangerous ease with which extreme order can give way to disorder and fragmentation.

The narrator's fear is a common one in this period of transition to modernity—the fear of losing oneself in a chaotic world. His natural response is to cling to the use of reason as a tool to bring under control what seems too large, too fragmented, too multiple. By describing reality, by penetrating behind appearances and weighing what is really there, he attempts to defend himself against this fear. He will advise his characters to exercise a similar prudence—to trust only what possesses some consistency, to calculate carefully what is real. Such positivism translates into a conservative ideology in which characters who do not want more than they have are rewarded with happiness. The ideology is borne out in a few minor characters who embody this ideal. One is the concierge of the Aransis palace, who, despite possessing substantial savings and an inheritance, lives in a modest nook in the corner of the palace and never abandons the humble position of concierge. He is always happy, active, and occupied. The other is Emilia Relimpio, who abandons *cursi* social climbing, marries a modest orthopedist, abandons all pretension, and is completely content in her domestic routine.

So the narrator preaches looking beyond appearances to an underlying reality, and thus retaining control (of life, of art). But several features of modern society conspire to render this attempt to penetrate appearances impossible. Most important among these is the entry of the masses into public life, which has enormous consequences for artistic representation. I will focus here not on the working class (also important in the novel) but on the formation of the petty bourgeois class of shop clerks that accompanies capitalist industrialization. T. J. Clark calls the emergence of this class one of the main determining circumstances of the art of the period. Clark has eloquently described the indignation of the Parisian *haute bourgeoisie* when petty bourgeois storekeepers started taking the same Sunday outings to the country as the former had always done (Clark, ch. 3). The anxiety produced by this new class of indeterminate contours was acute; it was a sector with no culture of its own, given to ideas above or below its station (Clark 236). And, owing to changes in economic structure, it was *mobile*, although by no means sure of its position. Since it is this class which identifies with the culture and commodities enjoyed by its "betters," it poses the most immediate challenge to the latter's lifestyle and worldview, and it becomes something of an obsession with the writers of the day.

How did this class of *parvenus* come to identify with the values of the upper bourgeoisie? One answer is mass culture. Jürgen Habermas points out that the first strata penetrated by new mass technology tend to be neither the upper nor the lower classes, but the upwardly mobile groups whose status is still in need of cultural legitimation (Habermas 173–74). This insecure class, then, is most susceptible to the ideas circulating in the print media, to which it has only recently had access. And the revolutionary government of 1868 itself had stated that the function of Spanish newspapers must be to spread enlightenment and educate the lower classes.[10] After 1868, newspapers proliferate, and their circulation increases. They come into the streets to meet the Spaniard, whereas before 1868 subscription was more common. And in the revolutionary years, one important idea in the press is *equality*. There is even a newspaper called *La Igualdad*, which had a relatively large circulation with respect to other Spanish papers of the day (Valls 180). The petty bourgeoisie has a special fervor, because it believes completely in its right to equal status with the wealthy but can only acquire the latter's trappings through immense efforts of will and self-sacrifice.[11] In Spain, an additional circumstance makes the petty bourgeoisie's position more tenuous, contradictory, and threatening: modernization is incomplete, so the prosperity generated by the new industries is limited. There is not enough pie to go around, so that the petty bourgeoisie will often be downwardly mobile, whereas in other countries it is more clearly on the rise.[12] The Spanish petty bourgeoisie will fight

10. The decree of October 1868 which lifted press restrictions began with a preamble declaring the spread of "enlightenment" through the press to be a mission of the government, and observed that "this sort of publication is a source of instruction for the common man. In Spain, newspapers are the books of the working class, and in these they find guidelines about their rights" (quoted in Valls 179–80).

11. In *La desheredada*, we see this desperate clinging to middle-class status in Don José's daughters, who only have one good dress between them but manage to adorn themselves so as to create an impression of wealth on afternoon strolls or at the theater.

12. For a discussion of uneven modernization in Latin America, see Ramos. Spain's failure to develop modern roads and railways would limit potential markets, as would its slow progress in industrialization. Widespread industry would have required a more educated labor force, which was impossible because of the lack of schools and

every step of the way to retain bourgeois identity. When there is not enough prosperity around, one's own place in the desired circle might only be assured by disqualifying others from occupying it; hence the mutual accusations of *cursilería* (tackiness, inappropriateness, kitsch, unfounded pretensions) thrown back and forth among the Spanish bourgeoisie of all strata.

Isidora is initially characterized as a member of the petty bourgeoisie, and her claim to nobility can be read as a kind of allegory of the powerful but frustrated aspirations of her class.[13] When Isidora arrives from the provinces, she is unaware of social conventions; we watch her absorb them on the streets of Madrid as she strives to erase her humble origins, to create herself, literally, out of whole cloth. In this she is representative of her petty bourgeois class. When Isidora goes to walk with Miquis in Madrid's Retiro Park, she at first wants to run barefoot among the foliage. In a chapter punctuated by references to the expulsion from Eden (the end of innocence), we watch her learn that here nature has been civilized, that one does not walk on the grass, and that one displays gloves and parasol as one does in the city. Soon, she will stare awestruck at the shop windows in the city center and buy the requisite gloves, parasol, and fan. When Isidora prepares for her interview with the *marquesa* at the palace, we

---

lack of resolve to build them. The Restoration brought a pact between the aristocracy and the conservative bourgeoisie which institutionalized this economic stagnation and hoped thereby to perpetuate the existing social structure. See Valls 186–87.

13. This allegory may be unconscious on the part of the narrator; it serves as an example of how changes in social structures find their way into novels in plots which are ostensibly about individuals with idiosyncratic foibles and defects. Isidora is, of course, shown by the narrator to have a character defect which he says is common among many Spaniards—excessive imagination; but this generalized characteristic appears, for the narrator, to transcend any particular historic or economic moment. It is present, we are shown, as far back as Don Quijote. The defect is thus shown as a timeless characteristic of Spaniards, an interpretation which is, of course, highly questionable. Galdós himself, in his "Observaciones sobre la novela española contemporánea" (1870), had presented the theory that Spaniards are congenital dreamers who lack all talent for observation. But he dismisses the idea that this is an intrinsic characteristic, arguing the "la citada disposición es más bien accidental, hija sin duda de condiciones del tiempo, que innata y característica" ("the aforementioned attitude is actually more a contingency, stemming from current conditions, rather than an intrinsic and innate characteristic") (Bonet 106). We may read *La desheredada* as an exploration of just what kind of "condiciones del tiempo" would lead a character like Isidora to live on dreams, rather than simply condemning her imagination as an individual defect.

watch her create whole narratives about her character through her clothing. She cannot look too well off, or she will seem dishonorable; she cannot look disheveled, or it will seem that poverty has eroded her noble essence. She must look modest, yet honorable and grave. The narrator concludes by telling us that she "rounded out her *personality* with the respectability of boots" (1072, italics mine).

Isidora has been learning the laws of what Guy Debord calls the society of the spectacle. This phrase refers to the penetration by consumer capitalism of areas of everyday life and leisure time which had previously been removed from the market and consumer logic. The parade of carriages on Madrid's Castellana Boulevard is a good example. Every day at a certain time the carriages arrive, full of bourgeoisie and nobles dressed to the nines. Members of each stratum of society aim to disguise their true, often sordid financial state and to convince every spectator that they belong to the stratum immediately above their true one. In the society of the spectacle the gaze of the Other is all-important. It is not only Isidora and her petty bourgeois comrades who create identities for themselves through attire but the entire bourgeoisie, each stratum pretending to the wealth of the stratum immediately above it.[14] Since wealth now counts as much as title, and since wealth is a recent phenomenon, even for many of the upper bourgeoisie, the sense of having no identity other than one's representation in public is acute (Valis, "Adorning" 8–9). And nothing is likely to diminish this insecurity—for everything depends on whether the Other "buys" the appearance, believes in an opulence which might be real or might be carefully simulated. But one *will never know* the Other's true opinion; one will remain tormented by the suspicion that the Other has actually found one *cursi* and is telling his friends so at that very moment. Thus, the identity of the bourgeois citizen will constantly shift, as he or she can be taken for a wealthy aristocrat one minute and reduced to an impoverished *cursi* the next.[15]

14. Alexis de Tocqueville, in *Democracy in America,* described already in the 1830s the confusion of ranks and the pretensions of wealth that accompany democratization, using the phrase "the hypocrisy of luxury" (Calinescu 226).

15. Angel Bahamonde has described the shifts in financial power between the nobility and the bourgeoisie during the nineteenth century. Marriages between the two classes became frequent beginning in the 1870s, and benefited both. The 1870s were thus a time of change in class relations that even modified the customs of the nobility.

The cultural phenomenon of *cursilería* has been explored in a fascinating study by Nöel Valis.[16] The *cursi* person, she explains, is "one who pretends to refinement and elegance without possessing them. . . . To be found *cursi* was to be found wanting—that is, lacking and desiring at the same time" (1, 5). Valis situates the phenomenon of *cursilería* in the context of Spain's transition from a precapitalist economy to a modern, industrialized one. Incipient modernity means that old forms are changing or taking on new meanings, creating confusion (1, 12). Modernity means, especially, the growing rights of the masses and their increasing participation in social and cultural events. But these petty bourgeois newcomers to the social scene have, as Valis points out, no firm identity based either on noble lineage or on a popular culture based in manual labor. Lacking identity, they anxiously adopt that of the aristocracy, imitating its customs.[17]

The narrator, as he unmasks for us different facets of the spectacle, creates a myth of modernity which, as T. J. Clark points out, was common in periods of transition such as the 1860s in France and the 1870s in Spain. At these times, the new idiom of the spectacle, still not fully standardized or familiar, mixed with older forms of sociability (64). The myth of the modern city results from such confusion about the rearrangement of life. The city is said to be the site of vice, vulgarity, and display—it is a city of falseness, where some pretend to be rich, and others imitate popular garb in a pretended identification with the "people." Says the narrator: "La confusión de clases es la moneda falsa de la igualdad ("The blending of social classes is like the counterfeit coin that passes for true equality") (1040).[18] Modernity is

16. Valis, "Adorning Women."

17. "They constructed their identities out of the artifacts of a specific culture, a culture belonging to the Other, to an Otherness perceived as superior in prestige and status" (Valis 9). Thomas Lewis describes the process whereby, during the Restoration, "the highest ranks of the bourgeoisie [were absorbed] within the ideology and ideological practices of the aristocracy" (321). Thus the bourgeoisie lacked an ideological justification of itself as a class: "the ideological problematic of the Restoration is defined precisely by the absence of an ideological practice capable of giving representational form, and hence, effective political presence, to the bourgeoisie *in its own right*" (Lewis 326). Lacking any sense of itself, then, the financially powerful but politically marginal bourgeoisie seeks its forms of self-representation in those of the upper class; the result is the spectacle.

18. Half a century later, Ortega y Gasset would express sentiments very much akin to those of this narrator:

the era of pretense and the era of confusion, where previously separate classes mix, old separations break down, people hide their origins, and all is illusion, ambiguity.[19] The city has become a "marketable mass of images" (Clark 49).

The narrator's myth of modernity emphasizes the eclipse of authenticity. Any *original* product, text, or person is engulfed by so many copies that the original is hopelessly lost, even contaminated, cheapened, by all those reproductions that glitter but are not gold. Over the course of the novel, a series of oppositions are created which reflect the narrator's nostalgia for the Old Regime (or at least his invented version of it). The Old Regime is associated with the high and the low—the nobility and the honorable, colorful common people; the New Regime is a false middle ground, neither here nor there.[20] The following oppositions structure the text:

| Old Regime | New Regime |
|---|---|
| intrinsic value (constant) | market value (fluctuates) |
| use-value | exchange-value |
| gold | paper money or credit; gilded surfaces |

---

Cities are bursting at the seams. . . . Hotels, full of people. Trains, full of travelers. Cafés, full of patrons. Boulevards, full of passersby. . . . Finding enough space, which never used to be a problem, is now every day a vexing dilemma.

. . . Random persons, who now make up this crowd, were always around, but never as a crowd. . . . Each one . . . occupied a place—perhaps his rightful one—in the country, in the village, in the town, in the neighborhoods of the great cities.

But now, all of a sudden, the only thing we see, everywhere, are crowds. Everywhere? No—only in the best places—the more refined products of culture, the places once reserved for a select minority.

. . . The masses trample on all that is different, distinguished, individual, qualified and select. (*La rebelión de las masas* 46–47, 52; translation mine).

19. On modernity and confusion in *La desheredada*, see Fernández Cifuentes. The confusion of classes portrayed in *La desheredada* may be a reaction not only to the growth of a lower middle class but also to the marriages between bourgeoisie and nobles, which had been rare before the 1870s (Bahamonde 374).

20. This interpretation is at odds with that of Labanyi, who reads *La desheredada* as an apology for social mobility based on free enterprise, a bourgeois meritocracy which should exist in Spain but doesn't. Labanyi sees Galdós as criticizing aristocracy and working class alike for their class exclusivism; she argues that the aristocracy is presented as an anachronistic carryover from the past. While such a position is undoubtedly backed up by textual evidence, it does miss the nostalgia which *also* pervades the narrator's discourse.

| | |
|---|---|
| honor (a fixed concept with fixed criteria) | adaptable "principles"; materialism |
| the interior; inner character; the referent | the exterior; fine clothing; the signifier |
| the original (handmade) | copies; reproductions with no original (made by machine) |
| the full (plenitude, integrity) | the empty (signifier without substance); the fragmented; the incomplete |
| distinctions; hierarchy | false equality |

Life under the New Regime is a sham where nothing is real. The spectacle does not even have real capital behind it, only credit, a situation emblematized by Joaquín Pez, with his distinguished appearance, fleeing from his creditors. The nobles are not "real" nobility but bourgeois capitalists hastily titled by Isabel II or her royal successors (Espina 208ff.). Ideologies, once passionately defended in Spain, have been replaced by a political farce in which there are "elections"—the *appearance* of democracy—but the outcome is predetermined by the corrupt political machine. Joaquín reveals that his father and the equivalent minister of the opposing party are really fast friends who exchange favors, even though in the Parliament (spectacle) they hurl accusations at one another. Even articles in the press are routinely manipulated, as critiques of the government or prominent businessmen often get toned down as a result of bribes.[21] Faith has been replaced by the display of wealth, and knowledge of a trade by an empty university degree. The masks and disguises sold for *Carnaval* in old Schropp's store serve as the emblem of Restoration Spain (1078).

The narrator represents Spain's position between the old world and the new as a series of contradictions which leave it no viable option, no idealized space or system toward which to move. Despite the association of the Old Regime with authenticity and nobility, the narrator is under no illusions about the viability of that system in the present. The spaces associated with the Old Regime have ceased to produce: economically (the *marquesa* lives and spends in Paris or

---

21. This kind of blackmail was so frequent that newspapermen counted on it as a supplement to their tiny salaries (Timoteo Alvarez 232ff.).

London; her house is shut tight and contains a dead world), and even semiotically—no signs are formulated by Old Regime façades. The *marquesa's* face "expressed *nothing*" as she stared at Isidora (1073, italics mine); Amadeo's palace remains *mute* as onlookers try to guess what is happening inside on the day of his abdication (1077, italics mine). The text stands, then, between a mute world beset by death (like the Aransis palace) and the world of the spectacle where every object has *too much* to say, most of it false. The old is ruined and may even be ordinary rather than exceptional (like the façade of the Aransis palace, 1042); the modern looks luxurious but is false, with a cheap veneer (like Isidora's furniture, 1084). The sadness of the old has yielded to the frivolity of the new; the Inquisition's disciplinary power is replaced by the subtler but lengthier torture of the factories. Where old is ruin and new is farce, no solution is forthcoming. Nowhere in the vast spaces of the text is there offered a glimpse of a better life, for inner spaces are ruled by discipline, and outer ones by spectacle.[22]

The narrator of *La desheredada* is caught between old, unproductive structures and new, hastily adopted techniques which leave old social problems unresolved while creating new ones. The ambivalence and shifting tone of *La desheredada* must be understood in terms of Spain's uneven modernization. An Enlightenment program of full liberty and democracy is still a dream in Spain, and the narrator clings to many aspects of the Enlightenment belief in reason, machines, progress. Part of him insists on sweeping aside the repressive, antiquated, stagnant structures of the Old Regime and sees a more thoroughgoing modernization as desirable. But the impact of the limited modernization that has occurred in Spain brings out his other side. He sees in Madrid an inferior, superficial modernization that creates a fake world of mass-produced objects. Many of the repressive Old Regime structures are left intact beneath the veneer of newness. Yet some of the most valuable aspects of the old world, notably the conditions it provided for the production of "high art," have, in his view, been annulled. The current uneven modernity of Spain is thus, for the narrator, worse than either complete modern-

22. The Castaño household is the only refuge we see; but it is boring and smells of rawhide; even this questionable idyll, however, is penetrated by the noise of the workshop (1132).

ization or no modernization at all. The perceived fakeness of the modern city produces in the narrator—as it does in so many cultural critics—a nostalgia for an invented past of authentic art and of obedient and colorful lower classes. The recognition that the old world is dead coexists in *La desheredada* with the feeling that some of the best aspects of Spanish society died with it.

The pages that follow focus on the side of the narrator that criticizes modernity and believes the modern world to be hostile to "high art." This reading will not do justice to the side of the narrator that believes in progress and mocks, condemns, or parodies the old world. I have kept my focus on the critique of modernity for several reasons. First, very little existing criticism on *La desheredada* situates the novel in the context of the modern city. Isidora's vanity and inability to see reality are described in criticism as being Galdós's view of the Spain of 1881; but the question of why the Spaniard of 1881 might have been prone to such defects is rarely addressed.[23] When history is brought in, it is most often the history of kings and politicians. In this kind of reading, Spain, represented by Isidora, loses its dignity at the hands of corrupt politicians and speculators, betraying the hopes it had in the September Revolution.[24] Literary history *is* discussed exhaustively by those critics who debate to what extent Galdós subscribed to naturalist determinism and to what extent *La desheredada's* characters had the freedom to make moral choices.[25] But changes in class relationships, technology, urban life, and cultural production are almost entirely absent from scholarship on this novel.[26] This is the more striking because the panoramic view

23. Much criticism has focused on Isidora's delusions and on the Cervantine opposition between illusion and reality that structures the novel. See, for example, Durand, "Reality"; R. Gullón, "Desdoblamiento"; Rodríguez and Hidalgo; Petit; Schnepf, "Mirror"; Torres; Austin; and Correa.

24. See Ruiz Salvador; Gilman; Dendle; Wright, "Representation"; and Casalduero.

25. See, for example, Rodgers, "*La desheredada* and Naturalism" and *From Enlightenment to Realism*; and Russell.

26. There are some important exceptions, which have proven invaluable for the present study. Castillo brilliantly explains the text's ambivalence toward the machine. Gold's work on the museum points to the impulse to collect that underlies the accumulation of intertexts and generic models in *La desheredada*, as well as its attempt to present the totality of the city. Fernández Cifuentes studies the problem of the confusion of signs and representation in the modern city. Andreu has studied in detail *La desheredada's* relationship to the serial novels of the time. She reveals the

of the city and its problems is the most obvious feature of the plot level of the text. And, as I will argue in chapter 2, the narrator's discourse keeps the question of art's relationship to the new mass culture constantly to the fore.

I see the narrator as having created Isidora precisely as an expression of his critique of modernity. First of all, she is the text's main example of indeterminacy. As we will see in chapter 2, although she is initially characterized as a social-climbing member of the petty bourgeoisie, she soon takes on characteristics which associate her with the nobility. It becomes impossible to decide what she really is, to which class she belongs. She thus illustrates the narrator's anxiety about the way the modern spectacle undermines the attempt to differentiate, to make distinctions. In the text's metacommentary on art in the modern world, Isidora again blurs boundaries. Sometimes she appears as a figure of mass cultural reproductions of fine works of art—a copy trying to pass itself off as an original. But at other times she functions as an expression of the narrator's nostalgia for what seems to have died with the old world—the possibility of producing authentic art. Isidora's role as a figure of high art will be explored in detail in chapter 2; but it is important to remember that ultimately her character cannot be defined as *either* high art or mass culture. She oscillates between the two, making impossible the very distinctions which the narrator is trying so hard to establish.

The spectacle and related aspects of Spain's modernity, then, combine to bring about the demise of the omniscient, positivistic model of narration. Mass production multiplies objects and, by concentrating industry in major cities, increases the size of the urban crowd; an overview of such a teeming reality becomes impossible to achieve. As mass production and the dictates of fashion create a drive to uniformity, both of dress and of conduct, the *differentiation* on which omniscient narration depends is undermined.[27] This is intensified by

---

substantial overlap in outlook between the narrator and the writers of moralizing serial fiction directed at women (see *Galdós y la literatura popular*, ch. 6). I will engage with several other critics of *La desheredada* individually in the pages that follow.

27. This is not to imply that no distinctions could *really* be made on the basis of appearances in the Spanish society of the day. Rather, I want to suggest that the narrator insistently represents confusion and simulation because of his fear that ultimately all class distinctions *will* break down and he will lose his privileged position. In his admission speech to the Royal Academy in 1897, Galdós would again emphasize

the charade of the spectacle, in which every effort is made to ensure that the difference between the lower middle-class citizen and his desired upper-class model *cannot* be detected. Elaborate calculation goes into generating an impenetrable, authentic-looking signifier; the prudent, reasoned appraisal of signifieds advocated by the narrator has become impossible. The signified appears to have been devoured in the madness of multiplication, just as the original can no longer be differentiated from the copy. This crisis of perception means that reality is no longer verifiable or describable through positivistic reason, whose limits it has exceeded. Enumeration of the unlimited is impossible; creativity and extensive use of metaphor will be required to convey the reality of modernity.

As background to my exploration of the narrator's response to modernity, I must explain the assumptions about narration that inform this reading of *La desheredada*. I have presented the narrator here as a being endowed with a psyche and afflicted by fears about the city's transition to modernity. But I also regard the narrator as the creator of the text's characters and of the world he narrates. I derive this dual view of the narrator from the work of Susana Reisz de Rivarola and Käte Hamburger. Reisz de Rivarola argues that what the reader of a fictional text is asked to accept as real is the voice of the narrator. For her, the narrator is

a voice which the producer [of the text] makes use of, a fictitious source of language that may, in some cases, cohere as a "person." . . . [T]he unreal thing presented most immediately as real by the author of a novel is not the world referred to in the novel's discourse, but the voice that sustains that discourse. (119; translation mine)

From Käte Hamburger's view of narration I want to draw only her notion that in the discourse of a narrator, "engendering [a world] and interpreting [it] are one single creative act" (Hamburger 189).

I will be arguing that the narrator speaks from a specific social

the tendency towards uniformity, as aristocracy and *pueblo* tend to melt into a middle class, as language becomes standardized and loses its local color, as even rural character loses its uniqueness. But here, Galdós insists that confusion is fertile terrain for art and that new and unpredictable social forms may emerge from the undifferentiated crowd. In *La desheredada* the focus is more on what is *lost* in the process. See "La sociedad presente como materia novelable," in Bonet 157–65.

position based on his class, his gender, and his "cultural capital." Much of his fear about modernity, in my view, results from his perception that this social position is now threatened. I regard this narrator as exceptional in several ways within the Galdosian corpus, so it will be useful to specify why I use the term *narrator* rather than *Galdós* and how this narrator differs from the "narrator-character" who comes to be a trademark of Galdós's novels later in the 1880s.

Galdós wrote novels for five decades. Because characters pop in and out of different novels, we are given the impression that Galdós is describing a world which exists outside his texts. And critics tend to imagine Galdós as an omniscient, infallible entity who stands above that world and has foreseen everything, right down to the foibles of each of his narrators. But this view of Galdós as the all-knowing father of his creation has its price. It can lead us to look for consistency within the Galdosian corpus, thereby missing the richness of difference, contradiction, change. And to make Galdós omniscient is to forego the attempt to explain what motivates an author to write. I prefer to see an author as an evolving human being who at different moments of life is moved to write by persons and social problems that nag at him until he explores them through fictional characters. The characters embody different facets of, or views about, the core problems.[28] By the time the text is finished, a process has occurred which is partly unconscious, in which the author has explored different possible solutions to the problems through the characters, and has drawn some conclusions about these problems (conclusions which do not necessarily solve them).[29] The dilemmas or obsessions which stimulate an author to write may vary greatly from one text to another, and the author himself may change widely as he writes a novel, coming to the next one in some measure a different

28. This idea is a variant of one proposed by Marthe Robert. See *The Old and the New* 18–19.

29. Germán Gullón, in *La novela como acto imaginativo*, acknowledges that not all in a novel is deliberate, stating that the author "tries to realize in the text intentions which are still uncertain" (24). Nevertheless, Gullón focuses on a Galdós who is aware of his own use of the imagination, who is, in *La desheredada*, in "complete control of his narrative faculties" (86). Without denying the conscious part of Galdós's genius, I want to take into account the workings of the *unconscious* in a literary text and the role of social class and gender in creating a set of assumptions which both author and narrator accept uncritically.

person.[30] The narrator therefore reveals to us a given moment of the author's psychological, literary, and political evolution.[31]

The narrator of *La desheredada* is an anomaly within Galdós's novelistic production in many respects. In my view, he is an uncomfortable creature, making the transition from the narrators of the more static novels of the 1870s—most of which take place in the provinces—to the narrators of the later 1880s who are more at home in the constantly changing streets of Madrid.[32] Galdós is best known for his fascination with the middle class ("la fuente inagotable," as he called it in "Observaciones") and for his exploration of the mixtures of high and low that give society its vitality. Later in the 1880s, he develops the sort of narrator now seen as his trademark—the narrator-character who knows the novel's characters personally and gets his news from them. This kind of narrator is on the same level as his characters, gossiping with them, becoming infected with their views and their characteristic phrases. The narrator-character mixes with his created world, allows his characters to change his way of thinking, and freely admits there are things he doesn't know.[33]

Yet in *La desheredada* we find a narrator who does not consider himself to be on the same level as his characters (despite a fleeting moment at the beginning of part 2 when he characterizes himself as a patient of Doctor Miquis).[34] He adopts a disciplinary stance toward his protagonist, sermonizing at her from above (ch. 20, "Liquidación"); he is not prepared to change his ideas in accordance with what she might teach him. This is in part a matter of class; the narrator wants to be seen as elite and therefore can't admit to learning any-

---

30. Ricardo Gullón points out how Fortunata takes the narrator of *Fortunata y Jacinta* by the hand and drags him into her world, so that he questions the assumptions underlying his bourgeois ideology. See *Técnicas de Galdós* 208.

31. Germán Gullón puts it in these terms: "Each real author creates as many doubles of himself, as many implied authors, as novels he writes, and in each one he has a different nature" (*El narrador* 19).

32. For an account of the evolution of Galdós's novels during these decades, see Gilman.

33. See R. Gullón, *Técnicas* 16–18, 116–18, 205–08. For a fascinating example of the way a narrator may change his attitude, see Turner.

34. For this reason, he rarely permits characters to tell their own stories to one another. Yet these "narraciones interiores," as John Kronik has called them, will be one of the defining features of *Fortunata y Jacinta*. See Kronik.

thing from an uneducated petty bourgeois character—and a woman to boot! The narrator does not identify with the rest of the characters either, with the exception of Miquis. The narrator is the mouthpiece of "high culture," creating his world with a literary vocabulary and a variety of generic models that situate him far above characters like *la Sanguijuelera*, with her colloquial expressions, or the bourgeois administrators who endlessly repeat the same catch phrases. Modern society is, in the narrator's view, a "fallen" world which has forgotten "high" culture and been taken in by the fake, mass cultural products made available by mechanical reproduction. This narrator, while reproducing the flavor of popular speech, sometimes represents that speech as an adulteration of a highbrow model; later Galdosian narrators will enjoy the texture of their characters' colloquial speech for its own sake.[35] Finally, this narrator is seduced by the idea of omniscience, by the role of the scientist offered him in the theory of Zola. He aims to represent the city in its totality—from the slums to the palace, from the insane asylum to the Retiro. To do so, he needs a bird's-eye view of the whole from above; he cannot limit himself to information gleaned from the characters. But the teeming city and its inhabitants, experts in manipulating appearances, will not allow the narrator to maintain that dream of omniscience, which he will have to let go over the course of the novel.

I read the narrator's insistence on literary models and his attempt at omniscience as defensive responses against the fear of being swallowed up in the modern city and losing his identity and his privilege. He insists on being "high," "above" his world, to save himself from the flux. When he sees art threatened with contamination by mass culture, he will try to imagine ways of saving it as well.

It is in this context that I situate the pervasive irony of this Galdosian narrator. *La desheredada* is a text often playful in tone, poking fun at different kinds of bombastic language and the people who use them, punning incorrigibly, parodying everything that comes to hand. The narrator uses irony in multiple ways, one being to estab-

35. The narrator of *La desheredada* puts forward the following view of language: "Donde suena un lenguaje soez sólo puede haber malas acciones y pensamientos poco delicados. Donde cantan las ranas, ¿qué ha de haber sino charcos y cieno?" ("Wherever vulgar language is heard, there can only be despicable actions and coarse thinking. Where frogs sing, what can there be other than mud and manure?") (1097).

lish a complicity between himself and his reader against a character's self-deluded opinion.[36] Almost nothing is accepted at face value, as any view is juxtaposed with others that negate it. The tendency of critics, in accordance with the common assumption of Galdós's superiority and omniscience, has been to glorify this irony, whether it comes from the narrator himself or from the character Miquis, who often acts as his spokesman.[37] Though I delight in the irony and humor which play a vital role in the novel, I see them as defense mechanisms which only partly conceal alternating tones of confusion, bitterness, and loss. My reading will isolate a wistful tone which has been ignored by criticism. It is a tone not commonly associated with Galdós, and I believe it is linked precisely to the narrator's stake in preserving a high culture which he suspects will soon be entirely obliterated.

This defense of the "high" against the "low," this desire to preserve a world slipping away and to maintain control of his material, is what creates a conservative tone and a pessimism about culture in *La desheredada*. Paradoxically, it also means that this early work by Galdós anticipates modernism more closely than his later works would. For modernism reacts against mechanization and mass culture by insisting on art for art's sake, a separate art about sad princesses in palaces, with elaborate allusions to the Western literary tradition.[38] I will be arguing that *La desheredada* is a remarkable text because it experiments with such a response to modernity and finds it a failure. In subsequent novels, Galdós will abandon the highbrow stance as unproductive, and bring his narrators into the streets to rub elbows with their characters. These narrators will gain authority from their closeness to events, while the authority of the narrator of *La desheredada* depends on his distance from them.

What follows in chapter 2 is an exploration of the narrator's experiment with the modernist utopia of a pure art that could help

---

36. For a detailed study of irony in *La desheredada*, see Urey, *Irony*.

37. For Urey, Miquis is "the voice of truth and of irony" (27). For my own, very different view of Miquis, see Sieburth, "Enlightenment."

38. The reference is to Rubén Darío, the Hispanic world's most famous modernist poet. His "Sonatina," from the volume *Prosas profanas*, begins: "La princesa está triste... ¿Qué tendrá la princesa?" ("The princess is sad... What can be the matter with the princess?") (*Poesía* 42).

counterbalance the chaotic, fragmenting forces of modernity and restore wholeness by linking the new world with the old. It is his last-ditch attempt to maintain his privileged position, linked in the text to the space of the palace. The second section of that chapter will then explain why the project of artistic purity could not be realized.

# Chapter Two

## Separate and Unequal: Literature's Polemic against Mass Culture in *La desheredada*

### The Search for Origins: Literary Family Romance in *La desheredada*

Para que la industria pueda hacerse pasar por noble, necesita fingir parentescos con el arte.

For industry to pass itself off as noble, it has to pretend it is related to art.
—Galdós, *La desheredada*

• • • **T**he plot of *La desheredada* tells us the story of the downward trajectory of a young girl; the narrator links Isidora's downfall to that of Spain. The bulk of the criticism on *La desheredada* has focused on this story and usually has reproduced the narrator's explicit, negative judgments on Isidora. I argue that *La desheredada* also tells another story, equally essential to understanding the novel, but virtually ignored by criticism until now. This second story determines most of the metaphors used in narration, much of the description of characters and space, and the generic models used to narrate the novel. It is a story about the problematic position of art and its producers in an age dominated by the criteria of utility, efficiency, and quantity. I will first present some evidence of the narrator's obsession with the problem of cultural production. One notices, first, that in *La desheredada*, among the objects that proliferate in such a terrifying way, *texts* of all kinds are the most frequently singled out.[1] Mechanically reproduced texts include newspapers, ballads, *aleluyas* (a series of illustrations which tells a story, with rhyming couplets captioning each picture), and Isidora's serial novels. In the handwritten variety we find Rufete's crazy decrees, the *marquesa*'s daughter's

---

1. This may respond to the proliferation of newspapers and magazines after 1868.

delirious, half-finished love letters, an asylum inmate's daily letter to the pope, the asylum secretary's continual, orderly writing, and countless others. And in fact, the very motivation for the plot is a problematic piece of writing—Rufete's falsified document of nobility. Writing is not the only cultural form to pervade the novel; pictorial art is also omnipresent, from the portraits hanging in the Aransis palace and the masterpieces in the Prado to the horrible prints which adorn the walls of the Relimpio household, the tasteless combinations of sacred and profane reproductions in the office of Manuel Pez, and on down to the *cromos* of lascivious priests which "inundate" the stores (1085) and Bou's lithographs of popular figures on shelf paper.

If the obsessiveness with which the narrator describes the cultural products which adorn every house in the novel were not sufficient evidence, the narrator smuggles metaphors from the sphere of culture into descriptions which have nothing to do with culture and even seem antithetical to it. The ragged boys of the poor city fringes march to fight each other, "playing . . . delicate Christmas sonatas, by pounding rhythmically on an oil can" (1021). The narrator regrets not being an epic poet in order to express with proper eloquence the fury of the puritanical Doña Laura when Isidora abandons the Relimpio household to sleep with Joaquín Pez (1080). When Isidora lives imprisoned by Botín, Don José complains daily to Mariano in the café, and the narrator inserts a completely ludicrous analogy with the shepherds and sheep of pastoral literature:

Durante algún tiempo, su único consuelo (de D. José) ha sido agregarse a Mariano en el café del Sur, y frente a él exhalar sus quejas, semejantes a las de los pastores de antaño; y así como las ovejas—dicho está por los poetas—se olvidaban de pacer para escuchar los cantos de los Salicios y Nemerosos, Mariano dejaba enfriar el café por atender a lo que don José refería. (1104)

For some time, Don José's only consolation has been to join Mariano at the Café del Sur, and to give vent to sighs and complaints similar to those of the shepherds of yore. And just as the sheep—or so the poets tell us—forgot to graze when they heard the songs of all those men named Salicio and Nemeroso, so Mariano let his coffee get cold as he listened to Don José's stories.

Even the brutish Mariano himself will be compared to a poet as he gradually acquires sophisticated knowledge about how others acquire wealth:

*Pecado* [Mariano] perfeccionaba su *intellectus,* enriqueciéndolo con luces nuevas acerca de la propiedad . . . , luces o ideas que burbujeaban en su cerebro, como los embriones de la belleza y el vago apuntar del plan artístico en la mente del poeta, al pasar de niño a hombre. (1120)

*Sinner* [Mariano] was perfecting his *intellectus,* enriching it with new knowledge about property . . . , illuminating ideas which bubbled in his brain, like embryos of beauty and the vague outline of an artistic plan germinate in the mind of the poet, as he passes from childhood to manhood.

The printer Juan Bou tries to speak delicately in front of Isidora, but his words resemble the sounds of an ox trying to emulate a nightingale; he is compared to "un epigrama escrito en octavas reales" ("an epigram written in iambic pentameter") (1123). Even the least aesthetically oriented characters, then, are incorporated into the pervasive metadiscourse on art which threads through the entire text. And much more obvious, yet almost entirely ignored by criticism, is the variety of genres which appear in *La desheredada,* both as modes of narration and in passing quotations. The picaresque novel, the Golden Age honor play, the church sermon, political speeches, melodramatic dialogue, popular rhymes, and serial novels are only some of the genres which constantly shock us with brusque contrasts and strange combinations. My reading is an attempt to explain this preoccupation with genre and the theme of art in a way that relates this metadiscursive carnival to the problems of modernity outlined above.

Since Isidora is one of the text's main vehicles for embodying the problems of art in the modern world, we need to explore the flexibility her character takes on over the course of the novel, the ways she acts as a vessel for multiple meanings about class and art. Isidora is initially presented to the reader as a *cursi*—that is, as a petty bourgeois social climber who strives to mask her plebeian origins and pass herself off as noble. In this role, she is condemned by the narrator for constantly fantasizing about her future life in the palace and neglecting practical matters in the real world. As the novel proceeds, however, Isidora overflows this limited definition. Her boundaries blur, and she takes on characteristics of the two classes, upper and lower, whose values are opposed to the bourgeois fakery that finds its expression in the spectacle. She begins to incarnate elements which the modern, rationalized society has shunted aside—beauty, poetry, passion, the imagination; this lends truth to the idea that she is "noble," even though she may not be of noble lineage. Many of her striking character traits, in fact, associate her much more deeply with the aristocracy than her dubious claims would warrant. She has innate good taste, unlike the tacky social climbers on the Castellana. Her beauty grows every day; her air of elegant superiority impresses even the judge at her trial. Male characters refer to her as a religious or mythical vision, as a divinity, as a queen. But at the end of the novel, when she is jailed, Isidora begins to feel a solidarity with the common people, unjustly persecuted as she believes herself to be. She adopts their language and gestures as she makes the decision to become a prostitute. Isidora's characteristics, then, potentially identify her with the whole social spectrum, from the *marquesa* to the ruffian Gaitica. One of her many functions is thus to blur class boundaries that the narrator would have wished to keep distinct. In her unique beauty and nobility, however, she enables him to criticize modern society.

The contradictory characterization of Isidora with regard to class has its counterpart on the level of culture. Insofar as Isidora is a petty bourgeois, social-climbing *cursi*, she is associated with the serial novels that repeat the stories of poor children who turn out to be noble and end up in palaces. In the second part of the novel, where Isidora's superiority is emphasized, she is associated with high art rather than with mass culture. As high art object, her fate is of prime importance to the narrator, for it is linked to his own fate as a would-be creator of high art in the modern age. The crucial question Isidora has been created to answer is whether art can survive in a world based on efficiency, utility, and materialism. As Isidora's claim to nobility begins to appear dubious, with the *marquesa*'s denial of any relationship, towards the end of part 1, the narrator, paradoxically, begins to insist on Isidora's beauty, uniqueness, and superiority. This is almost invariably accompanied by metaphors of art objects or references to a romantically coded and transcendent natural setting like the sea.

The creation of Isidora as art object begins with an important frontal attack on the opposition between art (seen as false) and reality, an opposition which characterizes positivism and the modern, rationalized society. In Isidora, declares the enthralled narrator, the ruby lips which poets have overused in verse could actually exist in reality (1013). Isidora, then, is living proof that art can exist in the real world. Later we learn that unlike the *cursi* Relimpio girls, Isidora's exceptionally refined taste is innate, not acquired by imitation. Her face, framed by chestnut hair, has tones of "poetry at twilight" (1072). Miquis compares her eyes to a deep and luminous sea (1072). Her manner constitutes its own title of nobility, and everything connected with her is exceptional ("selecto") (1106). Her hairdo is a "masterpiece," a "symphony" of hair (1113). Her neck and shoulders are of the Venetian school (1110). In the museum, she feels a kinship with the female figures painted on the canvases (1143). Her beauty shines out, *framed* by "fine muslins" (1121).

Noël Valis has described the tendency of the Spanish novelists of the 1890s to make of their female protagonists at once art objects (passive) and artists who actively seek to create their own lives. In both roles, she says, they are set apart from their surroundings, superior, superhuman. Their apartness *frames* them, creates a fragment within the novel—a work of art—which becomes increasingly isolated from the external reality described. This fragmentation corresponds to that of the modern world and to the new tactic of the modern writer, who abandons the idea of representing the whole of reality in his novel. Reality has become equivocal; the novelist responds by concentrating on the female figure, the work of art, which he may want to frame and set apart in order to save it from the flux.[2] I want to argue that *La desheredada* unwittingly anticipates the modernist experiment which isolates art as a separate world of refuge, as exceptional and qualitatively unlike the surrounding reality. I would argue that the narrator as modern writer creates Isidora as just such a separate art object but then sets her adrift in that "fallen" surrounding world, with its deceptive fakes, its materialism, its disciplinary structures. The test question is whether Isidora—and the work of art—can survive in all their uniqueness in such an environment. Isidora's task as artist (as "writer" of her own life, creator of her own destiny) is to create conditions in which she can remain an *objet d'art*.

The work of art, it is clear, cannot exist within the limits of the schemes of rationalization, of calculation. Isidora as work of art exists as what lies outside calculation and cannot mix with it. Her

2. Valis, "Novel into Painting".

beautiful eyes are a mystery that Miquis's positivist university professors cannot explain (1009–10); her dreams can scarcely find words to express them (1012); her imagination reaches "incalculable limits" (1017). Forced to add up receipts from the pawnshop, she becomes pale, her pulse falters. The narrator glosses:

Desdichadas las almas que siendo hermanas de lo infinito tienen que entroncarse a la fuerza con estas miserias del planeta llamadas cantidad, relación, gravedad. Verdaderamente, ¿qué cosa más contraria a lo infinito y a lo ideal que aquellos nefandos papeles? (1091)

Unhappy are those souls which, being spiritually akin to the infinite, are forced to take into account more earthly, grubby concerns, like amounts, proportions, gravity. Truly, what could be more contrary to the ideal and the infinite than those abominable promissory notes?[3]

The realm of calculation (the society of the spectacle), shown as degraded, is thus inimical to art, which must remain separate in order to exist. In literary terms, the novel, to exist as an art form, must keep its distance from the genres of rationalization (mass-produced by machine) which threaten to engulf it just as the *cursis* on the Castellana threaten to engulf Isidora and render her distinction invisible.

*La desheredada* is a text obsessed with origins, both familial and literary. The fact that it is impossible to state categorically to which class Isidora belongs leads us, on the level of narration, to consider her parallels to the modern writer. As Hauser indicates, the artist in the modern world is cut off from the bourgeois class of which he had earlier been the spokesman, and which no longer needs him. Below the bourgeoisie, he finds the uneducated classes which cannot read him yet (Hauser 4:132–33). His position is indeterminate, his institutional support (in Spain) almost nonexistent, yet he identifies with the most exquisite products of culture.

Where did this indeterminacy come from? In the plot, the loss of a clear identity is formulated as the crisis of the family.[4] Parents in this

3. The ironic tone behind most of these remarks might make us dismiss them as jokes; but the number of such comments and the insistence that there is something transcendent about Isidora point to another possible reading.

4. Galdós had seen this crisis as a key problem for the novel to explore at least since his programmatic statement of 1870, "Observaciones sobre la novela española contemporánea": "[M]ientras en una parte la falta de creencias afloja o rompe los lazos morales y civiles que forman la familia, en otras produce los mismos efectos el fana-

novel are either dead (the marquis of Aransis, Rufete, Virginia, Fran-
cisca Guillén), derelict in their parental roles (Rufete, José Relimpio,
Modesto Rico), or so puritanical that they bring on rebellion and
crisis (the *marquesa*, Laura Relimpio). The results are fragmentation,
loss of identity, and illegitimacy of all kinds. In the course of the
novel, we witness the disintegration of the Rufete and Relimpio families. And the madness which threatens the whole society is defined
from the beginning as being related to the disappearance of the family or the confusion of lineage. We are told the cause of incarceration
of only two asylum inmates (Rufete and Canencia), and the dementia
of both involves confusion about family ties.[5]

On the plot level, the roots of this text go back to sexual promiscuity and missing parents, forcing a search for identity, for origins, on
the part of the orphaned protagonist. If sexual promiscuity creates
confusion on the plot level, its equivalent on the level of art is mechanical reproduction, that procedure which creates "illegitimate"
copies, obscuring the original.[6] The artist, alienated from a public
sphere inundated with fakes, asserts his fundamental difference from
this "degraded" present and claims to be part of a superior sphere, the
direct inheritor of a glorious past cultural tradition.

The search for origins, then, drives the text on the levels of both
plot and narration. Both Isidora and the narrator have a stake in the
success of the enterprise of reconstructing the links between the old
world and the new. This utopian desire by the narrator corresponds
on the level of plot to the events of part 1, where Isidora does what is
necessary to reach the palace, to reconstruct the noble family. The
end of part 1 (her expulsion from the palace) and the whole of part 2

tismo y las costumbres devotas." ("On the one hand, the absence of belief in anything
weakens or actually breaks the ties of moral and civic responsibility that bind the
family together; while on the other, an excess of belief, fanaticism, and religious ritual
produce the same effects.") Quoted in Bonet 113.

5. Canencia "[c]ame here because of arguments and lawsuits with his children"
(32).

6. According to Díaz, the sophistication of reproductive techniques, "que hacía
posible difundir auténticas obras de arte, en cada número de una revista, divulgó por
toda Europa la modalidad que con el vocablo 'Ilustración' en su rótulo, manifestaba
la supremacía que otorgaban a la parte artística" (369) ("which made it possible to
disseminate authentic works of art in each issue of a magazine, caused a new kind
of publication to spread throughout Europe. The word 'Illustration' in its title proclaimed the priority it gave to the artistic aspect.")

form the story of the contamination caused by the failure of this endeavor. On the level of discourse, however, the utopian desire for a pure art uncontaminated by modernity is confronted from the beginning by reminders of the inevitability of contamination. From the start, the will to purity and the evidence of its impossibility exist in tension. In the present context, however, I will describe the positive and the negative moments separately, to avoid the risk of this reading becoming as chaotic as the novel itself.

Throughout this section, I draw substantially on Julio Ramos's analysis of the intellectual project of José Martí, which bears a remarkable resemblance to that of this Galdosian narrator. Martí saw literature in the modern world as a compensatory mechanism whose privileged vision could restore origins and family, link up fragments, and integrate old traditions with new inventions. The major difference between Galdós and Martí lies in the conclusions they drew from the inevitable failure of their common quest; these will be discussed in the third section, where I analyze the means by which art is contaminated in *La desheredada*.

Isidora, as we have seen, is a figure of the work of art. Adrift in the modern world, she must find a way to retain her special beauty and distinction without becoming contaminated by the fallen world of fakes and *cursis*. She must do this by establishing her origins, her right to exist in the palace. As she becomes active to ensure this outcome, her qualities as *artist* are revealed, qualities which she shares with the narrator. She is capable of imagining places, people, and language, creating novelistic scenes in her head (997). She knows how to capture a person's character in a few quick, colorful details (1006–07), making it unnecessary for the narrator to add anything to her description of Botín (1111, 1113). Most of all, she knows how to create *herself* artistically (which, as we shall see, the narrator is also doing), and the narrator describes this ability as related to her *birth*. The talents enumerated below as Isidora's are those needed by any modern writer aiming to create beauty and coherence out of the current chaos:

Con ella *nació*, como *nace* con el poeta la inspiración, aquella facultad de sus ojos para ver siempre lo más bello, sorprender lo armonioso y elegir siempre de un modo magistral . . . (1039, italics mine)

With her *was born*, as inspiration *is born* with the poet, that aptitude for seeing always what is beautiful, surprising into existence what is harmonious, and therefore making inspired choices. (italics mine)

The narrator never states explicitly that Isidora's claims have no foundation; indeed, he defends her distinction more and more as she loses all hope of realizing her claims. As the outcome of her lawsuit looks more dubious, the narrator gives us Isidora's thoughts about her merits in the free indirect style:

Ella era noble por su nacimiento, y si no lo fuera, bastaría a darle la ejecutoria su gran belleza, su figura, sus gustos delicados, sus simpatías por toda cosa elegante y superior. (1134)

She was noble by birth, and even if she weren't, her great beauty, her figure, her refined taste, her affinity for everything elegant and superior, would be enough to grant her a title.

While the narrator maintains an ironic distance from Isidora's vanity throughout the novel, he is not simply mocking Isidora's words here. He has too often insisted in his own voice on Isidora's beauty, distinction, and good taste. He compares her to a duchess (1085) (a title higher than that of the *marquesa*), asserts that she wears her title on her face (1106). Why such a strong defense of Isidora? Because her quest to be recognized as special and unique even though she lacks the conventional qualifications is an enterprise which exactly reflects his own.

Art at this historical juncture is on the defensive. The press threatens to co-opt it and make it serve utilitarian ends. A glance at the leading newspapers of the period (*La Correspondencia de España* and *El Imparcial*) is sufficient to understand the danger. Installments appeared daily, at the bottom of the third and fourth pages of the newspaper, and they were often cut off unceremoniously in mid-*word*. They generally droned on for eight months or more. In Spain, the lack of a bourgeois revolution in the late eighteenth or early nineteenth centuries had meant that art and literature had not had a period of separation from noble or state patronage in which to exist alone in the field of culture before the technological revolution brought the wave of industrialized serials. When the Old Regime finally did fall, art was forced to hit the pavement running to keep from being drowned in the flood of newsprint. Yet because of the lack of a developed book market, "high" art depended on the same newspapers that spread the hastily cooked up serials. The up-and-coming writers of the day got their apprenticeships and made themselves known to the public by writing in the Monday literary section of *El Imparcial.* Their novels often appeared in installments either before or after appearing in book form. Just as Isidora looks very much like another petty bourgeois social climber, so the would-be highbrow novel looks suspiciously like the mass culture of its day. In fact, according to Montesinos and Ribbans, *La desheredada* itself was first published in installments, months before its appearance in book form.[7]

Marthe Robert argues that Freud's family romance of the neurotic is the driving impulse that characterizes the diverse genre known as the novel.[8] The novel, she points out, was an upstart genre with respect to poetry and drama. Its tendency to make ample use of sex and violence made it doubly suspicious. As she indicates, long after readers had made clear their preference for the novel, some of its most illustrious practitioners still felt the need to apologize for it or even to attack it. Our context in the present study makes it easy to define the "original sin" of the novel, aside from its refusal to obey the kinds of restrictive rules that governed poetry and drama. The novel is the first genre to depend on the printing press for its diffusion. From its birth in *Don Quijote,* the modern novel constitutes itself as a critique of the less highbrow products of that same press (the novel of chivalry), yet defends itself as high art, claiming to be an epic written in prose.[9] But the novel's position has been contradictory from the start. As Bakhtin points out, the novel is born as a deflation of the epic, lyric poetry, and other "high" genres. It is by nature a *mixture* of genres, containing both high and low and glorying in the dialogic conflicts that result.[10] Perhaps for that very reason, though, it was long considered suspect by church authorities, and "lowbrow" by the literary establishment. During the nineteenth century, the novel gradually acquired prominence in Spain in a variety of subgenres—historical

7. See Montesinos 2:1; and Ribbans.

8. Robert, *Origins of the Novel,* introduction.

9. "[T]he epic can be written in prose just as it can in verse" (Cervantes, pt. 1, ch. 47, 567; trans. mine).

10. See *The Dialogic Imagination.*

novels, domestic fiction, epistolary novels, translations of foreign romantic novels, and the like. As Catherine Jagoe indicates, the domestic fiction written by women did much to achieve respectability for the novel form in the 1850s and 1860s. Jagoe argues that Galdós's "Observaciones" (1870) is a hidden polemic against female novelists and readers which tries to take back the novel genre and claim "high" status for it by advocating a more "virile" kind of novel—that is, the realist novel. She reads *La desheredada* as a cautionary tale about the potential dangers of female readers like Isidora and of the implausible serial fiction they consumed.[11] Within the web of associations established in *La desheredada*, as we shall see, the novel as a genre is represented as tainted by its links to the female sex and to mechanical reproduction; the two come together in metaphors of promiscuity, illegitimacy, and monstrous birth. The narrator thus finds himself in the awkward position of desiring the privilege and prestige of the "highbrow" writer while producing a text in a genre traditionally associated with deflation and linked, in modern times, to mechanical reproduction and mass culture. While his text bears witness to the impossibility of divorcing the novel from the "low," from mass culture, he nevertheless does his utmost to establish its legitimacy as a work of "high" art.

What means does our modern narrator use to carry off the family romance of the novelist? Like Freud's neurotic, he denies his lowly parents and invents higher ones. In this case, the novel minimizes its kinship with the press (its birth by mechanical reproduction), and claims filiation with the Bible, the epic, and the genres of the Golden Age. The "father" whose presence persists over the entire text is his most illustrious predecessor in the genre, Cervantes. Just as Isidora tries to hide her provincial origins and her lack of education, then, the narrator risks becoming a cultural *cursi*, playing down his text's mechanical origins and proclaiming himself the child and heir of the classics.

The narrator makes use of an array of "legitimation strategies" to give himself the desired authority. Most of these have been described by Ramos in connection with Martí and other fin de siècle Latin American writers; some are unique to our particular, playful narra-

11. See "Disinheriting the Feminine."

tor.[12] One way to impose order on the cultural chaos, says Ramos, is to assert a clear opposition between "real culture" (high art) and "false culture" (mass culture). The crisis of values of the modern world (materialism, promiscuity, etc.) can then be blamed on the spread the hastily cooked up serials. The up-and-coming writers of self as saving the world from this crisis (Ramos 202–03). The narrator of *La desheredada* creates this opposition by asserting his difference from the "organic intellectuals" who administer the new society and write for its information industry.[13] These administrators are represented insistently as of inferior birth, revealing the narrator's obsession with the filiation he wants to prove. (Such jibes at competitors are equivalent to Isidora's scornful judgments on the *cursis* she encounters in Madrid.) The worst offender is Don José's good-for-nothing son, Melchor, who malicious tongues report is a *tresmesino*—an infant born after only three months of pregnancy (1040). When we meet him, he has just had a second birth; he is "recién salido del vientre de la madre Universidad" ("newly issued from the womb of Mother University") (1035). But, like the other "organic" intellectuals in the novel, he is "as denuded of knowledge as he was swathed in conceitedness" (1035). A "fount of ignorance" (1041), he speaks with a repertoire of clichés and formulas (1041), and what he produces are advertisements inviting the public to invest in nonexistent inventions or projects, or, alternatively, sensationalist newspaper articles accusing the government of corruption. Melchor is likened by the narrator to a spanking new boat, recently painted, which now must float itself on the seas of ambition (1041). He is like a product of the new mechanical age—shiny and attractive, but lacking substance. Even more significantly, he is compared to an artist, in the field of *smoking*. No one can blow a smoke ring like him, and his

12. Page references to Ramos will be given where the strategies are ones mentioned by him.

13. The term *organic intellectuals* is drawn by Ramos from the work of Antonio Gramsci. It refers to those who have a directive, technical, organizing capacity in a given kind of economic system. In the modern world, these directors are specialized professionals—engineers, lawyers, professional politicians, and such. Men of letters, whose mode of knowledge precedes the new system, are called by Gramsci "traditional" intellectuals; the clergy also fall into this category. See Gramsci, "Intellectuals," in *Selections from the Prison Notebooks* 3–23.

pipe, after he blows smoke on it and polishes it, looks like the purest ebony (1042). But there is nothing behind the smokescreen of clichés of the organic intellectual. The narrator applies such conclusions to all doctors recently *incubated* in the university (1120).[14]

Other, more successful professionals are similarly attacked. The commissioner satirized for his inefficacy in combating juvenile delinquency is called the *author* of countless bureaucratic documents (1030). Muñoz y Nones, the notary, has never opened a book other than the *Ley de Enjuiciamiento Civil* (1119). But the most important family of organic intellectuals is the Pez family. Through the quick multiplication common to fish and machines, they have monstrously created an entire new world of fakery which has obscured the old one created by God. The narrator makes the point by narrating the Pez story in the language of Genesis 1, the originary text par excellence. The family metaphor is belabored, as Pez is the *father* of bureaucratic forms, brought up in the *maternal* Spanish administration. Pez has never opened the leather-bound, gilt-edged books in his office (1059), and his children, all employed in the administration, don't bother to report for work since they are ignorant of every aspect of the job (1056). In this world, the narrator tells us, hard work and talent open no doors; only connections bring opportunities. The narrator thus explains his own marginalization while deploring the false world (the "family" of a subhuman species—fish—that populates Spain's administrative class) that has displaced the old ways. Given the many characters in this novel who have never opened a book, we conclude—as the narrator wants us to do—that he is the only one who has read the Bible and still remembers that there was another, authentic world before this one.[15]

The narrator attacks many of these "organic intellectuals" (Mel-

14. See Hernández Sandoica on the lack of participation of the Spanish universities—that of Madrid included—in the cultural and scientific developments of the nineteenth century.

15. The ideology being conveyed through characters who only own highbrow books for status, but never read them, is that "nobody reads the good books *any more*." In fact, as we saw in our rapid survey of the nineteenth-century reading public in Spain, the circle of highbrow readers had been extremely small and was now growing, precisely through the greater access provided by the new press. The apocalyptic idea that modernity means the end of true culture has been traced by Patrick Brantlinger as far back as the Greeks, though parallels with the decline of the Roman Empire reached fever pitch in the nineteenth century and have continued to this day.

chor, Botín, the Pez family) for being materialistic, shameless social climbers. This obscures his own, more subtle cultural social climbing. At the same time, he represents the new, rationalized discourses of modernity as clichés, formulas, stereotypes. Botín's soporific political speeches, Bou's socialist clichés, Isidora's serial novels, the language of the newspaper—all are parodied. Many of the organic intellectuals speak almost exclusively in clichés, and every character who works at the printing press has his mind colonized by the catchy rhymes he is printing and by Bou's oft-repeated, pompous phrases. The organic genres of rationalization, then, are shown to be of inferior or monstrous birth, and as empty, repetitive, and fake—like the mass-produced statues of Don Quijote which Isidora sees everywhere (1059).

The narrator is stacking the deck against modernity by leaving out of this cultural panorama any modern writing that might qualify as "high culture." The Spanish novelists of the 1870s, including Galdós himself, were in fact producing some work of high quality, but they are excised from the frame of *La desheredada*. Nor are we ever given an inkling that the newspaper prints literary material, for that would recall this text's lowly origins, which it seeks to repress. The cultural panorama represented, then, is apocalyptic—on the one hand, the vapid genres of mass culture; on the other, the novel we are reading, which forms a solitary bulwark against the demise of culture and memory. Thus, although the market and the newspaper were what had permitted members of the bourgeoisie like our narrator to become writers in the first place, these writers nevertheless represent newspaper language as antithetical to literary discourse (Ramos 101–02).[16] The social-climbing narrator has thus created a space for himself by "killing off" his competitors. The only other "traditional" intellectuals who receive fleeting recognition in the novel are the schoolteachers. The narrator depends on them to teach the literary tradition that will create a reading public for his work. Where the organic intellectuals create (and then are incapable of resolving) the problems of modernity, the schoolteachers may help to solve them.

16. Another example of a skewed representation of current culture can be found in Alas's *La Regenta*, written a few years after *La desheredada*. All of its characters read, but no modern Spanish literature exists, and the classics are left unread except by the protagonist and her spouse, who misinterpret them.

The dedication page of the novel polemicizes against the former while desiring the success of the latter:

. . . convendría dedicar estas páginas..., ¿a quién? ¿Al infeliz paciente, a los curanderos y droguistas que, llamándose filósofos o políticos, le recetan uno y otro día?... No, lás dedico a los que son o deben ser sus verdaderos médicos; a los maestros de escuela.

. . . It would be appropriate to dedicate these pages—to whom? To the unfortunate patient? To the quacks and druggists who, calling themselves philosophers and politicians, give him new prescriptions every single day? No, I dedicate them to those who are, or should be, his real doctors—the schoolteachers.

The narrator links the cultural level of characters to the circumstances of their birth (tresmesino, etc.). He is a class snob, nostalgic for the (invented) days of true aristocracy. The masses, who are familiar with either no high culture or only the degraded copies they encounter through the printing press, are seen as enemies of culture. And the "purity" of the nobility is eroded by marriages to corrupt commoners. Joaquín Pez, titled the marqués viudo de Saldeoro, and Sánchez Botín, a conde o barón consorte, have both married noblewomen strictly for money. It is implied that Joaquín's young wife was long-suffering as he philandered; the charitable wife of the satyr Botín is planning to found a new hospital (1104). The noblewomen, then, are sympathetic figures; the fault lies with their husbands, who are of inferior birth. Most importantly, both of these "hybrid" marriages are sterile. The narrator, by contrast to these "false" nobles who are really only ignorant bourgeois administrators, can present himself as truly having a link with the past of high culture—the literary tradition that includes the Bible and the Spanish Golden Age.

The narrator aims to narrate in a way uncontaminated by the rationalization and corruption of the market. His narration, if it is to be distinguishable from the mass culture he claims is not his kin, must differ markedly from the varieties of fiction commonly available.[17] This is achieved, first, through intense stylization. Galdós took perhaps more care with the style of La desheredada than with any other of his novels; Montesinos reports statements by Galdós

17. Lest there be any confusion, the narrator refers to his text as an historia, not as a novela. The word novel connotes serials, or installments, and poor quality.

about having taken special care with this novel (ix), finding that it took him longer to write because his writing had become more reflexive (2). This attention to style can be read as a response to the pressure of the flat, standardized discourse of information that surrounds the narrator (Ramos 110). If language has been instrumentalized in the modern world, the narrator's discourse will fight the linear pull, the ostensible transparency of the language of information, by creating a vertical axis of signification whereby a word alludes to another text, or comments on itself. This slows the "consumability" of the text, since the words are now important for their own texture and particularity. Metaphors beautify even the most sterile aspects of modernity, like Don José's numbers, compared to grains of sand by the sea (Ramos 114). Play with words or styles is rampant. Consider the narrator's introduction of a man who will turn out to be a good-for-nothing alcoholic as "un rico mercader americano" ("a rich American merchant"). He explains:

Entiéndase bien que lo de rico se le aplica por ser tal su apellido (se llamaba Modesto Rico), y lo de americano por tener un establecimiento, no en las Américas que están de la otra banda del mar, sino en aquellas menos pingües y lejanas que se extienden por la Rivera llamada de Curtidores... (1018)

Please understand that I've applied the word "rich" to him because it was his last name (he was called Modesto Rico), and the word *American* because he had his store, not in the Americas across the seas, but on those less prestigious and faraway shores that are found along the bank of the river called the Tanneries.

Chapter 12 begins without warning, with a quotation from Genesis, and the narrator launches with gusto into the style of the preacher: "Dear brothers and sisters . . ." (1053). Later, we reach a chapter called "Flamenca cytherea" (Gypsy Venus), and the narrator stops the presses to reflect on such a title:

La unión nefanda de estos dos vocablos, bárbaro el uno, helénico el otro, merece la execración universal; pero no importa. Adelante. (1112)

The abominable union of these two words, one barbaric, the other Hellenic, deserves universal execration; but it doesn't matter. Onward.

The narrator thus forces his reader to reflect not only on his choice of particular words, but on their origins as well. Language asserts its own intrinsic value.

Most important, however, is the narrator's more extended experimentation with genre—his writing of one chapter as a picaresque novella, another as Genesis 1, still another with elements of the Golden Age honor play, and one which consists of a reworking of Don Quijote's letter of advice to Sancho when the latter becomes governor of the island Barataria (pt. 2, chs. 42, 43). We are now in a position to offer some reasons for this constant experimentation. First, it should be noted that the genres rewritten in part 1 of the novel are exclusively old-world genres, mainly those of the Golden Age.[18] The narrator is trying to specify his lineage, the literary parents whose heir he wishes to be. One could almost read these overt allusions as a call to the parent for recognition through similarity, much like Isidora's appeal to the *marquesa* in the palace: "I am the living portrait of my mother" (1075). The narrator, to establish the legitimacy of his claim, clothes himself in Golden Age genres throughout part 1, just as Isidora carefully dresses herself before entering the palace. The signifier, for both, is the key to success.

Aside from proving himself to those cultural "fathers," the narrator is also trying to give himself a role in the modern society which has disinherited him. He needs a means to exist; he needs to prove his value in a world judged by standards of utility (Ramos 205ff.). The use of earlier genres is a way of specifying the tradition he represents, and of proving that the kind of knowledge which those literary prisms can provide about society is much more profound than the "organic" knowledge of dry statistics and forms. Thus, in two cases, he juxtaposes narration in a traditional genre with the description of "organic" administrators. In chapter 6, the picaresque mode provides a moving portrait of the plight of the poor and the living conditions which lead them to crime. At the close of the chapter, the commissioner of Beneficence is introduced and satirized mercilessly as he bumbles about, organizing commissions which never produce anything. Chapter 12 is the biblical story of creation—of the useless, "organic" bureaucracy run by the Pez family. The narrator's use of these strong authorities, then, asserts his capacity to explain modern

18. The reworking of Isidora's serial novels of poor women who end up living in palaces occurs throughout the novel, but it is done subtly; again, the novel does not wish to betray its kinship with mass culture. It is only mentioned openly in terms of parody, the narrator's story defining itself as the *antithesis* of Isidora's novels. The actual areas of overlap between the two will be discussed later.

life and identify its problems. They also indicate that he can narrate modernity from a distance, through the filter provided by the genres of another age. He has a bird's-eye view which gives him authority; he appears to narrate not from within the contaminated modern reality but from another place entirely (Ramos 192ff., 209).

Finally, the constant change of narrative voice makes the narrator hard to pin down. If he is a fugitive from the modern disciplinary structures that seek to create uniformity, the unexpected changes of register and literary model may function as changes of disguise would for a criminal seeking to avoid prison. In the narrator's case, the prison would be the drudgery of churning out a certain number of words a day in a never-ending serial novel.

## Beethoven

Si la ciudad, profundamente antiorgánica, descalabra con su ciencia y con sus máquinas las antiguas estructuras, ¿qué lenguaje podría dominarla, representarla, mediante un cuadro capaz aún de articular la totalidad?

If the city, profoundly antiorganic, dismantles the old structures with its science and machines, what language could dominate the city, represent it in a picture still capable of expressing its totality?
—Julio Ramos, *Desencuentros de la modernidad en América Latina*

Isidora's utopia is the palace, her "patria perdida" (1123). There, she imagines, lies a wholeness, a completeness which includes motherhood, friends, travel, and other things lacking in her alienated modern existence (1006). On the meta-artistic level, in her status as art object, the palace would shelter her from contamination by the market.

Since the narrator presents the palace to us in chapter 9 as a building of nothing more than ordinary appearance which houses no extraordinary art treasures and is permeated by sadness, death, and the heritage of fanatical religion, it would be easy to conclude that the narrator does not share his protagonist's stake in the palace or her identification of it with utopia.[19] But this would be too hasty a clo-

19. Martha Krow-Lucal believes that the thrust of the Beethoven chapter is to parody the *marquesa*'s worldview. In her daughter's room, accompanied by beauti-

sure on a space which is, in fact, as crucial for the narrator-critic of modernity as it is for his protagonist. For it is in the palace that he will find confirmed his own dream—that art can solve the problems of fragmentation and uniformity rampant in the modern world and reconnect it with its past. The characteristics of the palace itself, bleak though they may appear, are actually essential to realizing this role for art. The narrator, in his panoramic overview of Madrid, has been seeking a space from which to speak without being contaminated by the market. But the novelistic spaces are permeated with the spectacle of capital—including the church. The museum is not satisfactory either, for the crowd may enter it at will, and it is too close to the centers of commerce. In fact, the narrator presents Isidora's impression of the museum *by comparison with* her reaction to the shopwindows—the museum is already tainted by the juxtaposition.[20] The palace, however, is a space on a separate plane from the rest of Madrid. No one can enter its gigantic door, and it refuses to become exchange-value, to signify to the outside world ("The house was mute" [1073]). Time has stopped within the palace; nothing is either sold or bought, so that the palace exists outside the circuit of consumption. Its very ordinariness is functional for the narrator, for the palace lacks all the glitter and ostentation associated with consumerism. Its austere, silent separateness provides a refuge from the fragmenting forces at work in the city. Finally, the mediocrity of most of the art works on its walls is a functional part of the narrator's family romance. If much of the old art is of poor quality, there is room for a new art which inherits and carries on the best of what is old.

And in the palace, we are presented with what cannot be found anywhere else in the novel—original art works which capture the essence of their real models. The first is the portrait of Virginia, the wayward daughter of the *marquesa*:

---

ful music which she is incapable of understanding, her melodramatic exclamations smack of the cheap neoromanticism to which the aristocracy still clings. But Krow-Lucal never explains why the description of Beethoven's music is so detailed and so exquisitely written.

20. Furthermore, as Eugenio Donato demonstrates in "The Museum's Furnace," the museum is the positivist's attempt at reaching totality by the presentation of an accumulation of ordered fragments, and it necessarily fails to reach its goal. For a discussion of the museum's links with the Spanish realist novel, see Gold, "A Tomb with a View" and "Show and Tell."

¡Era tan parecida; era la pintura, como de Madrazo, tan fina, tan conforme con la distinción, elegancia y gracia del original! (1045)

It was so like her! The painting, like those of Madrazo, was so fine, so faithful to the distinction, elegance and grace of the original!

The portrait captures the character of Virginia, the depth of her emotion, only partially disguised by a jocose expression. The *marquesa* cannot stop looking at it, and reacts emotionally with compassion for her daughter's suffering—precisely what she had lacked during her daughter's lifetime. But it is in music that the deceased Virginia will have her emotions expressed in all their complexity and will be given a celestial promise of pardon and peace (1046). And it is also in a description of the music of Beethoven that the narrator will express his desired solution to the problems of the modern world and to the crisis of art.[21]

My reading of the narrator's treatment of Beethoven picks out an earnestness and a longing in his discourse. I wish to minimize neither the irony which pervades the discourse of *La desheredada* nor the cynicism which prevents the narrator from wholeheartedly setting up the past of the palace as a viable alternative to the present fakery and confusion. But critics have until now glorified Galdosian irony in a way that assumes a narrator who has little at stake in the demise of old illusions or in the downfall of his protagonist. I think we can understand the narrator's irony and playfulness better if we see it—much like the jocose expression on Virginia's face in the portrait—as a way to fend off his sadness at the political and cultural state of the country and his uncertainty about the fate of art now that palaces no longer provide protection. Thus even as he condemns the *marquesa* and the old world she represents, the narrator recognizes that the end of that world may have negative consequences for art. The presence of the lengthy description of the sonata in this chapter cannot be satisfactorily explained with reference to irony. For me, it represents the formulation of a narratorial ideal of art which cannot be realized outside the palace; it is an ideal which dies hard, and the dominant tone of the chapter is one of loss.[22]

21. Vernon Chamberlin has studied both Galdós's fascination with Beethoven and the symphonic structure of *Fortunata y Jacinta*, in *Galdós and Beethoven*.

22. Morag Shiach very usefully reminds us that nostalgia may be for a state which never actually existed. He notes that cultural critics from the late eighteenth to the

Virginia's son (the *marquesa*'s grandson) is a precocious virtuoso pianist. He is the only character in the text who can bring true art to life, because of his nobility and his separation from the world, ensconced as he is in the palace.[23] These characteristics are the ones the narrator feels he needs to have in order to produce great art under current conditions; the grandson is thus a figure of the narrator's desired role. And several pages of this chapter, written with exquisite care, evoke the Beethoven sonata which the grandson plays while the *marquesa* enters her daughter's room/tomb for the first time since Virginia's death nine years before. Certain passages of the sonata description are crucial for the understanding of the narrator's artistic utopia:

Una sola idea, tan sencilla como desgarradora, aparecía entre el vértigo de mil ideas secundarias, y se perdía luego en la más caprichosa variedad de diseños que puede concebir la fantasía, para reaparecer al instante transformada. Si en el tono menor estaba aquella idea vestida de tinieblas, ahora en el mayor se presentaba bañada en luz resplandeciente . . .

De modulación en modulación, la idea única se iba desfigurando sin dejar de ser la misma, a semejanza de un histrión que cambia de vestido. Su cuerpo subsistía, su aspecto variaba... Sentíase después acosada por bravío tumulto de arpegios, escalas cromáticas e imitaciones, y se la oía descender a pasos de gigante, huir, descoyuntarse y hacerse pedazos... Creyérase que todo iba a concluir; pero un soplo de reacción atravesaba la escala entera del piano; los fragmentos dispersos se juntaban, se reconocían, como se reconocían, como se reconocerán y juntarán los huesos de un mismo esqueleto en el Juicio final, y la idea se presentaba de nuevo triunfante como cosa resucitada y redimida. Sin duda alguna una voz de otro mundo clamaba entre el armonioso bullicio del clave: "Yo fui pasión, duda, lucha, pecado, deshonra, pero fui también arrepentimiento, expiación, redención, luz y Paraíso." (1045)

---

mid-twentieth century "always seem to identify themselves as just a little too late: too late to find truly authentic texts, too late to escape compromise and fragmentation." He suggests that recent history consistently becomes saturated with intense longings and projections—even among television critics of the 1980s who idealize the television of the 1950s as "somehow nearer to the essence of television [than] the trivia and gloss of television in the eighties" (Shiach 12).

23. The narrator here links the creation of art to the protection from the market offered by the palace. Carmen Martín Gaite's novel offers a very different view of what conditions give rise to good art. For a comparison of the aesthetic theories offered by the two texts, see "Preserving a Precious Past" in ch. 5, below.

A single theme, as simple as it was heartrending, would appear amidst the whirlwind of a thousand secondary themes, and then be lost in the most capricious variety of patterns that fantasy could conceive, only to reappear, transformed, in the next moment. If in the minor key that theme was clothed in shadows, now in the major key it appeared bathed in shining light . . .

From modulation to modulation, this single theme lost its shape, without ever ceasing to be what it was, the way the same actor changes costume. Its substance remained, but its appearance varied. Then it saw itself assaulted by a tumultuous onslaught of arpeggios, chromatic scales, and repetitions, and it was heard descending by giant steps, fleeing, being torn apart, and falling to pieces. It looked as if everything had come to an end. But then a shudder passed through the whole keyboard. Splintered fragments came together in mutual recognition, just as the bones of a single skeleton recognized each other, and will recognize each other and become joined on the final Day of Judgment. And the theme reappeared triumphant, as something resurrected and redeemed. Amidst the harmonious uproar of the tonic key one heard, without a doubt, a voice from another world crying: "I was once passion, doubt, struggle, sin, and dishonor, but I was also repentance, expiation, redemption, and the light of Paradise."

The passage expresses clearly the narrator's hope for art's role in the world. It maintains that among all the chaotic variety of phenomena that the modern world contains, there is a common essence or "idea"—the musical theme. Although the essence threatens to disappear among the "thousand secondary themes" and the "capricious variety of patterns," it does not in fact get lost. Below the changes of clothes, the body remains the same ("Its substance remained, but its appearance varied"). Thus the fear that appearances (signifiers) have done away with the underlying essence (the signified) is allayed; amidst all the multiplicity, the unique survives.

Then the ultimate threat of modernity appears—fragmentation. The musical idea, like that body under the clothing, is torn apart and smashed to pieces ("descoyuntarse y hacerse pedazos")—the narrator's fear is realized. This is the situation in which the narrator has found the world. The old lies in ruins, it has fallen to pieces like the particles of dead flowers and clothes which surround the *marquesa* during this scene. The new is divided into copies among which the unique essence is diluted. All is a shambles. It looks like the end ("Creyérase que todo iba a concluir"). But suddenly the piano reacts, the fragments recognize each other, and the idea is reborn, triumphant and redeemed. The narrator uses verbs of past and future to refer to the possible time of such redemption ("como se reconocían, como se reconocerán"), situating unity and totality both in an invented, utopian past, and in a future achievable precisely through art like Beethoven's.

In the final sentence of the quoted passage, the modern work of art evokes its origins, just as Virginia's illegitimate son unknowingly evokes his mother. Art affirms that it has sinned—and one suspects that the suffering born of the sin gives it the depth necessary for artistic success—but it has also expiated the sin and found redemption. This is the hope of the critic of modernity. Though his novel may be a hybrid of high art and tainted, mass cultural origins, he will earn the right to the status he was initially forced to usurp, as the metaphoric work of integration brings redemption to those who read or receive his art. This is the role of the grandson, who is forced to practice ten hours a day (1044) to expiate his illegitimate origins, but who in return is able to produce true art, an art which seems in the chapter to have brought redemption to his mother. The duality of sin and expiation, then, is essential to art as represented here. Those who have sinned and repented have a privileged view which enables them to envision the redeeming essence under the apparently degraded appearances.

Redemption requires the reconciliation of the point of view of the sinner with that of her judge. Virginia's passion must be recognized in all its profundity, which the marquesa had failed to do. But the marquesa's viewpoint is crucial too. If the cause of the chaos of modernity is represented in this novel as the destruction of family and lineage through sexual promiscuity, then Virginia's sin takes on monumental proportions. It is responsible for nothing less than the crisis of modernity, the death of the old world (now mummified in the palace) and the loss of identity of the modern subject. The old world, as a result of the sins of its subjects, is destroyed through a second flood—this time a flood of machine-produced goods and faked identities rather than a deluge of water. This is why art's role is so crucial. It must expiate the sin, effect reconciliation, and bring the old world back to life, linking it to the new one and restoring meaning to modern existence.

How does art bring about redemption? It reunites the appearance and the essence, the new world and the old, which the spectacle had torn asunder. It can always detect the presence of the signified, and proclaims that it exists intact despite the changing appearances. Where the discourses of rationalization can do no more than attest to fragmentation through statistics, and are unable to repair, redeem, or reintegrate anything over the course of the novel, true art has the metaphoric capacity to integrate the *varied* in the *one* (Martí, quoted in Ramos 191), and thus to provide meaning and redemption:

Las sabias formas laberínticas del canon sucedieron a la sencillez soberana, de donde resultó que la hermosa idea se multiplicaba, y que de tantos ejemplares de una misma cosa formábase un bello trenzado de peregrino efecto por hablar mucho al sentimiento y un poco al raciocinio. (1046)

The knowing, labyrinthine forms of the main theme took the place of that sovereign simplicity, so that the lovely theme was multiplied, and from so many copies of the same thing was formed a beautiful weave, having a rare and wonderful effect because it appealed more to feeling than it did to reason.

The one and the many here are not in conflict—together they produce beauty. And they unite emotion and reason. Emotion has been obscured in mass-reproduced art (as it is represented in this novel), since copies of classic art are used only as status symbols, for calculated effect. Art reintroduces true emotion, uniting it with a kind of reason not degraded by calculation. In terms we would use today, art integrates human faculties through its appeal both to the conscious mind ("raciocinio") and to the unconscious ("sentimiento"). In this way, it provides an antidote to the alienation of the modern subject.

Several aspects of the narrator's own artistic project parallel the effects which art produces in this scene. As Beethoven works the miracle of reuniting fragments, the narrator writes a passage about the music dense in metaphors, bringing together diverse phenomena which together illuminate the transcendent similarity that exists beneath their varied appearances. To reach true meaning in the modern age, the narrator must privilege metaphoric narration over a more literal relationship of word to thing. This is because the literal, "informational" level of language has been so denatured by rationalization that it lacks all credibility and can no longer communicate.

The description of Beethoven's music is in several respects a figure for the novel we are reading. The music book which contains it is described as "grand," "jumbled," "obscure" (1049)—like the long text of *La desheredada*, a pastiche of discourses which poses formidable challenges to its reader. Like the theme of the music, the narrator's voice changes in tone and register. It puts on different *masks* ("Enmascarándose festivamente" [1046]) and endless disguises, like the actor constantly changing his costume. These masks and disguises are, of course, the genres. Paradoxically, the different masks work to preserve the unique essence underlying them; both Beethoven and the older genres provide stability in a world of flux.

A chain of resurrections occurs in the chapter. On the plot level, the *marquesa* reopens her house, symbolically, for *three* days. And she enters her dead daughter's room, comparing this act to opening a tomb (1043). Once the tomb is open, the daughter (who died "like a poor martyr" [1046]) is brought to life by the portrait and by Beethoven. When she returns to rest, it is with the certainty of salvation given in the music (1046). On the level of discourse, we watch Beethoven resurrect the atomized world and its meaning by reuniting the scattered fragments. Finally, on the meta-artistic level, the narrator's carefully wrought description recreates Beethoven's music and makes its redemptive power available to a public *outside* the palace. This is the narrator's most important claim for the utility of his own art—it alone can bring authentic art to life, take it out of its deep freeze in the palace, and permit it to act in the world again.[24] And this is, in fact, what the narrator does by writing the story of Isidora—again, on several levels. On the level of plot, by insisting on Isidora's special distinction, he is asserting that Isidora incarnates in the modern world something precious, something essentially similar to what the nobly born Virginia embodied in the old world, and that this is true regardless of Isidora's lack of title. In Isidora's allegorical function as work of art, she brings to life the old world of classic art, performing the miracle of uniting art with life and thus becoming "the living portrait of [her] mother"—a *live* art work which, unlike the painted portrait of Virginia, can leave the palace.

---

24. I do not mean to suggest that the public of 1880 would have perceived Beethoven's music as "old" or "antiquated." But it seems important that the palace refuses to acknowledge any developments after the Romantic period. And we see no examples in the text of what the narrator would consider "authentic art" that were produced after Beethoven's death in 1827. The narrator is keeping later "high culture" outside the frame of his text to strengthen his critique of the current, unevenly modern situation of Spain.

Finally, on the level of narration, the Golden Age genres used to narrate this modern story function in a similar fashion: "high" art is brought to life, and into action, in a modern setting. The old genres, then, act as connective tissue between the old and new worlds, running counter to the tendency of modernity to bulldoze the old and forget it was ever there.

Literature in the modern world has taken on functions, salient in this scene, which were once carried out by the Church—to represent origins, sin, and redemption; and to serve as a refuge from the corruption of the market (Ramos 206ff.). The church service itself, however, has by now been reduced to the repetition of empty formulas.[25]

The plot through chapter 9, then, holds out hope for modern society. The theme of redemption is strong, as the possible parents of Isidora are redeemed in death and reconciled with God, the *ur*-parent. Rufete dies kissing the hand of a priest (996); Virginia died, according to her mother, "reconciled with God, reciting prayers and kissing the holy image of our Redeemer" (1046). The narrator as critic of modernity, then, claims that the fragmentation associated with modernity is caused by the forgetting of origins/parents. Isidora's possible progenitors had forgotten God until the moment of their deaths; other parental figures have also been forgotten.[26] The narrator waxes nostalgic for important public figures, such as General Prim, who led the September Revolution, and even Isabel II, who represented a genuine kind of royalty no longer in existence. These parental figures had incarnated values other than materialism, efficiency, or self-interest. Finally, in this narrator's version, culture is in crisis because society has forgotten the artistic progenitors who created real, original art, as opposed to the sterile copies of the modern world. This forgetting of parents has caused the split between old world and new. But just as

25. "Y con . . . prisa [Isidora] bosquejaba la señal de la cruz sobre la frente, cara y pechos, y . . . atropelladamente mascullaba un padrenuestro" ("Distractedly, [Isidora] made the gesture of crossing herself and hastily mumbled the words of the Lord's Prayer") (1031).

26. Catherine Jaffe points out that this forgetting, or severing of parent-child ties, works both ways. Rufete has denied his relationship to his daughter and has prevented his wife from being a true mother to her either; the *marquesa* does not tell her grandson that the ring she gives him was really left to him by his dead mother, thus preventing him from remembering her as she wanted. Finally, Relimpio, a "padrino" (godfather) to Isidora, fails to advise her or provide for her ("Mothers and Orphans" 32, 35).

Rufete and Virginia do finally remember their origins, so the narrator will carry on the work of his literary ancestors and thereby reunite the two worlds. Paradoxically, resurrecting artistic ancestors is what will enable modernity to create something original and new (like the novel we are reading). For there is something dead and ghostly about modernity as represented in *La desheredada*—it can make more and more reproduced copies of already-existing works but can create no culture of its own. The narrator's text, by contrast, is a new and living creation. In sum, the narrator, by showing the miracles Beethoven can perform, has created a function for his own marginality in modern society. In order to redeem modern life, he must remain as distanced from it as possible, looking at it through the prism of his cultural heritage.

This brings us to the question posed by Ramos in the epigraph to this section. What is the language that can express such redemptive totality? The narrator has chosen music as its best medium, and we may well ask what makes music privileged among the arts. Music, at the time of *La desheredada*, was different from painting and words in that it could not be mechanically reproduced. Edison had invented the phonograph in 1877, a scant four years before the publication of *La desheredada*, and it would take decades before it became widely used. Beethoven's music, in this text, can only be performed (and its message can only be conveyed in words) by one who possesses a special nobility, like Virginia's son—the proof is that the bourgeois Miquis, for all his quick wit and knowledge, can only butcher the piece when he gets into the palace on false pretenses one chapter later.

### The Demise of the Dream of Purity:
### Art and the Market

The dream of the palace will never come true for Isidora. The *marquesa* refuses to admit her, arguing that her resemblance to the wayward Virginia is purely coincidental. But Isidora is a work of art, like the novel we are reading. Her failure to be recognized as belonging in the palace thus entails the failure of the novel to achieve "high" literary status and protection from market forces. It is, in other words, the demise of the narrator's family romance. Isidora's failure is specifically shown as a literary one, as she speaks in the language of the seventeenth-century honor play ("soy quien soy" [1074]), and the *marquesa* calls her performance "well-rehearsed farces, or a chapter in a novel." Isidora, and the narrator's text by implication, has been rejected because of her tainted birth, her lowly, mass cultural origins.[27]

The palace shuts itself off in muteness, refusing to establish a connection to the surrounding world, to the present. The grandson, practicing the piano ten hours a day and never leaving the palace, is unlikely to produce descendants. The sterile mummification of the palace and its culture are seen within the frame of *La desheredada* as the death of art, since true culture has not been passed on to any member of the bourgeoisie. The bourgeois world portrayed in the novel, as shown in the previous section, is one of "organic intellectuals" who consume culture only as a status symbol, and who are incapable of *producing* any authentic culture of their own. Just as Isidora (the art object) must now find a way to exist in that world without losing her beauty and distinction, so the novelist is now abruptly deprived of patronage and is expelled, without protection, into the market. He, too, is disinherited.[28] The symptom of art's new orphaned status is the lack of the noble benefactor to whom Golden Age authors dedicated their texts. Our narrator's uncertainty is palpable: "it would be appropriate to dedicate these pages—to whom?"

Given the pressures of the commercialized world which surround it, this unprotected art must withdraw as much as possible from public life in order not to be contaminated. This art insists on beauty, style, refinement, uniqueness—all that differentiates it from the standardized products of the market. But such separateness is highly problematic, and to a large extent, *La desheredada* is nothing other than a reflection on the dilemmas it poses. Many episodes of the novel contain explicit discussion of the role of art in society. Other plot events can be read as symbolic enactments of cultural theories. And Isidora herself is so consistently likened to a beautiful art object in the second part of the novel that her trajectory, from her expulsion

27. Isidora is called an "impostor" during the scene, much as the serial novel appears as an impostor in the world of literature.

28. I use the pronoun *he* for the disinherited novelist because I hope to establish in this book that this apocalyptic view of modernity and mass culture is very much a male myth.

from the palace to her stay in jail, can be read as a kind of cultural allegory of the fate of high art in the world of the market.

The consideration of the function of art in *La desheredada* anticipates many of the arguments of Herbert Marcuse in his 1937 essay "On the Affirmative Character of Culture."[29] For Marcuse, culture has come in bourgeois practice to constitute a mental and spiritual world superior to, and segregated from, the rest of civilization (94–95). It is the sphere that addresses human longings that cannot be satisfied in the rationalized world—longings for justice, beauty, community, and the like. In short, culture is in charge of human claims to happiness. Art exists, then, to mitigate the contradiction between an insufferable existence and the need for happiness to make such an existence bearable (118–19). Artistic beauty provides a false resolution of the contradiction, giving the illusion of providing present happiness. Those who consume it find their longings momentarily satisfied and want to repeat the experience (119). Thus, in a positivistic world where the existing system is seen as the last word, people are taught that their dreams can be realized only internally, through injections of culture into a soul divorced from everyday life. The real world is considered unredeemable, and thereby exonerated, free of any pressure for change. In this way, "affirmative culture" reinforces a bad social order.

The narrator of *La desheredada* is ambivalent about what art's position should be. On the one hand, he would like to see true art isolated from the madding crowd, protected in the palace. On the other, he recognizes the limitations and the irresponsibility of an art that does not act in the world. The separateness of art from public life is shown as reprehensible in *La desheredada* in a variety of ways. Art—in the person of Isidora—appears disoriented, lacking social function, after it is disinherited by the aristocracy:

Toda aquella tarde [Isidora] estuvo pensando en la clase de ocupación que más le convendría; pero sus grandes cavilaciones no llevaron luz ninguna a la confusión y perplejidad que en su mente reinaba. (1095)

That whole afternoon, [Isidora] thought about what kind of occupation would best suit her; but her grand reflections didn't shed any light on the confusion and perplexity reigning in her mind.

29. See *Negations* 88–133.

Part of the problem of the status of "high" art in general, and literature in particular, may be the lack of a public sufficiently educated to
consume it. While the highbrow readership is not nonexistent, as *La
desheredada* implies, it is nevertheless the case that in 1888–89 only
sixteen thousand students attended university, of a population of
over seventeen million.[30] An art that cultivates a polished style and
literary allusions seems condemned to irrelevance—a fact bitterly
underscored for Galdós when *La desheredada* itself was received
with silence from the critics. Given the obtuseness of most of Spain's
literary critics of the period, it seems possible that the complexity of
this work left them uncomprehending.[31]

The one important function which art seems able to fulfill is that
of the pleasurable escape which makes reality bearable. The quintessential example of this is the medical student Miquis's plan to learn
about the most varied and unpleasant kinds of illnesses, become an
expert, and earn enough money for a (daily!) subscription to the op-
era, "para que su espíritu, cansado del excesivo roce con lo humano,
se restaurase en las frescas auras de un arte divino" ("so that his
spirit, worn down by excessive contact with humanity, would be
restored by the refreshing aura of a divine art") (1012). The music of
Beethoven played by the *marquesa*'s grandson also seems to call at
times for "pleasure, dancing, drink, and the ability to forget one's
troubles" (1046); the name of the grandson's huge dog, Saúl, seems
deliberately chosen to underscore the consolatory function of art in
the funereal interior of the palace.[32] But such examples present several problems in the context of *La desheredada*. One is that the consolatory, compensatory function of art proves identical to that of
mass culture—momentary escape and fortification so that one may
return to work ("el martirio") refreshed. Art's very separateness from
the rationalized world ends up reinforcing the system it sought to
escape, as Marcuse argues. And the more remote it becomes in form

30. Botrel, "L'Aptitude à communiquer: Alphabétisation et Scholarisation en Espagne de 1860 à 1920."
31. Leopoldo Alas, "Clarín," was a bright light in the critical gloom, denouncing
other critics for their silence and praising *La desheredada* for its innovations (Alas,
*Galdós* 104ff.).
32. The biblical King Saul was afflicted with terror when the spirit of the Lord
departed from him; David played the harp for him, and Saul found relief (1 Sam. 16:14–
23).

and style, the more art's function becomes similar to that of the *plots* of the serial novels. The countesses, jewels, and palaces found in stock serial plots appeal to the public with their exoticism. Yet "highbrow," modernist literature also uses exoticism to dazzle its readers. This may be an exoticism of form (for example, the return to the medieval *alejandrino* verse form), or an overlay of classical allusions which transport the reader to far-off lands and ages. It seems that both "highbrow" and "lowbrow" readers like the exotic escape, but the "highbrow" reader might not like to acknowledge his similarity to the consumer of serial fiction.

A second problem for this separate, autonomous art is that, as an indispensable outlet providing escape from a repressive system, it becomes analogous in function to prostitution, legal at this time. Nowhere is this identity so apparent as in Isidora's relationship with Botín. This authoritarian lover buys her the most beautiful and refined clothing but forbids her to wear it for anyone else. He will be refreshed by her as art object and as sexual object, but he insists on keeping her shut up in her apartment because of his jealousy and fear of scandal. He orders her to attend mass regularly, because "it's best not to give the working class ['el pueblo'] a bad example" (1110). Pleasures such as art and sex, then, only remain so as long as they are exclusive, unavailable to the commoner, and as long as they are clearly separated from everyday life, which continues to be based on discipline. By complying with this role, art strengthens the status quo.

This escapist function of art, embodied in Isidora, has other negative consequences. Art becomes irresponsible, for in order to pursue beauty, it must turn its back on the ugliness of the problems of the world. We are repeatedly told of Isidora's indifference to, and ignorance of, politics. She is initially indifferent to the coming of the Republic, overshadowed for her by her appointment with the *marquesa*. While Don José waxes sentimental at the site of the assassination of General Prim (an event considered by the narrator to be the beginning of Spain's dishonor), Isidora ignores the bullet holes. Later, she is impatient when Joaquín describes the political corruption of her hated lover, Botín. But, as her down-to-earth, plebeian aunt reminds her at the beginning of the text, to disown the ugliness and the lowborn aspects of life will condemn her to living a life of lies (56). In fact, art's main preoccupation as an autonomous object is nothing other than *itself*. This is the allegorical significance of Isidora's passion for looking at herself in the mirror, a process often punctuated by narratorial references to art:

Contemplóse en el gran espejo, embelesada de su hermosura... Allí, en el campo misterioso del cristal azogado, el raso, los encajes, los ojos, formaban un conjunto en que había algo de las inmensidades movibles del mar alumbradas por el astro de la noche. Isidora encontraba mundos de poesía en aquella reproducción de sí misma. (1134)

She gazed at herself in the great mirror, enchanted by her own beauty. Deep within the mystery of the silvered glass, the silks, the lacework, and her eyes formed a whole which whispered something of the shimmering immensities of the sea lighted by the starry night. Isidora found a realm of poetry in that reproduction of herself.[33]

This ignorance of everything other than itself makes art vulnerable to deception, as when Isidora sees only the beauty of the parade on the Castellana and remains unaware both of how falsely contrived that beauty is *and* of the unjust social structure that has created it. To ignore the problems of the world seems to constitute an affirmation that nothing is wrong. Ironically, an autonomous art ends up duplicating the function of the press under Restoration censorship, which was strict until 1883 (Valls 192): by not addressing real political and social issues, it seems to affirm that they do not exist.

Such considerations reveal the dialectic of an autonomous art. On the one hand, the creation of a separate, imaginary world constitutes a protest against a reality which offers no possibility for a better life.[34] Its function is particularly radical as it operates in Isidora, who is determined to use the imaginary world to transform actual reality.

33. Catherine Jaffe asserts that Isidora uses the mirror to become something she isn't, to the point of losing a sense both of her own identity and of the sordid, surrounding reality which ultimately will undermine the beauty of her image in the mirror ("El motivo del espejo"). I would add the allegorical reading that art's obsession with its own beauty will necessarily entail the forgetting of its real role in the world and a vulnerability to the world's ugly aspects.

34. As Rubén Darío says in the "Palabras liminares" which preface *Prosas profanas:* "veréis en mis versos princesas, reyes, cosas imperiales, visiones de países lejanos o imposibles: ¡qué queréis!, yo detesto la vida y el tiempo en que me tocó nacer" ("In my poetry, you'll find princesses, kings, imperial things, visions of faraway lands or invented ones. What would you expect? I loathe the times and the age into which I had the misfortune to be born") (36).

Yet the minute that such an imaginary world becomes a static refuge rather than a program for change, art has abdicated its responsibility toward public life and begins to condone injustice. It then tends to be seen by various sectors of the public as irrelevant at best, guilty at worst.

The irresponsibility that taints a separate, autonomous art is accompanied by the charge of inauthenticity or hypocrisy when we begin to question how separate art can really be from the market. For in fact, an art not subsidized by patrons must exist in the market like any other commodity, despite its avowed disinterest in the material sphere (Habermas 29). Thus, when Isidora suggests that she and Joaquín should escape and live hidden in a cottage separate from society, a disillusioned Joaquín answers that only birds, who know nothing of the minting of money, can make such nests. Isidora's belief in such solutions, he concludes, comes from novelists, who are "falsifiers of life" (1141). As an ordinary commodity, art cannot make ends meet in Spain's limited market, as Joaquín declares: "Writers, artists, industrialists, and even the shopkeepers are all dying of starvation" (1109). And an art committed to seeking beauty requires substantial material support, for it is irresistibly drawn to what is fine and exceptional, and it consumes more than it produces. Isidora cannot resist buying roses, although she has a limited stipend from her uncle; later she reflects, "if I deny myself everything I suffer too much, and if I don't I'm dishonored" (1143–44). Joaquín, another lover of finery who lacks practical sense, declares that poverty makes impossible both art and dignity (1141).[35] This love of refinement and lack of common sense makes art vulnerable to being co-opted by "protectors" who are entirely devoid of the noble ideals art claims to incarnate. In order to remain free and untainted by the sphere of rationalization, Isidora refuses to work; but in fact she is forced to accept the

35. Several characteristics of Joaquín make him analogous to the artist who wants to live in a higher sphere. As he describes himself, he lives in an ideal world, is unable to comprehend the dictates of positivism, aspires constantly to the infinite; his immoral conduct is the result of his irrepressible fantasy life, which precludes action in the practical world of rationalization (1111). This, combined with his handsome appearance, make him similar enough to the work of high art that, when we judge him guilty for his parasitism and lack of useful productivity, we may be uncomfortably close to making a similar judgment on art. Joaquín, like art, believes his profligacy is innocent: "I haven't taken anything from anybody" (1111).

protection (and restrictions) of those who are powerful in the commercial sphere in order to maintain her separateness. Art, in the person of Isidora, submits to the patronage of unscrupulous government officials (Botín, whose name means "booty"), the owner of a printing press who denounces beauty as superfluous (Bou), and petty administrators who use beauty to gain status (Melchor). Art, to maintain its standards of beauty, must sell itself to the highest bidder, and thereby abandons its claims to moral superiority and to the transcendence of material wants.[36]

Given the flexibility of the capitalistic system, it is difficult for art to remain separate from the rationalized sphere, even with the protection it enjoys. Because of its stylistic refinement and the exclusionary nature of its cultural allusions (understood by only the few), art objects become attractive to the bourgeoisie as luxury items that will validate their owners (Valis) by producing a veneer of culture to complement their wealth.[37] The beauty of art is thus reduced to exchange-value, becoming a mere signifier of refinement. Art ob-

---

36. Interestingly, these claims of moral superiority and disinterest in material gain are taken up by the developing working-class press in its accusation that the bourgeois "grand press" has sold out; Josep-Francesc Valls quotes *El Socialista:* "[O]ur 'industry' isn't like any other. It's a *disinterested business not aimed at productivity.* To us, the propagation of ideas is everything and the personal profits nil. If the working-class press stopped honoring its doctrines and instead devoted itself to the exploitation of sensational scandals, the adulation of the powerful, and commercial advertising, it would become part of that journalistic industry which makes the bourgeois press an *indecent courtesan who sells her favors* to the crooked politician, the speculator, and the lucky gambler" (Valls 196, n. 33, quoting V. Bozal; trans. and italics mine).

37. The connection between art and luxury is explored by Máximo Manso, the protagonist of Galdós's next novel: "El lujo es lo que antes se llamaba el demonio, la serpiente, el ángel caído, porque el lujo fue también querubín, fue *arte, generosidad, realeza* y ahora es un maleficio mesocrático, al alcance de la burguesía, pues con la industria y las máquinas se han puesto en condiciones perfectas para corromper a todo el género humano, sin distinción de clases." ("Luxury is what used to be called the devil, the serpent, the fallen angel, because luxury was also at one time a cherubim; luxury meant *art, generosity, royalty,* and now it has cast a spell on the middle classes, it's available to the bourgeoisie, because industrialization and machines have reached the point where they have corrupted all of Humanity, without regard to class.") (*El amigo Manso,* quoted in Andreu, *Galdós y la literatura popular* 101; italics mine). It seems that luxury was authentic and desirable when it was exclusive, and it was then synonymous with *art;* but the democratization of luxury is a symptom of corruption. Isidora, as art object and luxury item at once, has become *too available.*

jects, requiring income, are vulnerable to this process and, ironically, fall victim to rationalization themselves, as we see on Manuel Pez's bookshelf, "all full of identical, gilt-edged books, which showed in the purity of their red and black leather spines that they had never been read!" (1059). The word *purity*, of course, becomes highly ironic in this context, since the description indicates that the would-be separate, "pure" sphere of high culture has in fact become incorporated into the sphere of rationalization and consumption. A converse movement also takes place: technology becomes aestheticized, mass-producing beautiful objects (Ramos 114–16). The distance that separates a beautiful piece of art from the sphere of everyday consumerism is thereby substantially reduced.

Beautiful art, then, is shown to depend on the backing of the very system it claims to transcend. The art object which hides its connection to industrial capitalism is not, in fact, so different from the *cursi* on the Castellana who pretends to have left behind his plebeian origins. The law of the spectacle, in which the relationships and conditions that produce an image are disguised and made to seem natural, is common to both (Kipnis 19–20). Matei Calinescu has explored the effect of mass production on aesthetics in his discussion of kitsch, which he sees as inseparable from modernity: "[Kitsch] appears at that moment in history when beauty in its various forms is socially distributed like any other commodity subject to the essential market law of supply and demand" (229).

One chapter of *La desheredada* is especially important for a consideration of art's role in an industrialized society. It is the chapter describing Juan Bou's lithography and printing workshop, where Isidora's brother Mariano comes closest to finding steady, palatable employment. The chapter contains explicit reflections on the culpability of bourgeois art, as well as detailed descriptions of the inspirations, means, and materials which produce industrialized art. The chapter is dominated by perhaps the most complex character in the book, Juan Bou. Assuming, as I do, that the narrator creates each character as a way to explore a specific facet of the contradictions which obsess him, it becomes possible to explain both the enormous significance of Bou's ideas in the context of the narrator's dilemma about the role of art, and the contradictory, ambivalent way in which Bou is presented to us.[38]

38. For this assumption about characters, see Robert, *The Old and the New* 18ff.

In many ways, Juan Bou is a caricature. Built like a tank, with a huge beard setting off one rotating eyeball and one paralyzed eyeball, Bou both parrots and misinterprets socialist ideas in a way that makes him apparently easy to dismiss. His egotism makes him think of himself as a great political hero, the supreme representative of the "people," the "Guiding Light of the Working Man" ("Obrero-sol"). Although he constantly advocates the end of private property and the abolition of money, he turns out to be quite glad to receive an unexpected inheritance. But the stacking of the deck against Bou's person and his ideas is but a measure of the formidable challenge they pose to the narrator as proponent of an autonomous art. First, Bou is the only character to earn an honest living through modern industry without depending on government subsidies.[39] (The few other characters in *La desheredada* to earn an honest living work out of the home in the preindustrial way idealized by the narrator.) Secondly, Bou's financial success comes from combining art with industry; he thus stands for everything abhorred by the purist narrator, with whom he also competes for an audience. Finally, Bou challenges the narrator by his ability to mediate between his bourgeois class of origin and the working class. Bou, however inauthentically, feels identified with a specific class, while the narrator, as we shall see, is rejected in various ways by all classes and cannot claim to influence any of them.

Prior to this chapter, art has already become a suspect entity, as far as the bourgeois disciplinary establishment is concerned, because it exceeds standardization and is not limited to verifiable truth. This disciplinary system will eventually arrest Isidora, the incarnation of art, and accuse her of falsification. In the chapter on Bou, art seems caught between the remaining two social classes and condemned by both. Having described the dark, dusty, lugubrious ambience of Bou's print workshop, the narrator comments:

se podría sospechar que el . . . arte había sido encarcelado allí para expiar las culpas que alguna vez, por andar en malas manos, ha podido cometer. (1100)

one might suspect that . . . art had been imprisoned there to expiate the sin that at some time, by getting into the wrong hands, it has committed.

What sins art has to expiate depends on which class is judging it, and in the present context, it could be either the upper or the lower. The

39. "He had no source of income other than his work" (1099).

metaphors of imprisonment to expiate sins and of getting into the wrong hands recall the aristocratic Virginia, imprisoned because of her affair with a commoner. The passage immediately preceding the quotation notes that the printing press in Bou's factory had once been used to print clandestine leftist material, "and it retained the appearance of those infamous plots planned under cover of darkness." This is immediately followed by a reference to the "horrible guillotine" which could cut off a human head as easily as it could cut paper for cigarettes (1100). The narrator then refers to the art of printing as the "sovereign instrument of the Divinity." All of this conveys an aristocratic view which fears the consequences of the use of printing by commoners (let alone the proletariat!) and sees art as irrevocably tainted by its contact with the masses.[40] In this view, art has become too lowbrow.

But the main accusations in the chapter are leveled by the proletariat through their mouthpiece, Juan Bou. Bou denounces the poets of the past for having told humanity lies and derailed it from the important issues of life (1103). In the present day, he says, art is simply a distraction for the upper classes, who have the leisure to enjoy it because they live off the labor of the poor:

Ellos no labran la tierra, ellos no cogen una herramienta, ellos no hacen más que pasear, comer bien, ir al teatro y leer libros llenos de bobadas... (1102)

They don't work the land, nor even take up a tool; all they do is stroll about, eat well, go to the theater, and read books stuffed with foolish ideas.

In this view, art has sold out to the rich; it is guilty by virtue of its irrelevance to social issues and by its inaccessibility to the working class. Don José has articulated a similar view in the palace, the space of high culture in the novel: "How can some have so much and others so little!" (1049). The rich and their high art are both guilty of callousness in the face of poverty. Bou goes further, lumping this kind of art together with bourgeois bureaucracy and proposing to destroy all papers: "Papers don't do a thing for humanity." He proposes to

40. To invoke the holiness of the original use of print—the Gutenberg Bible—is to express nostalgia for the "good old days" when high culture was clearly distinguishable from low "pulp." But this ideal past is a myth, for Don Quijote already challenged those who said that the plots of the lowly novel of chivalry were implausible by recalling the presence of giants in the Bible (Cervantes, pt. 2, ch. 1, 50); the distinction between high and low was already problematic in the early seventeenth century.

offer lawyers, judges, and administrators a hoe or a plow to earn their living: "but pushing papers won't get you a meal here, gentlemen . . ." (1101). Bou here advocates a return to use-value and an abolition of exchange-value which coincides in part with the narrator's condemnation of the society of the spectacle. The crucial difference is that for Bou, the sphere of exchange-value includes art, while the narrator believes that art can redeem the fallen, commercialized world by being "above" it.

Bou calls the upper classes "sanguijuelas del país" ("leeches off society") (1101), and this obviously gets under the narrator's skin, for he obsessively returns to the issue of how he and his readers are implicated in this accusation. The pronouns *nosotros* and *vosotros*, almost entirely absent from the rest of the novel because they break the mimetic illusion, are recurrent and prominent in this chapter:

> Nosotros, los que no tenemos las manos llenos de callos, no éramos pueblo; vosotros, los propietarios, los abogados, los comerciantes, tampoco erais pueblo. (1098)
>
> Su señora (de Bou) . . . era una sanguijuela del país, como vosotros, los que esto leéis. (1098)
>
> . . . en cuanto a todos nosotros, que no tenemos callosidades en las manos . . . (1101)

> Those of us who don't have any callouses on our hands—well, we're not working class; you, the property owners, the lawyers, the merchants, you're not working-class people either.
>
> [Bou's] wife leeched off society, just like you who are reading this.
>
> . . . as for all of us, who have no callouses on our hands . . .

*Nosotros*, while it refers to the bourgeoisie, obviously includes the artist, who also lacks the calloused hands needed for inclusion in the "people." And *vosotros*, "you who are reading this," refers to the writer's audience. The narrator here admits that his art is addressed exclusively to a bourgeois audience; Bou has unmasked the fact that art, in its proclaimed indifference to the worldly sphere of politics, has in fact abandoned the lower classes. (We might recall for comparison the age of Shakespeare and Lope de Vega, when the common people attended theatrical performances along with the nobles.) According to the proletarian view, then, the sins that art is expiating by being jailed in the cramped confinement of the printing press are the sins of luxurious irresponsibility which perpetuate social injustice. High art has here been "disinherited" yet again, by the only social class which remained as a potential audience for the future—the working class. The narrator may indeed ask to whom he should dedicate this novel.

We have seen how an art removed from social concerns can be seen as irresponsible, and how that supposedly separate art is actually dependent on the ever-expanding commercial sphere for its support. We now need to explore the effects of technological change on the whole arena of culture. For technology creates new relationships among different kinds of cultural phenomena, and these relationships make the separateness of high art merely a dream, a component of an invented past.

As we see in the chapter on Bou's printing workshop (as well as elsewhere in the novel), the mass culture produced by machine creates a conduit which brings into contact spheres of culture that were formerly separate. The folklore of each portion of Spain, for example, had previously been localized in specific regions, with costumes worn on given holidays and local traditions passed on to those who lived in the area. But Bou has made his money by marketing that kind of rural, community-based culture to an urban bourgeoisie with no knowledge of the land and no characteristic culture of its own (Clark 229–30). In accordance with the new fashion of aestheticizing the many consumer goods that created bourgeois comfort, Bou was the first to print popular figures like *majas* and bullfighters on shelf paper and to sell it on a massive scale (1099). Regional culture, alive and subject to creative modification in its local context, is here reified and sold as a cliché, an exotic object which permits the bourgeoisie to be tourists without leaving their homes.

With the criterion of profit uppermost, Bou acquires a printing press as a mere supplement to his lithographic sales. He prints the ballads and rhymes sold in the streets by blind men on a large scale, so that the blind men and stores can acquire them more cheaply than ever. We may assume that more people will be able to consume this kind of cultural product given the cheapness of its production by machine. In his most mercenary moments, Bou works with the corrupt Melchor on posters for the offices of mining and railway concessions which want to encourage development. On the posters are pictures of nuns leading beggars to an ideal charitable hospice with

Greek columns, conveying, as the narrator says, "the idea that they were working there to alleviate the lot of the needy" (1116). The public, thus sentimentally engaged, will buy lottery tickets to finance a development which has nothing to do with sheltering the poor. Here, the representation of the poor through a superficially "classical" art makes them mere instruments for the enrichment of a few developers; their misery has been exploited to garner funds for the rich. Art, far from constituting an end in itself or a separate sphere, is but a means to a commercial end. Other aspects of the new relations between the lower class and culture are more threatening to the narrator. Previously, the culture of the common people was an oral culture, exemplified in the figure of Isidora's aunt, Encarnación Guillén. She is a picturesque character, offering popular remedies for ailments, peppering her speech with religious metaphors and proverbs, and trying to keep the family together rather than bettering herself. But the illiterate Encarnación is aging, and her relationship to culture has been displaced by that of the proletariat, which is linked to the printing press. The press was a key instrument of the bourgeoisie in its struggle for power, and the working class is now learning to make use of it, attaining what the narrator calls a "literary fever" (1099) as it makes its demands in clandestinely circulated newspapers. The narrator is more comfortable with the poor as a colorfully illiterate mass than as a demanding proletariat beginning to exploit the channels of culture formerly confined to the upper classes.

High art is also implicated in the new relationships between class and culture. We may consider the Aransis palace to be the space of high culture in the novel, a cultural space which the bourgeoisie and the working class, galvanized by their faith in total equality, are determined to occupy. After the Beethoven chapter has established the traditional link between high culture (the palace) and an elite aristocracy, two later scenes chronicle the assault on high culture from below. The first is the tour of the palace which Miquis arranges for Isidora through his relative, the doorman. Once inside, Miquis and Don José condemn the elaborate splendor of the palace, given the number of homeless people. A portrait of Sister Teodora de Aransis, mother superior of a convent, is evaluated by Miquis and Don José solely in terms of the sexiness of the nun; Don José intimates that he would court her if she came back to life (1049). The reverent distance between art object and spectators is thus abolished. But the main damage to high art is perpetrated by Miquis, who insists on playing the music of Beethoven left open on the piano. Beethoven has made access to his music difficult through "lots of lines, dots, flourishes, accents, and scrawls," indicating that only the "expert musician" should try them. He has also placed numerous flats in the key signature, as the narrator says, "like a scarecrow to keep the laymen away" (1049). But Miquis plays anyway, producing mainly wrong notes, "hoarse sounds," and incomplete phrases, a pathetic caricature, "as if sublime poetry were reduced to puerile doggerel" (1049). With this artistic metaphor, the narrator shows how high culture is denatured and diminished through its appropriation by those (the bourgeoisie) who lack the cultivation to preserve its sublime character.

The second contamination of the palace involves the irreverent abolition of an even greater distance, that between the culture of the aristocracy and the uncultured working class. It occurs when Bou, brother-in-law of the doorman, receives permission to tour the palace with Isidora. Ascending the staircase at the entrance, Bou hums inane popular rhymes, which contrast in the reader's mind with the classical music previously associated with the palace. Inside, unaware of Isidora's connection to the Aransis palace, Bou insults the portraits of knights and nuns, telling them that if they were alive he would make them sweep the streets. He throws himself into chairs to test their comfort, achieved, he says, through the suffering of the poor. He takes valuable art objects in his clumsy hands, caressing the cheeks of golden nymphs, fingering porcelain knick-knacks and almost breaking them. He repeats that all of this splendor belongs to the people. Isidora, of course, is horrified; and so, though to a lesser extent, is the reader. For Bou threatens not only the wealth of the aristocracy here, but also the sphere of high culture, which he does not understand. The aura of the work of art, defined by Walter Benjamin as "the unique phenomenon of a distance, however close it may be" (Benjamin, *Illuminations* 222), has been very graphically eliminated here, as Bou, representative of the masses, feels entitled to bring all works of art within his strangulating grasp.[41] Where the

41. Fernández Cifuentes uses Benjamin's term *aura* to describe Isidora's beauty but does not develop a comparison between her and the work of art (302).

bourgeois Miquis profaned traditional culture by trying to appropriate it, Bou makes clear his desire to eliminate it altogether.[42] Not
even the private Aransis palace, then, is protected against the contaminating fingers of the masses. And the museum, too, has been
brought within reach of the masses not only by its free entrance
policy but by the reproductions of its paintings in illustrated magazines (1098); it now exists on a continuum with that most ephemeral
of pictorial arts, lithography, carried out so efficiently by Juan Bou.
Clearly, high art cannot hope to remain intact and separate in the
wake of the vast changes in political and cultural relationships.

Walter Benjamin's famous essay, "The Work of Art in the Age of
Mechanical Reproduction," sums up the changes that dislocate high
art from its traditional functions and contexts. Mechanical reproduction has separated art from its basis in cult and ritual—site of its
original use-value—which over the centuries had been secularized
into the cult of beauty. Rather than having to seek out the revered
work of art in ritualized institutions like museums and churches, the
viewer can wait for the reproduced work of art to seek him out in a
shop, after which he may hang the piece in his living room. Tradition
is shattered as the original presence and unique history of the work of
art becomes irrelevant. The distance imposed by such factors disappears, and the reproduction is placed in contexts which abolish all
reverence, like Velázquez's Christ hanging among nude females in
Pez's study. According to Benjamin, the idea of equality makes the
masses want to bring things closer spatially and to overcome the
uniqueness of any phenomenon by accepting its reproduction (Benjamin, *Illuminations* 223).[43] And in photography, he points out, authenticity ceases to be a factor altogether, since it is not applicable to

42. Bou may be feeling the power of the aura and become destructive out of insecurity; whatever his motivation, the existence of a sphere of high art is threatened.

43. "Once kitsch is technically possible and economically profitable, the proliferation of cheap or not-so-cheap imitations of everything—from primitive folk art to the
latest avant-garde—is limited only by the market. Value is measured directly by the
demand for spurious replicas or reproductions of objects whose original aesthetic
meaning consisted, or should have consisted, in being unique and therefore inimita-
ble. No one today is surprised that any masterpiece, say Michelangelo's *Moses*, is
available for 'home use' in copies of different sizes and materials (from plaster, plastic
and china to real marble)" (Calinescu 226).

photographic prints. We can add several consequences of the mass reproduction of art works to Benjamin's considerations. When works of art meet the viewer in his living room, their function as exchange-value becomes accentuated; they can be used as a prop in the eternal act of "putting on class" (Clark 234). A work of art that as a solitary object might have contained a critique of the social structures of its day, now can easily become an instrument of conformity. It can be reified into a cliché, like the statue of Don Quijote on Pez's book-shelf, a statue Isidora scorns because "you see it everywhere" (1059). From the point of view of the narrator as critic of modernity, *La desheredada* is the story of the final shattering of the aura of the work of art. The aura remained in only two elements of the text—the palace and Isidora, the object of awestruck admiration. But the palace is invaded by the plebs, and Isidora deliberately destroys her own aura at the end of the text, as she embraces prostitution and expresses her desire to be nameless, not to be Isidora any longer. (It may be the willful destruction of the artistic aura that gives Isidora's last appearance its intense impact on the reader, the sense of irrevocable loss.)

The mass reproduction of "high" art is an indication that the distinction between high and mass culture is no longer (if it ever was) a viable way to understand the modern world. We have already noted that the serial novels read by Isidora and "high" art perform some similar functions in *La desheredada*; both are means of escaping from routine or from suffering, only to return to them fortified. And both seek to forge links between the old world and the new, to comfort the consumer by proclaiming (either through content or through style) that the rift is neither total nor irreversible. The research of several scholars underscores the impossibility of separating *La desheredada*, with its high artistic aims, from the serial novels it would like to denounce. Alicia Andreu notes that some of the moral aims of the writers of commercial literature were shared by Galdós—notably the goal of correcting social ills by creating exemplary plots with a concealed didactic function (*Galdós* 98). Galdós also shared with serial writers a preoccupation with excessive materialism, which they linked to women (101), and their belief in the need for more education as a safeguard against this temptation (104). Andreu points out that the notary's advice to Isidora—that she embrace a humble existence without ambition—reproduces the class prejudices of conservative serial writers, who believed that a woman must never aspire to leave her class (125ff.).

The kinds of overlap in content and function revealed by Andreu are reinforced by an overlap in *form* discovered recently by Geoffrey Ribbans. Ribbans's research indicates that *La desheredada* was first published in sixteen installments, by advance subscription, and that these installments came out three times a month, from March to August of 1881 (Ribbans 4). These installments were paginated continuously so that they could easily be published in book form. Ribbans's examination of the first book edition of the novel reveals several characteristics which suggest that it had previously been published in parts (for example, the size of the pages was different from usual editions of Galdós's novels, and each new chapter begins on a separate page) (5). Ribbans participates in the long critical tradition that considers Galdós an exalted writer who by definition can have no connection with the lowly serial novels hastily cooked up for the lower classes, so he is at pains to create categories within serial publications that would separate Galdós from the dross:

es cierto que existían marcadas graduaciones de calidad dentro de la lozana fronda folletinesca. . . . [I]mporta señalar que en este caso se trata de otra variante menos deleznable, la novela por suscripción adelantada, que . . . no deja de ser en gran medida aceptable por tener una relación más directa con la publicación en forma de libro. . . . Está muy lejos, pues, de la forma corriente y vulgar de la novela de entrega: una narración descuidada, con frecuencia anónimas, de pocas páginas, repartidas sin adelanto entre las clases urbanas más modestas. (Ribbans 1, 2, 4)

it is true that there were notable gradations in quality within the luxuriant foliage of serialized fiction. . . . It is important to point out that in this case we are dealing with another, less ephemeral variant, the novel by advance subscription, which is surely much more acceptable because it has a more direct relation with publication in book form. . . . It is very far, then, from the common and vulgar form of the installment novel: a careless, often anonymous narration, consisting of only a few pages, distributed without advance subscription among the most modest urban classes.

Ribbans further asserts that the kind of works promoted by Galdós's character José Ido del Sagrario in *Fortunata y Jacinta* are not novels but "thick tomes with titles on the topic of women like *Famous Women, Women of the Bible,* and *Famous Courtesans.*" He comments: "It makes one sad even to think of *La desheredada* in such company" (11, n.6).

I have quoted Ribbans at length because the assumptions underlying these passages testify to the great success that Galdós and his contemporaries had in distancing themselves from the serial novel through constant polemicizing in essays, which created apparently sharp divisions: book vs. installment, "serious" writer vs. hack, male reader vs. female, and so forth.[44] But as shown above, the distinctions do not stand up, and when we clear away the polemics, what we find is: (1) that at this time serial novels can easily become books, and vice versa; (2) that the sloppiest serial novel exists on a *continuum* with the most polished literary productions; and (3) that writers at both ends of the continuum share both common themes and common publication opportunities. Finally, to bring in only briefly *La desheredada's* connection to folklore (about which further study is necessary), it has been observed that the gang fight of chapter 6 is based on a popular nineteenth-century *aleluya* called "La pedrea."[45]

Naturally, Isidora is the character who undermines the high/mass opposition, just as she challenges class boundaries and other cultural constructions. Isidora is on the market in part 2, has sold herself to the rich and powerful; yet her beauty and distinction remain, challenging the narrator's apocalyptic view. Mass reproduction means that art will never be entirely separate; yet if it is exceptional like Isidora, it will not get lost in the crowd either. The novel, too, must accept itself as the product of industry *and* as the mouthpiece of an older literary tradition. The ideal of autonomy must give way to a more flexible view of art's existence in the real world of mass culture, where it risks being contaminated but stands to gain a wider audience. Art is now part of a world where heterogenous objects mix in a carnivalesque hodgepodge, like the shop windows Isidora examines:

[Isidora] deteníase también a contemplar las encías con que los dentistas anuncian su arte, las caricaturas políticas de los periódicos, colgados en las vidrieras de los cafés; los libros, los cromos, los palillos de dientes, las aves

44. On the realist novel's condemnation of women readers, see Jagoe, *Gender*, ch. 4.

45. Carmen Bravo-Villasante, "El naturalismo de Galdós y el mundo de *La desheredada*," *Cuadernos Hispanoamericanos* 77 (1969): 479–86; mentioned in Bly, *Vision* 110.

disecadas, las pelucas y postizos, las condecoraciones, las fotografías, los dulces y hasta los comercios ambulantes en que todo es *a real*. (1032)

[Isidora] would stop to look at the false teeth dentists use to advertise their art; the political cartoons from the newspapers, hanging in the windows of cafés; the books, lithographs, toothpicks, stuffed birds, wigs, hairpieces, medals of honor, photographs, candies, and even the street vendors, where everything costs a quarter.

The form of *La desheredada* itself stands as a testimony both to the failure of the project of purity *and* to the fact that art and the machine are not really as incompatible as the narrator's ideology would have us believe. The pressures of the marketplace are most evident in part 2, after the hope of palace patronage is dashed. The dominant intercalated genres of part 2 are all mass cultural genres, where in part 1 they had been old-world, Golden Age forms. In part 2 we find chapters of melodramatic dialogue, current political speeches to Parliament, popular rhymes, socialist rhetoric, the serial novel, and, of course, the newspaper. The first chapter of the second part proclaims the dual allegiance of the novel. On the one hand, the model of *Don Quijote*'s second part is emphasized from the first, as the narrator loses track of his protagonist until he gets sick and is treated by Dr. Miquis, who begins to talk about the events of the first part of the book and brings the narrator up to date. But the bulk of the chapter owes allegiance to another model—the newspaper, which in this period gives most news in short paragraphs of only a sentence each, without organization by subject matter.[46] The narrator imitates journalistic style as he intercalates the political events of 1873–75 with the vicissitudes of Isidora and other characters. High art has become obsessed with the discourse of mass culture, its omnipresent Other. In fact, one could say that *La desheredada* presents in its form a battle between traditional forms of literary discourse, "lined up" in part 1, and the technologized discourses of modernity, emphasized in part 2. Although the old is often rewritten with reverence and the new par-

46. Another moment of direct confrontation between old and new forms of discourse comes in the creation sermon of part 1, in which the narrator combines the rhetoric of the pulpit with the suspense tactics of the *folletín* to end the chapter: "En el capítulo siguiente veréis, ¡oh amados feligreses!, lo que pasó" ("In the following chapter you will see, oh my dear parishioners!, what happened next") (1058).

odied, the symmetry of structure gives them a symbolic equivalence as they struggle for supremacy in this highly dialogic novel.

We can attribute the heterogeneity of form in *La desheredada* not only to the lack of secure institutions where literature could find at least partial shelter from mass culture (a developed book market, a university free of political and clerical repression),[47] but more generally to the incompleteness of political, social, and economic change in Spain over the previous century. Much of the social structure of the Old Regime survives, along with its mode of production, in the late nineteenth century; the project of Enlightenment is still incomplete and continues to voice its critique of archaic structures; industrialization exists in partial form; a parliament coexists with de facto decision making by a select oligarchy. This incompleteness, found in every sphere of Spanish society, finds its reflection in a narration built of fragments of codes, and in a narrator who is himself divided between the positivistic faith in reason and the disillusioned critique of modernity.

The narrator as critic of modernity had created a utopian role for art in which it would resolve contradictions, reconnect the old and the new, and reconstitute the family, fragmented by modernity. This utopian possibility was affirmed in the music of Beethoven. But by the end of the novel, the fabric of society has unraveled to such an extent that it cannot be repaired. Social disparities are vast, and tensions have been raised to such a pitch that anarchists regularly set off bombs outside wealthy palaces, and Mariano even tries to kill the king, society's ultimate father. The symbolic "family" of society cannot be put back together; Mariano goes to his death without clemency from the king, and no Beethoven can reconcile their positions as the sonata had been able to reconcile Virginia and the *marquesa*. The literary genres of the Golden Age attempt to narrate the present using the codes of the past, but they come up short, unable to describe modernity. They end up juxtaposed with modern discourses in a text which, rather than presenting a model of coherence, seems monstrous and threatens to overflow its bounds. And the dreams of a return to those literary origins dissolves on other grounds as well, for the genres of the Golden Age to which the narrator looks for his origins are themselves uncertain of their status. That period was

47. For the Latin American version of this situation, see Ramos, chs. 3 and 4.

itself a time of massive changes which shook established certainties to their foundations. In the seventeenth century, the growth of trade and the rise of a pragmatic merchant class, the challenge to Catholicism from outside the country, and the beginnings of experimental science all made for a questioning of received ideas. The family and the clear lineage idealized by Galdós's narrator are not to be found in Golden Age literature. The picaresque antihero has left his parents, or never knew them, and tries to climb the social ladder although he comes from the gutter; Don Quijote's true origins are unknown, and he invents his own lineage, while the manuscript which tells his story is of even more uncertain provenance. Lineage was an obsession during the period, since the Inquisition demanded proof of purity of blood; yet everyone knew that genealogies were often falsified, since so many families had Jewish ancestry. Perhaps the honor plays, which provide models for the *marquesa*'s conduct, can be read as attempts to combat uncertainties about lineage by inculcating fear of the consequences of (female) infidelity; at any rate, they provide no model of familial bliss. And the authenticity which our modern narrator seeks in a preindustrial age was hardly to be found at a time when Spain's vast imperial possessions coexisted with constant internal bankruptcy, when penniless men of noble title considered it dishonorable to work but feigned the appearance of riches while often going hungry. Signifiers were composed just as consciously in the seventeenth century as in the nineteenth, leading Don Quijote, after being fooled by his eyes many times, to decide "que es menester tocar las apariencias con la mano para dar lugar al desengaño" ("one must touch appearances with one's own hands in order not to be deceived") (pt. 2, ch. 11). So the search for origins proves to be a question of infinite regress, a guaranteed failure. And, as the description of the Aransis palace indicates, the sought-for origins may turn out to be uninhabitable, dark, cold spaces ("only what has been renovated is habitable" [1042]). Or they may be uninteresting, like the paintings on its walls. Or they may just be ruins, like the room which was Virginia's tomb. So art must abandon the dream of returning to a past it has largely invented, and re-theorize its relation to society.

The dream of purity has been proven unrealizable. We may find the contamination of art figured discursively in the fate of gold, that guarantee of authenticity which is also beautiful. Gold is repeatedly contaminated or diluted in the discourse of *La desheredada*. The *marquesa* still wears golden glasses (1073), but the gold on her daughter's fine furniture has turned to black (1044). When Isidora leaves the palace, a metaphorical description of a sunset reflects the failure of the dream of purity: "The sparks of melted gold got gradually paler, or sank, leaving behind them a pale, greenish trail" (1076). Isidora's very name contains the verb *dorar*—to gild; and the bed, which is for the narrator the symbol of Isidora's dishonor, is made of copper, described as golden in color (1089). The most graphic illustration of what has happened to gold is found in Joaquín Pez's title of *marqués viudo de Saldeoro*. Joaquín is gold-colored salt, as his comely appearance is but a veneer of both inconstancy and bankruptcy. And of course, Spain's earlier bankruptcy during the "Siglo de Oro" makes that name ironic as well. By the end, Isidora's search for the gold of an inheritance and the narrator's search for purity, beauty, and authenticity have turned to salt; *la Sanguijuelera* sums it up for her niece: "The bit about your inheritance has dissolved like salt in water" (1164).

Julio Ramos writes about José Martí's exile in New York, which exposed him to the same kind of urban fragmentation that torments our narrator. Martí is a foreigner in this setting and is able to propose solutions to the crisis in terms of a Latin American identity based on family and tradition, a "we" ("nosotros") that he could contrast to the alienated, amoral "they" of the United States. Art, by preserving tradition and espousing this Latin American viewpoint, could claim to provide an alternative to the damage inflicted by modernity. Galdós is not so sanguine in *La desheredada*, for he is at home, has no "outside" alternative to embrace. For the narrator, the conclusions to be drawn from the plot of *La desheredada* are apocalyptic: art, the only possible redeeming force in society, has been irrevocably contaminated. Isidora, by abolishing her identity and embracing the uncertain freedom of prostitution, appears to have gone farther than the narrator can tolerate; she might be proposing a militant kind of art which attempts to subvert the current, corrupt bourgeois society by playing on its weaknesses from the margins. She knows that she cannot remain pure while doing this, but she seems ready to take the leap. That this move represents for her a kind of political action in solidarity with a group is evidenced by her repeated use, in the text's final pages, of the word *nosotras*; it refers to a group of women who will take vengeance on bourgeois men by using the weapon of their own body. Isidora had never used a first person *plural* before, focused as she was on her own needs. The narrator, however, cannot follow her down that path, for he still recognizes himself as part of the bourgeoisie with uncalloused hands which he refers to as "nosotros." A few years later, in *Fortunata y Jacinta*, Galdós appears more ready to contemplate an art connected to the lower class, an art that might effect change in bourgeois society. In *La desheredada*, however, his narrator can only lament his impotence—he cannot keep art pure, he can find no refuge, and he cannot even control the ultimate destiny of his own protagonist, who disappears, beyond his view, into the streets.

# Chapter Three

Fusion of Genres, Distinction of Genders: A Recipe

for Partial Social Change in Galdós's *Tormento*

• • • Significant numbers of Hispanic novelists of the nineteenth and twentieth centuries have followed the lead of Cervantes by introducing popular genres into their own texts for the apparently comical and innocuous purpose of parodying their artificial conventions or their facile moralizing. But the insertion of a popular genre into the novelistic frame seems to open a crack in the novel's very foundations. Once the conventions and ideology of the popular genre are questioned, a chain reaction is set off. First, it becomes clear that the popular genre (in the case of *Tormento*, the sentimental serial novel, or *folletín*) does not exist in a vacuum, but is rather a product of, and commentary on, a particular social and political system. If the popular genre is read as the fantasy of the dominant class about the workings of society (Dorfman), then to question the *folletín*'s conventions is also to question the regime in which it flourishes. The heyday of the *folletín* and the *novela por entregas*, according to Jean-François Botrel, can be located between 1850 and 1870, coinciding with the latter years of the reign of Isabel II (1833–68).[1] Since Galdós began to

---

1. From 1833 to 1843, until Isabel was declared of age, the country was governed by the regency of her mother, María Cristina.

write fiction in 1870, we can read *Tormento* (1884), set in the watershed year of 1868, as a kind of capsule history of the change in novel writing in Spain at that time, as well as the history of two regimes. In his 1870 essay "Observaciones sobre la novela española contemporánea," Galdós presented himself as leading the way in the reinvention of the realist novel, which he described as almost moribund since the late seventeenth century.[2] In so doing, he used the ingredients of the *folletines* he read in childhood, combining them with the demystifying strategies of Cervantes and the techniques of Balzac and Dickens (Gilman 24, 111–12, 201–02). In fact, one of Galdós's first fictional works, "La novela en el tranvía" (1870), is a Cervantine burlesque of the *folletín* and its readers; Galdós opens a space for his own future writing by belittling the competition. To locate the action of *Tormento* in 1868, then, is to remind his readers of the 1880s of the path he has traveled and the battles he has fought to attract a reading public since 1868.

To parody the *folletín* is, in *Tormento*, a vehicle for a thoroughgoing denunciation of the political and economic system in which it flourished—the reign of Isabel II. But the chain reaction of deconstructive questioning does not end here. By foregrounding the artificiality of the conventions that govern both the plot of Ido's *folletín* and the social norms of Isabelline Spain, the novel forces its reader to wonder as well what conventions govern the narrator's text. If the narrator discredits the Old Regime, what does he put in its place? To what extent does his discourse depart from the conventions of the *folletín*? To what extent has Restoration society shaken off the repressive rules of the Old Regime? In short, what political and social norms are buttressing *realism* as their mode of cultural expression?[3]

Let me begin by specifying the assumptions that will ground my

2. Catherine Jagoe, in "Disinheriting the Feminine," argues that Galdós and other male realists redefined the novel in such a way as to erase the many highly respected and widely read idealistic novels written by women between 1850 and 1870. The realist aesthetic, she suggests, was a way for men to define, and take control of, the terrain of "highbrow," "serious" literature.

3. Alicia Andreu notes that "the linguistic and ideological codes of both texts (the *folletín* and the realist text) confront one another in a Galdosian metatext, creating, through their textual dialogue, a conflict of codes that mutually deconstruct one another" (*"El folletín:* De Galdós a Manuel Puig" 541).

discussion of the dialogue of genres in *Tormento*. I will be considering the serial novels written by Ido as belonging to the genre of romance, as described by Northrop Frye. Genre here is considered as a
*mode*, which informs a number of fixed forms of narration; such
diverse texts as the adventure story, the historical novel, the spy
story, the love story, or science fiction may be characterized by the
patterns of the romance mode.[4] For Frye, the realist mode of narration privileges characters over plot, asking what will happen if particular characters encounter one another. Romance fiction, by contrast, is structured as a series of discontinuous events that happen to
characters; it is marked by implausible coincidences, extremes of
good and evil, constant surprises, and suspense.[5] For Frye, romance is
a wish fulfillment, or utopian fantasy, which aims at the transformation of the world of everyday reality (Jameson 138). While the events
of the story concern the "real world," the struggle played out in the
plot is between higher and lower kinds of worlds, between angelic
characters and demonic figures. The action often takes place in a
world related to that of the unconscious (Frye 57–58); the narrative
movement will rise into wish fulfillment or sink into anxiety and
nightmare. Descents involving changes of identity and imprisonment in dark, small spaces are frequent. For female characters, the
defense of virginity is central, as is the goal of marriage.

The utopian struggle to achieve a better world and to keep it uncontaminated by the imperfections of the real world is central for
Frye (58). But chivalric romances (and a good deal of later romance
fiction) also rationalize existing or past social structures. A dialectic
is thus established:

[T]o recreate the past and bring it into the present is only half the operation.
The other half consists of bringing something into the present which is potential or possible, and in that sense belongs to the future. This recreation of
the possible or future or ideal constitutes the wish-fulfillment element in
romance. (Frye 179)

*Tormento*'s dialogic juxtaposition of romance conventions with an
empiricist, positivist point of view will bring to the forefront both

4. See Jameson, "Magical Narratives" 138–40.
5. As Ortega y Gasset puts it, "the interest which such reading provides comes
precisely from its inverisimilitude" (*Meditaciones* 104).

of these contradictory tendencies of the romance mode, tendencies which Jameson has called *reification* and *Utopia*.[6]

José Ido del Sagrario, the character who writes serial novels in *Tormento*, cultivates many of the subgenres of romance. He first tells us about an adventure story, set in the Spain of Felipe II, with chases, underground tunnels, princesses, Moors, lascivious nuns, and sacks of gold. But he is also writing a love story which is an apology for feminine virtue and domesticity, designed to serve as an example to his female readers. It will be useful for my later argument to recall the work of Nancy Armstrong on conduct manuals, and that of Doris Sommer on nineteenth-century Latin American love stories. Armstrong reminds us that in presenting a certain kind of woman as a desirable marriage partner, conduct literature is at the same time working to consolidate a certain kind of political and economic system. Sommer studies Latin American novels which constituted "foundational fictions" in their respective countries. She notes that this romance form is boldly allegorical, with the lovers representing particular regions, races, parties, or economic interests (Sommer 5). We will see that in *Tormento* the romance mode functions both as an apology for an existing social structure *and* as a utopian protest against that structure, a wish for something better.

The kind of discourse to which romance is juxtaposed in *Tormento* also requires characterization. It is a narration wedded to reality, based on principles of positivistic philosophy and experimental science. Here, as Ortega points out, the characters and events are deliberately ordinary and unremarkable; the reader's interest is captured by how the story is told. This kind of narration exists precisely as a parody of romance, as a deflationary pinprick that bursts the bubble of dreams and wishes. But such a discourse has limitations, both literarily and politically; *Tormento* foregrounds them. The novel begins with a melodramatic theatrical dialogue featuring José Ido. We first meet the narrator, who is Ido's competitor, in the second chapter, where he quite deliberately launches into a detailed account of the most prosaic of events—the Bringas family moving into a new house and unpacking their belongings. This unexciting chapter accelerates the process by which the discourse of rationality, observation, and

6. See Jameson's article by that name.

"common sense" becomes itself an object, rather than remaining a discourse to be taken at face value as authoritative. Bakhtin explains: "Under conditions of the novel every direct word . . . is to a greater or lesser degree made into an object, the word itself becomes a bounded image, one that quite often appears ridiculous in this framed condition" (*Dialogic Imagination* 49–50). The hybrid combination of romance and what we may call "rationalist" discourse in *Tormento* is precisely what guarantees the reification of the narrator's viewpoint:

We must note that where hybridization occurs, the language being used to illuminate another language . . . is reified to the point where it itself becomes an image of a language. The more broadly and deeply the device of hybridization is employed in a novel . . . the more reified becomes the representing and illuminating language itself, until it finally is transformed into one more of the images of languages the novel contains. (Bakhtin, *Dialogic Imagination* 361)

Nineteenth-century science and philosophy, by attempting to explain in material terms even the emotional and imaginative side of human beings, and by privileging what exists over what might potentially be brought into being, had, as Ortega says, made of reality a prison, and denied human need for dreams and adventures:

A poco que vivimos hemos palpado ya los confines de nuestra prisión. Treinta años cuando más tardamos en reconocer los límites dentro de los cuales van a moverse nuestras posibilidades. Tomamos posesión de lo real, que es como haber medido los metros de una cadena prendida de nuestros pies. Entonces decimos: "¿Esto es la vida? ¿Nada más que esto?" (*Meditaciones* 122)

No sooner do we start living than we've already felt along the walls of our prison. It takes us thirty years at the most to recognize the limits imposed upon what is possible for us. Taking possession of the real is like measuring the length of the chain attached to our feet. That's when we say: "Is this what life's about? Nothing more than this?"

Galdós will emphasize precisely the stifling, limiting nature of reality in his narrator's description of Isabelline Spain. The function of adventure will seem especially crucial: "Adventure shatters that oppressive, insistent reality as though it were a pane of glass. Adventure is the unexpected, the unforeseen, the new. Every adventurous episode is like a rebirth" (*Meditaciones* 122). The realist novel will constitute itself precisely as a combination of discourses, in which the positivist allegiance to reality is always tempered by experiments with other kinds of texts, be they romances, saints' lives, or socialist propaganda. Thus the narrator's text in *Tormento* will soon begin to incorporate elements of romance; by the end of the novel the two discursive viewpoints which are contrasted at the beginning are fused in a new kind of mixture.[7]

By bringing out the dialectic between complicity with existing social structures and protest against them in *both* generic modes, *Tormento* provides a valuable corrective to the ways fictions defined as "high" and "low" have until recently been analyzed. Critics of mass cultural texts have most often focused on their ideologically conservative elements, the way they offer artificial solutions to real and complex problems. In the case of "high" cultural texts, as Tony Bennett has shown, Marxist critics had invented new reasons for endorsing the same canonical works valued by bourgeois criticism. They focused on the ways in which their favored texts had gained distance, or "relative autonomy," from dominant ideologies. Yet highbrow texts, as Bennett points out, are far from immune to the political and social system in which they appear. And mass cultural texts frequently play with, parody, or foreground ideology.[8] Jameson observes that all texts arouse real anxieties and dreams, utopian impulses, which they may then either contain in artificially tranquilizing endings (ideology) or use in a negative critique of existing social structures (Jameson, "Reification" 141–48).

In the case of *Tormento*, we witness the positivist narrator's merciless parody of the ideological plots of the sentimental *folletín;* his discourse acts as a negative critique of the social structures which the *folletín* whitewashes. Yet the narrator's discourse itself is revealed as limited, bound to the same social structures it denounces, and is shown to participate in some of the same facile distortions found in mass cultural texts. And the *folletín,* in turn, is revealed to possess a positive, utopian side, for it is a text belonging to the romance genre, which is not bound to represent the real and is free to represent a new, imaginary society, to hold out hope for change (Frye; Jameson, *Political Unconscious*). In its ending, *Tormento* uses this

7. For a different approach to narration in *Tormento,* see Germán Gullón, "Tres narradores en busca de un lector," in *El narrador en la novela del siglo XIX.*

8. See Bennett, "Marxism and Popular Fiction."

revolutionary thrust of romance to point the way toward a new society unencumbered by the repressive conventions that have governed both Isabelline and Restoration Spain, and both the sentimental *folletín* and the narrator's demystifying discourse. It is this questioning of two eras and two genres—and the insistent signalling toward a third, ideal option—that I propose to chart in this chapter.

Alicia Andreu has outlined how the narrator parodies the *folletín* of the *Mujer Virtuosa* (*Galdós* 71–91). The main object of the narrator's satire is the stereotype of the poor but virtuous women who manage to *"live by their work"* (20).[9] (Galdós italicized these words to reveal them as a cliché.) Refugio is the mouthpiece for the narrator's demystification: "What are my fingers made of now? Sewing so much has turned them into sticks of wood. And what have I gotten out of it? I just get poorer and poorer" (45). Through the character of Amparo, the narrator further shows that the very qualities which nineteenth-century society reinforces in a woman, the very characteristics of the *Mujer Virtuosa*, are the ones which bring about a woman's dishonor in the "real" world. These are, above all, weakness, or fragility, and submissiveness. Amparo's sin, her inability to resist Polo, is described by the narrator as "incomprehensible fragility" (55); Amparo herself states, "I'll try never to be so weak again—yes, weak, for that's my worst sin—being good, and terribly afraid" (57). If the *folletín* makes a clear division between "good" and "bad" characters, the narrator points out the impossibility of separating good from bad by playfully changing Amparo's name to Tormento whenever she is with Polo. Whereas the *folletín* would have split off Amparo's sexuality to create a separate "evil" character called Tormento, Galdós makes clear that any "real" character is a mixture of qualities; hence the narrator alternates the names Amparo and Tormento within a single page (91ff.). The Amparo/Tormento duality belies the polarizations of Ido's *folletines*, where women are described *either* as "pretty, single, chaste" (13) *or* with words such as "crime," "torment," "sacrilege," and "deceit" (84). Finally, the narrator parodies the formal conventions and style of the *folletín* through suspenseful or melodramatic chapter endings (chs. 9, 16, 26, 27, 34); hyperbolic terms such as "beast" (96), "monster" (90), "angel" (95), "executioner" (93), and "scoundrel" (75); and names laden with symbolic overtones.

9. Page references are to Benito Pérez Galdós, *Tormento*, in *Novelas* 2:11–124.

The function of the *folletín* in Isabelline society is clearly laid out by Ido in the first chapter; it is to serve as a moral example and to reinforce conventional morality, to assuage the reader's conscience, to protect the reader from what he or she doesn't want to see: "Incredible things happen that can't appear in a book, because people would be shocked" (14). The critical function of the narrator's discourse, by contrast, is to point out what the *folletín* has glossed over: the dark side of life, the cases that cannot be dismissed as well-deserved punishment, the ideology underlying the *folletín* itself. The *folletín* bases its portrayal of characters on a direct correspondence between outer beauty and inner virtue, a correspondence which dates back to the epic. The narrator attacks precisely this signifier-referent homology as he unmasks Isabelline society. The mission of his discourse is to reveal all the ways in which the signifier is contrary to the signified, or inadequate to represent it.[10] Thus Rosalía looks like a duchess when dressed for the theater but in private wears an old housecoat and has tousled hair.[11] Marcelina's perpetual attendance at mass hides her utter selfishness: "I would really like to help the sick, scraping sores and smallpox scabs, cleaning out wounds, but I haven't got the stomach for it. Every time I've tried it, I've gotten sick" (99). Amparo's beauty and modesty make her appear virtuous if one "reads" her, as Caballero does, through the codes of the *folletín*; but her mere bodily survival is based on the support she received from Polo, motivated partly by the sexual favors she bestowed on him. As far as language is concerned, quantity of words is in inverse proportion to substance. Ido writes three *folletines* at once and never stops talking; Paquito Bringas knows no grammar, geography, or mathematics, though he speaks like a politician and "wrote treatises on the *Social Question* which astounded his young classmates" (28). In sum, the appearance of order (political and moral) masks moral and physical disorder in all spheres.

Fredric Jameson, in *The Political Unconscious*, outlines three horizons, or frameworks, in which a cultural text can be read. The second of these is the social; the text is seen as an example of the

10. See Fernández Cifuentes on the sign in Galdós. Hazel Gold explores the gap between signifier and signified as the distinction between *teatralidad* and *vida* ("Vivir un dramón").

11. Chad C. Wright has studied the importance of external appearance in *Tormento*.

relationship between classes, and the critic seeks to unmask the belief system, the "class fantasy," which the ruling class uses to legitimize its dominance over the other classes (83–88). In the case of
*Tormento*, the social system which "torments" Amparo and Polo is
an old one; the belief system by which it operates can be seen as
several overlapping legitimation strategies which keep certain sectors of society in power even though their economic productivity has
long since declined. The first kernel of belief (or *ideologeme*) which
legitimizes the Isabelline social structure is the concept of *honra*,
dating back to the Golden Age. For my purposes, *honra* is comprised
of several elements:

1. external appearance rather than actual wealth determines status;
   value therefore placed on self-display

2. dishonor is attached to manual labor

3. dependence on titles, lineage, and crown favor

4. value of purity of blood over wealth

5. for women, the repression of all manifestation of sexual desire, intra-
   or extramaritally

The second legitimator of the Old Regime is the Church, which
preached the "immorality" of both sexual and materialist desires and
taught the poor to renounce material wealth in favor of rewards in
the afterlife.

Isabel II's reign is characterized by the uneasy coexistence of Old
Regime structures (among them, a monarch who dissolves Parliament at will and refuses to name liberal prime ministers; hated taxes
on basic goods and services; press censorship; and Church influence
over affairs of state) with fledgling industry and the gradual rise of a
middle class that could compete with the nobility for control of the
greatest percentage of the national product. The system looks back
nostalgically to the glorious Spain of the *Reconquista* and Counter-
Reformation. (Can it be a coincidence that Ido and Felipe go for a
drink at the *café de Lepanto*, "a depressing, poor, broken-down establishment that has already disappeared from Santo Domingo Square,
leaving no trace of its former glory" [11]?) Since social status still
derives from titles, appearances, and *relaciones* rather than from
wealth, the old institutions have managed to retain hegemony even

in the mid-nineteenth century, when their inertia and lack of productivity are longstanding. By defining consumption as immoral, the system restricts the growth of capitalism and uses a combination of real and promised rewards to keep the lower-middle and working classes from developing materialist desires. Ido's *folletín*, in which the two penniless orphan girls reject the money of the *marqués* for the sake of their honor, connects money and sexual license and attaches a social stigma to both. Ido is a spokesman for the ideology which seeks to convince the poor that their own *honra* (originally based on purity of blood) is more important than material wealth: "Where will you find honor? In poor people, working-class men, beggars. Where do you find chicanery? Among the wealthy, the nobility, ministers, generals, courtiers" (13). Ido's *folletines* reproduce the uneven modernity of Isabelline Spain, sometimes looking back nostalgically to the world of nobles, Inquisition, and palaces, and sometimes functioning as an apology for bourgeois domesticity.

The lower middle class (and some of the lower nobility, now bankrupt) is in some respects in the most awkward position of all because of the enduring aftereffects of the ideology of *honra*, particularly the dishonor once attached to manual labor. *Honra* requires them to appear impeccable at public functions and to frequent the fashionable theater and summer baths, yet their economic situation is really quite precarious. Refugio unmasks the penury of the Bringases:

en aquella casa no hay más que miseria, una miseria mal charolada... Parecen gente, ¿y qué son? Unos pobretones como nosotras. Quítales aquel barniz, quítales las relaciones, ¿y qué les queda? Hambre, cursilería. Van de gorra a los teatros, recogen los pedazos de tela que tiran en Palacio, piden limosna con buenas formas... (38)

in that house there's nothing more than stinginess, a wretchedness poorly painted over. They look so high and mighty, but what are they? Just poor folk like us. Take away the varnish, take away their social contacts, and what have you got? Hunger and pretentiousness. They mooch tickets to the theater, they gather up bits and pieces of cloth discarded in the palace, and they go begging in style.

The Isabelline regime, by the time we meet it in *Tormento*, is shown as surviving by strict rules of containment of desire. Hegemony in *Tormento* depends on retention, both of money and of sexual fluids; the flowing of either is seen as a prescription for personal and social disaster, or worse, a sin.[12] Francisco Bringas is the most fervent representative of this system. The main verb associated with Bringas is *componer*, to fix up what is old and outworn so that it will continue to function; this activity can be seen as a figure for the tactics of the old political system.[13] Rosalía's strategy for success is to receive while never giving; she gets hand-me-downs from the queen and gifts from Agustín. The family as a whole maintains its social position through ascetic practices such as eating less and cutting out coffee and wine (88). The female representatives of the Isabelline system are ostentatiously chaste; Rosalía takes pride in being "honrada" (30), while Marcelina Polo considers Madrid her convent and behaves accordingly (98). The narrator longs for a more open system, where deferred gratification would not be the norm. He departs here both from the practices of Spain's bankrupt Old Regime, which cannot afford to be generous, and from the bourgeois capitalist belief in thrift.

Nancy Armstrong has shown how a new conception of what made a woman desirable, propagated through conduct books, helped to create a certain ideal of domestic life. The domestic model, she argues, was operative in creating the middle class as a group which identified itself as having interests in common. The ideal domestic woman was, of course, the "angel in the house," the *Mujer Virtuosa*, who shunned display, was modest and submissive, and was firm only in the hand with which she ran her comfortable yet frugal household. We will see later where the narrator stands in relation to this ideology about women. For the moment, let us note that the virtuous orphans of José Ido's *folletín* are examples of the modern, capitalist ideal of domesticity. In Spain, the situation is less simple than the gradual displacement of the aristocratic model by the domestic one, as Armstrong describes it for England. Rather, in the 1860s, we find

12. We recall the fate of Alejandro Miquis in *El doctor Centeno*. He was subject to a condemnation and lack of charity which effectively killed him; his sin was to expend both money and semen. See Pérez Galdós, *Novelas* 1:1312–1468.

13. In this context, Chad Wright's observation that Amparo's sewing means, as Barthes says, "mend, make, repair," is highly suggestive. Sewing, repairing the status quo, is the activity by which women keep together the tattered institutions which make them slaves. But sewing will also undermine the system when it becomes tied, in the Rosalía of *La de Bringas*, to an appetite for luxury (Wright 31; Barthes 169).

the awkward coexistence of a regime still based on display and royal favor with the popularity of serial novels derivative of European literature of domesticity.

In *Tormento*, social life is shown still to revolve around the court and people of title. Ironically, the *folletín's* domestic angels may well have functioned in Spain to *buttress* certain aspects of the Isabelline regime. In the European context, to inculcate frugality and self-sacrifice into the middle-class woman often meant maximizing the income brought in by her husband so that the family could live comfortably and accumulate wealth. In Spain, however, readers of *folletines* often belonged to the sector of the population clinging desperately to an ideal of middle-class status while actually being threatened with downward mobility because of insufficient economic development. For readers who, like Amparo, lacked a secure provider of income, Ido's *folletín* preached a continued abnegation which would leave Spain's limited available wealth securely in the hands of the aristocracy and its hangers-on.[14] Thus the old institutions, paradoxically, benefit from the new consumer technology, which produces the *folletín* to perpetuate the old message of repression of desire, both sexual and material. The way in which the Isabelline system is able to make use of a discourse which arises from a very different ideological matrix, and manages to mask the discontinuities between the two legitimation strategies, resembles the work of Bringas with pieces of the palace rug acquired at different times:

Yo empalmé tan bien el pedazo que te dieron hace dos años en Palacio con el que lograste hace un mes, y casé con tanto cuidado las piezas, que no se conoce la diferencia de dibujo. (18)

I took the piece they gave you two years ago at the palace, and the one you got a month ago, and I lined up the pieces so carefully that you can't see the difference in the pattern.

Amparo initially appears to conform completely to the model of

14. Catherine Jagoe: "The rapid rise to dominance of the angelic ideal is, in part, due to the fact that it could easily be enlisted to serve a wide range of political agendas. It figures in the writings of radical liberal intellectuals . . . , as well as conservative liberals. . . . It was also attractive to anti-democratic writers, who represented female purity and piety as bastions against a rising tide of immorality in the public, male sphere. . . . The *ángel del hogar* was presented as a remedy against the threat of democratic social change . . ." (*Gender* ch. 1).

the *Mujer Virtuosa* outlined above. Her work for Rosalía gives her little remuneration, and like all ideal nineteenth-century women, she eats almost nothing (29, 39; Michie, 12–29). The hegemonic society can offer her only one solution to the problem of survival—she can become a nun, with the aid of a dowry from Isabel II; it is noteworthy that such a solution also enforces her sterility, thus controlling the growth of a population of have-nots.[15] Amparo thus represents the lower middle class as victim of the traditional institutions of religion and *honra*; given her sin against these structures, her life is "anxiety, fear, constant trembling" (54).

*Tormento*, then, associates Isabelline Spain with repression at many levels. Social mobility is made impossible by the system of *relaciones*; sexual repression is ensured through the Church; women face repression based on gender; cultural expression (the *folletín* and the newspaper) is censored. The narrator spatializes the repression of desire in the dark, claustrophic rooms where the action of the novel takes place. Limited opportunities combine with the dominant rhetoric to create a stifling feeling:

[Polo]— . . . ¿A ti no te molesta esta sociedad, no te ahoga esta atmósfera, no se te cae el cielo encima, no tienes ganas de respirar libremente?

[Amparo]—Lo que me ahoga es otra cosa...

[Polo]—...La conciencia, sí... (55)

[Polo]—Aren't you sick of this society? Stifled in this atmosphere? Isn't it as if the sky were closing in on you? Don't you wish you could breathe freely?

[Amparo]—What's stifling me is something else.

[Polo]—Yes, your conscience.

Agustín Caballero is the antithesis of the representatives of the embattled monarchy, possessing money but lacking social graces (Durand 517). Initially, as a capitalist, he represents salvation for bankrupt Isabelline Spain, for he offers an infusion of money while accepting the sexual restrictions enshrined by the Church. Rosalía represents the old system; she is attracted by Agustín's richness while being scandalized by his social ineptness and his constant pur-

15. Ido's imagined title for Amparo's story gives voice to the hegemonic solution: "*Del lupanar al claustro*" ("*From the Brothel to the Cloister*") (120).

chasing of new commodities. Rosalía is defined from the beginning as suspicious of capitalist development, presented in spatial terms:

Todo lo que no sea este trocito no me parece Madrid. . . . Cuando paso dos días sin ver la plaza de Oriente, Santo Domingo el Real, la Encarnación y el Senado, me parece que no he vivido. . . . Cuando oigo hablar de las familias que se han ido a vivir a ese barrio, a esa Sacramental que está haciendo Salamanca más allá de la plaza de toros, me da escalofrío. ¡Jesús, qué miedo! (19)

Nothing outside of my little neighborhood seems like Madrid to me. . . . When I go a few days without seeing the Plaza de Oriente, the Royal Chapel of Santo Domingo, the Church of the Incarnation and the Senate, it seems to me I haven't been living. When I hear about these families that have gone out to live in that wilderness that Salamanca is building on the other side of the bullring, it sends shivers up my spine. My God, it scares me!

Agustín's emphasis on home comforts over external pomp offends Rosalía because it shows up her own willingness to endure Spartan discomfort at home in order to attend the palace dances. Thus upon visiting his home, Rosalía tells Agustín, "This kind of luxury is an insult, and brings on revolutions" (72). Yet Rosalía is so attracted by the riches that Agustín brings that she imagines him marrying her six-year-old daughter. (Since Rosalía's family is a parodic reflection of the Bourbon dynasty—her children bear the names of the royal family—Rosalía's dreams of an alliance with Agustín can be read as the Crown's desire for capitalist support).[16]

For the narrator, Agustín's brand of capitalism offers a breath of fresh air to the literally obscurantist Spain portrayed in *Tormento*. In the present tense which denotes his own opinion, the narrator establishes oppositions between Rosalía's society and his own ideal, which corresponds to Agustín's capitalism: laziness vs. the vigor that comes from honest work; and connections vs. individual initiative (20–21). Agustín's critique of Spanish society is also that of the narrator:

—¡Hacerse monja! Eso es de países muertos. ¡Mendigos, curas, empleados; la

16. As Charnon-Deutsch points out, Rosalía's house is "a miniature, although somewhat shabby, Palacio" ("Inhabited Space" 36).

pobreza instituida y reglamentada!... Pero no: usted está llamada a un destino mejor, usted tiene mucho mérito. (33)

"Become a nun? That only happens in dead countries. Beggars, priests, office workers—poverty institutionalized and regimented! But *you* are destined for something much better; you deserve much more."

(The word *mérito* is noteworthy since it is foreign to the system of *honra*.) Agustín's house is described three times, once by Felipe and twice by the narrator; the latter's fascination with the "miraculous" modern conveniences and tasteful decorations of the house is evident (41–42; 68–69; 88–89). The narrator takes particular note of the "comfortable layout" of the house, which contrasts with "that Latin-style luxury which sacrifices people's comfort and cultivates vanity and outward appearances" (68). The brightness and ventilation of the rooms represent an enlightenment which offers escape from the omnipresent darkness (Charnon-Deutsch, "Inhabited Space" 40–43).

Rosalía's hostility toward Amparo from the beginning of the novel can be read as a defensive reaction on the part of petty bourgeois adherents of Isabel II against the rise of another petty bourgeois sector with different values. Since the Bringas family has come to depend as much on Agustín (capital) as on *Palacio* for its survival, its stake in Agustín's marriage is enormous.[17] His announced marriage to Amparo is a grave blow to the system of *honra* described above. By withdrawing his support from the conservative petty bourgeoisie (the many families who try to "net" him for one of their daughters), he dashes their hopes for a new, unlimited source of wealth which would enable them to continue the policy of continual *receiving*. His marriage to Amparo is scandalous. Its revolutionary effect on the economic system is implicit in the contradiction between Amparo's two last names: Sánchez (common people) vs. Emperador. Second, the marriage represents the alliance of two economic sectors which together could pose a threat to the Old Regime; it thus carries the country further down the path toward revolution. For these reasons, Rosalía cannot accept the news, even though she herself is not sure why she is so upset:

Representóse a la hija de Sánchez Emperador disfrutando de los tesoros de aquella casa sin igual, y consideraba esto tan absurdo como si los bueyes

17. Agustín literally supports the government by lending it money (43).

volaran en bandadas por encima de los tejados, y los gorriones, uncidos en parejas, tiraran de los carros . . . no acertaba a explicarse el motivo de su despecho. "Porque a mí, ¿qué me va ni me viene en esto?... Conmigo no se había de casar, porque soy casada; ni con Isabelita tampoco, porque es muy niña." (72–73)

She imagined the orphaned daughter of Sánchez Emperador enjoying the treasures of that splendid house, and it seemed as absurd to her as if the oxen were flying in flocks over the rooftops, while the swallows, yoked in pairs, pulled the carts . . . She couldn't understand why she was so upset. "After all, what's this got to do with me? He wasn't going to marry me, because I'm already married. And he wouldn't have married Isabelita either, because she's just a child."

Economically, it would appear that the narrator sees in unrestricted capitalism a remedy for the ossification and penury of the Spain of Isabel II. On the level of narration, the techniques of realism, by unmasking the repressive social conventions which underly the *folletín*, fulfill a similar progressive function: they point toward postrevolutionary transformation. But the Restoration and the discourse of positivism are not presented in *Tormento* as satisfactory alternatives to the Isabelline regime. The problem is that the desired revolution was incomplete, and the Restoration which put an end to the chaotic changes in government between 1868 and 1874 meant an alliance of bourgeoisie with nobles in which many aspects of the Old Regime were allowed to survive. *Tormento*'s narrator tells us from the beginning that Restoration society is not all that different from Isabelline society ("there hasn't been much change in the last sixteen years" [20]), and may in some ways be worse ("Now parasitism has changed in character, causing greater harm" [30]). In this context, where true restructuring is lacking, Agustín's capitalism cannot create a more just society. The narrator underscores this by showing Agustín not simply as an alternative to Isabel II, but in many respects as her *mirror*. Rosalía praises the charitable generosity of Isabel: "She is so charitable that if it were up to her, she'd give away all the nation's wealth in alms. She receives so many requests and petitions from the needy every day" [23]. From Felipe we learn that Agustín also fulfills this function: "At all hours of the day there are people asking for alms, because my master is very charitable" [42]. Felipe's ensuing description of the many kinds of people who beg at Agustín's door makes us wonder whether the capitalist system which has made him rich will really help the lot of the poor; we suspect that begging at one palace will be the same as begging at the other. (Felipe calls Agustín's house a "palacio" and declares, "An empress has to live here" [42].) Agustín and Isabel are again shown as mirror images when Rosalía decides that Agustín, rather than *la Señora*, could provide Amparo's dowry (23). When we recall that Agustín's fortune comes from supplying the troops of the Confederacy in the American Civil War (34), we can no longer avoid the conclusion that capitalism will entail exploitation as surely as the postfeudal regime of Isabel II. Two final parallels establish Agustín as a mirror image of Isabel II. Rosalía, who wears the queen's hand-me-downs and walks on an old carpet from the palace, also enjoys the use of the contents of Agustín's "palace"; Bringas informs her, "That silly man [Agustín] told me you could have the use of everything that was bought for the wedding" (124). We see that the conservative petty bourgeoisie will profit from either regime.

Just as the Restoration is represented as *continuing* many aspects of the earlier regime, so the narrator's discourse is revealed to be saturated with devices and assumptions deriving from the *folletín*. In Galdós's early "La novela en el tranvía" (1870), the implied author claims to be able to localize the *folletín* in the deluded imagination of his protagonist, much as Cervantes does at the beginning of *Don Quijote*. In these two texts, it is assumed that the protagonist's version of events (giants, countesses) can be separated from the "reality" presented by the narrator (windmills, laundresses). The reader can thus dismiss the *folletín* as the mere hallucination of a single character. In *Tormento*, however, the *folletín* informs the behavior and thoughts of many of the characters. Agustín's thoughts about Amparo all derive from the *folletín*; Polo's celebration of Amparo as a "saint" (52) and an "angel" (95) correspond to her melodramatic thoughts of him as a "monster" (90), a "wild animal that no one can capture" (90). But most significantly, the melodrama and clichés of the *folletín* enter the *narrator's* discourse—the events presented to the reader as *real* are presented according to the conventions of the very genre which the narrator has been parodying as false. Thus the narrator calls Polo "barbarian" (91), "beast" (92), and "brute" (92), and heightens the sensationalism of Polo's imprisonment of Amparo with lines like "How horrible her panic was!" (93).[18] Even more telling is the narrator's description of Amparo's physical features at the end of chapter 20, a veritable litany of clichés. The evident dependence of the narrator's story on the *folletín* causes the reader to question how "real" its "realism" can be.[19]

This dependence of realism on the *folletín* becomes more apparent when we consider aspects of the *folletín* which are incorporated into realist discourse *without* parody. This is the case with the bulk of socially dominant ideas regarding women. The narrator's portrayal of women in *Tormento* reproduces almost unquestioningly the dominant discourse on women of the time, a discourse unceasingly propagated in conduct manuals and *folletines*. As Nancy Armstrong has argued, discourse on what makes a woman desirable is inseparable from political and economic questions. In the case of the domestic woman, as Armstrong demonstrates, the creation of such an ideal in conduct manuals actually preceded, and helped to create, the idea of a middle class having common interests and based on a rigid separation between the public, male sphere, and the domestic sphere governed by the female (Armstrong, ch. 2).

In Spain, as befitting a country without a highly developed book market, the ideology of domesticity was propagated largely in magazines. Most often, it was conveyed in domestic novels written by women, in which the fictional plot functioned as an instrument of the didactic message. Among Pilar Sinués de Marco's numerous works were a bestseller called *The Angel in the House* (1859) and a text called *Daughter, Wife and Mother: Letters for Women about Their Duties to Family and Society* (1863) (Jagoe, *Gender* ch. 1). Other female writers of conduct literature included Angela Grassi, Pilar Pascual de San Juan, and Faustina Sáez de Melgar. Men, of

---

18. Douglass Rogers discusses the development of Galdós's treatment of popular literature since "La novela en el tranvía" (139). For a discussion of melodrama in *Tormento*, see Percival.

19. Alfred Rodríguez, in a very suggestive study, describes the deliberate mixing of genres in *Tormento* as a setup for the reader. The reader is led to postulate a simple binary opposition between Ido's *folletín* and the realist novel which pokes fun at it. But it then turns out that the realist novel itself is saturated with scenes and devices characteristic of the *folletín*; Amparo's "suicide" is but one example. See Rodríguez 79–80.

course, contributed articles to magazines for women, in which they sermonized on desirable female behavior.[20]

Conduct manuals and *folletines* brought the domestic woman into being by discrediting the earlier ideal of the aristocratic woman. By the second half of the nineteenth century, the manuals' work was done in England. The domestic woman had been accepted as "natural," her characteristics were part of common sense (Armstrong 8–9). But in Spain, the ideal of aristocratic display persisted along with the many political and economic structures of the Old Regime which survived well into the Restoration. The frivolous *cursi* who puts her body on display is a staple of realist literature; display had taken on a new function, indicating bourgeois economic success. But the narrator appears in *Tormento* to prefer an English model of bourgeois domesticity to the Spanish spectacle. He also laments the fact that so many facets of the Old Regime still survive in the Restoration, unaffected by the Revolution of 1868. So the narrator's characterization of *Tormento*'s women still retains a polemical tone. Rosalía and Amparo are created in opposition to one another, with Rosalía being associated from the outset with the body (she is "one of those fleshy beauties" [16]) and Amparo characterized first in terms of inner qualities like good sense and tolerant character (22); she is described physically only much later (67). Rosalía is the aristocratic demon of the conduct manuals who incarnates the opposite of everything the domestic woman represents. Her house is crammed and inhospitable; she loves to display her body, even at the cost of feeding her children. The supposedly "natural" sex roles are reversed, as it is Bringas who stretches and administers the family money, and Rosalía who would love to spend it. Her formula for success is the old one of proximity to those with title and wealth; the narrator refers to her similarity with *duquesas* and *marquesas* when dressed up (13, 20). Her love of display and material things is shown to lead to her sexual dishonor in *La de Bringas*. The man of good sense, in the terms of the conduct books, will reject such a woman, however beautiful or wealthy, as a drain on his pocketbook and disrupter of the tranquility of his home life. Like Agustín, he will prefer a woman, however poor, who is submissive and hardworking, lacks any selfish desires, shuns public

20. For a review of conduct literature in Spanish magazines, see Andreu, *Galdós*, ch. 3, "Manual de conducta."

display for the privacy of home, and consumes as little as possible (Armstrong 73). That Amparo and Rosalía are competing for dominance is made clear from the treatment accorded to their last names by the narrator. Rosalía, who prizes titles, invents an undeserved, sonorous name for herself—that of Pipaón de la Barca. The narrator explains to the reader how the title is falsified and punishes Rosalía for her presumption by calling her *la de Bringas*. One would think the narrator stood for exactitude regarding last names, but in fact, in his treatment of Amparo's names, he invents a lineage for her that surpasses Rosalía's. Amparo's father's names are Sánchez Emperador; her mother's are unknown. Spanish custom would dictate that Amparo retain only the Sánchez of her father's name, adding one surname from her mother. But the narrator not only uses the name Emperador for Amparo, he suppresses the plebeian-sounding Sánchez and *modifies* the name Emperador to call Amparo "la Emperadora," a name which belongs to Amparo no more than Pipaón de la Barca belongs to Rosalía. Amparo, then, is the domestic *emperatriz* who deserves Agustín's palace (42). Furthermore, when Amparo's beauty is described, a neighbor declares that if Amparo were properly attired and taken to a noble *salon*, "neither duchesses nor princesses could compete with her" (37). Amparo has thus surpassed the highest title associated with Rosalía. The narrator has manipulated titles to show the superiority of his domestic woman to the ideal woman of Isabelline Spain.

The conduct books develop the domestic woman as resolutely middle class. A family's financial comfort is indicated by its ability to live on the husband's income alone. Because domesticity, seen as "natural" to women, becomes synonymous with virtue, the lower-class woman who must leave the home to seek a living is considered immoral; in Armstrong's words, "the figure of the prostitute could be freely invoked to describe any woman who dared to labor for money" (118).[21] It is this class-based conception of sexuality that lurks behind the characterization of Refugio, who leaves the home to serve as a model to painters. Refugio's view of the world is given ambivalent treatment by the narrator. On the one hand, he supports her discourse when she demolishes the myth that one can be penniless and

21. Says Jagoe: "The same discourse which desexualized the women of the middle class hypersexualized working-class women" (*Gender* ch. 1).

yet be the angel in the house: "[My fingers] have turned into sticks of wood from so much sewing. And what do I get out of it? I just get poorer and poorer" (45). He also seems to sympathize with the predicament of the middle-class girl who is now poor yet cannot share the values of working-class men; as Refugio puts it, "Am I supposed to marry a mover?" (45). Since it is clear that Amparo's dishonor has come quickly through a combination of poverty and simple submissiveness, one might expect the narrator to valorize a woman with a stronger will. Yet the conduct-manual view that woman is by nature submissive is so ingrained that the more decisive woman must of necessity be associated with immorality. So it is with the portrayal of Refugio, whose strong will is shown as inseparable from the promiscuity and antidomesticity associated with the lower classes. Her house is constantly messy and "unlivable"; her money and energy go into dressing up to display her body; like Rosalía, she is domineering and manipulative. Her face has a "spicy appeal" (37), exciting sexual desire, while Amparo's "deeper" beauty provokes in Agustín a wholesome love devoid of passion. (Polo's wild passion for Amparo contradicts this picture, but is presented as a moral disorder that requires a cure.)

The final polemic conducted on behalf of the domestic woman is the discrediting of the Old Regime single woman who devotes herself to God. As Armstrong has shown, the conduct books preach that woman's natural duty lies in the practice of secular morality (106). To sacrifice oneself for one's family is "natural"; to sacrifice oneself for God is seen as selfish. Hence the treatment of Marcelina Polo, the religious fanatic, who is shown as much more "immoral" and destructive than Amparo although she remains virginal. Ultimately inhuman, she is described as made of mahogany (100).

The portrayal of women in *Tormento* points up broad areas of coincidence between the views of the narrator on the one hand, and those of José Ido's *folletín* (written as a moral example) and the conduct literature of the day on the other.[22] However, realist authors were at pains to condemn the *folletín* publicly and to conceal areas of overlap such as this. I will return to the question of women later, as I

---

22. Alicia Andreu, in *Galdós y la literatura popular*, has also pointed out many respects in which Galdós's views overlap with those of the writers of *folletines*. See especially the section entitled "¿Rechazo de la literatura de consumo?" (95–109).

attempt to evaluate the possible utopian features of the novel's ending. For the moment, I want to point out that within the reality of
Spain, both that of Isabel II and that of the Restoration, the polemic
by both Ido and the narrator in favor of the domestic woman has only
served to paint women into a corner. Within the context of a middle
class that is weak, precarious, and often downwardly mobile, to ad-
vocate the model of the woman who stays at home seems to be to
preach starvation. The narrator is honest enough to show that within
the framework of Isabel's regime, the "angel in the house" who manages to combine chastity with submissiveness cannot exist except on
paper in a *folletín*.[23] He separately acknowledges that society has not
changed much in the sixteen years since 1868 (20). The question of
how real women were supposed to skip through a minefield in which
they would be guilty either of strong-willed antidomesticity or of
sexual dishonor (or both) remains unexplored. Or can the narrator be
suggesting that women's only hope is that society might forgive the
woman who resembles the domestic angel for the dishonor that may
have befallen her through poverty and submissiveness?

Let us now leave the level of plot to consider the ways in which
imagery and narrative strategies seem to undermine the foundations
of the belief in scientific observation that grounds the narrator's discourse. Several factors cast doubt on the narratorial omniscience, the
powers of observation on which positivism and experimental science
depend. Multiple contradictions and incongruencies prevent the
reader from putting the pieces of this textual puzzle together to form
a coherent whole (Urey 47ff.). Most obviously, there are chronologi-
cal problems. The first scene seems at first glance to correspond to
Felipe's visit to Amparo in chapter 11, especially since Felipe reiter-
ates Ido's invitation to come chat after he delivers his envelope (14,
43). Felipe tells Ido in chapter 1 that the Bringases cannot attend the
theater performance because one of their children is sick (13); yet
the only time we see the Bringases with a sick child, they *do* go to the

---

23. *Tormento's* female characters are generated through two oppositions: "submissiveness vs. strong will" and "sexual virtue (*honradez*) vs. sexual dishonor." Rosalía
and Marcelina combine *honradez* with a strong will which, for the narrator, is negative. Refugio combines the two negative poles of strong will and quite deliberate
dishonor. Amparo combines dishonor with the positively connoted submissiveness. It
is only the fictional "angel in the house" who can combine the virtues of *honradez* and
submissiveness.

theater (ch. 8). The envelope of chapter 1, according to Felipe, contains *billetes de teatro*; but in chapter 11, the envelope he brings contains money—in contrast, we are told, to other envelopes: "She knew in her heart that it did not contain theater tickets, as it had other times" (41).[24] Even within chapter 11 itself, the chronology does not hold together. When the bell rings, Amparo is surprised, "For ten o'clock had already gone by, maybe even ten-thirty" (40). Yet Felipe, at the end of his visit, says that the time is "a quarter to nine" (43). Chronology fails on another occasion. In chapter 13, Amparo leaves her house at ten o'clock and arrives at Polo's at eleven (47). Amparo then shops for food, cleans the house, brings in the *carbonero* and the *aguador*, washes the dishes, sets the table, and makes lunch. The narrator then comments: "So lunch, which could have been ready at eleven, took three quarters of an hour longer" (53). Other details contradict one another. Of Bringas we are told: "He didn't subscribe to any newspapers" (30); yet we later see the newspaper arrive (63).

The stock conventions which the narrator uses in characterization also seem to unravel before the reader's eyes in *Tormento*. Amparo's presence in Rosalía's house is described as follows: "We see her there, always the same, her mood unchanging." Yet a few lines later we are told that she "smiled slightly if Rosalía was in a good mood, and was submerged in deep sadness if the lady of the house was sad or angry" (22). Agustín is described as "incapable of making conversation on pleasant, superficial topics" (24), but as he attempts to declare himself to Amparo, the narrator comments, "For a man of few words, it feels comfortable to simply answer and follow the course of light conversation provided for him" (32).[25] Such phrases, which are easily believed when taken singly but are contradictory when combined, seem to undermine the edifice of positivist reliability. The realist novel points up fissures and discontinuities, undoing the kind of work done by Bringas on the pieces of palace carpet—work which would gloss over inconsistencies.

24. Rodríguez points out that in no other novel does Galdós combine generic ambivalence with ambiguous narrative chronology, and that in no other case does the generic hybridization occupy the first pages of the work, "which, because of their location at the beginning, determine the tone of the work" (68).

25. These incongruencies were pointed out to me by Patrick Hub in an unpublished Duke University graduate paper of December 1988.

The narrator bases his claim to legitimacy on his powers of observation; the novel claims to be a mirror of society. Yet the tactics which *Tormento*'s narrator uses to demystify the *folletín* are ones which undermine such a claim. For by showing the dark side of the bright, optimistic surface of the *folletín*, the narrator has created a world in which it is simply *too dark to see*. The *folletín* is associated with clarity and light in the "clear image" that Agustín has of Amparo in his imagination, an image that corresponds point for point to the *folletín*'s "angel in the house" ("He saw her clearly, as clearly as if he had her in front of him" [35]). The narrator's response is to emphasize that, because of the darkness, the lovers are in fact unable to see each other: "It was already getting late, and they couldn't see each other well enough to make out one another's emotions" (63). Agustín and Amparo meet each other in the hall, "as dark as an animal's cave" (64).[26] In fact, Agustín's imagination *replaces* the light of the sun as he tries to look at his beloved in the darkness (64). The *folletín* supplies light; the narrator blots it out with darkness. The fact that darkness impedes observation is underlined from the first lines of the novel, in which the two cloaked men bump into each other in the darkness and are so unable to see that they do not realize that they know each other well (Charnon-Deutsch, "Inhabited Space" 42). The persistent darkness eventually gives the spaces of the novel the tone of a nightmare world characteristic of romance, reproducing Amparo's intense perception of the world as a hostile place.

Having questioned the viability of the Restoration and positivism as true alternatives to the regime of Isabel II and the *folletín*, the text of *Tormento* continues its dialectical interrogation by criticizing the entire realm of Isabelline culture. This realm includes the existing political system and its social norms, as well as the writing which occurs under its protection. *Tormento* thus confronts directly the double bind of criticizing culture while at the same time being itself a cultural artifact, irrevocably implicated in the system it denounces. We can explore this contradiction by considering the production of language in *Tormento*, by the characters and by the narrator. In *Tor-*

26. The insistence on darkness is omnipresent. Rosalía cannot see Caballero kissing her daughter across the room (27); the dining room is "dark as night" (65); Polo's house is a "dead, lugubrious dwelling" to which Amparo brings light (52). Charnon-Deutsch explores how the characteristics peculiar to each house relate to its inhabitants ("Inhabited Space").

*mento*, the production of language, whether verbal or written, conforms to the rules of censorship; what can be said is what does not question or exceed the existing norms. This applies equally to love and to politics. Love is represented in the verbal loquacity and written fecundity of Ido's discourse—the *folletín*. Politics is represented in the imitative speeches of Paquito Bringas and Joaquín Pez, and in the censored periodical which Polo reads. Love is linked to politics in a reference to Agustín, who has memorized his speech to Amparo "like an orator on his way to Congress to make a speech" (35). This language which conforms to the dominant ideology is associated with the color white. Amparo says of Agustín: "Certainly, he had read her thoroughly; but God had willed that, as he turned the pages of her soul, he should see only the white, pure ones, not the black one" (74). The *folletín* is associated with blindness, with not seeing the dark page. The narrator's discourse, of course, exists to reveal the presence of the dark page—not only Amparo's sin, but the dark side of every character, of society, and of everyday life in dark houses, far from bright palaces.

Since, in the world of *Tormento*, language can represent only what exists within the system, within the dominant culture, the only way the narrator can signal the presence of elements that exceed or contradict that culture is through darkness.[27] All that which is in the realm of Nature, all that which does not find resolution within the system, is represented through darkness. Darkness, then, signals *difference*. Such elements, unaccounted for within the system, include desire (Amparo's *página negra*), malice (represented in the fanatically religious Marcelina Polo, described as "black from head to toe" [85]), and other political systems (Rosalía, anticipating revolution, "saw the future as black" [77]). Polo dreams of being so far from his culture that at twelve o'clock noon he can say " 'Now it must be twelve o'clock midnight in that horrible place called Madrid' " (58). Again, the vision of a different way of being entails darkness in the domi-

---

27. In *Tormento*, we rarely witness street scenes, and those we do see occur almost exclusively in darkness. This is in contrast with the bulk of the *Novelas contemporáneas*, where the descriptions of different sectors of Madrid and of the hustle and bustle of city life are a Galdosian trademark. But few *Novelas contemporáneas* are set prior to 1868. The correlation between the confinement to inner spaces, the darkness, and the political system is all the more striking when compared to other works by Galdós.

nant culture. When not described as darkness, what is not included in the system is described as madness. *Tormento*, referring to her affair with Polo, tells him, "That madness is done and over with" (48). Reading Polo's letter from the country, in which he rejects culture in favor of nature, Amparo decides, "He's crazy" (80).

The realist novel is faced with a dilemma. As a book, it is, by its very nature, tied to culture. As Polo puts it:

¡Malditos los que en el laberinto artificioso de las sociedades han derrocado la naturaleza para poner en su lugar la pedantería, y han fundado la ciudadela de la mentira sobre un montón de libros amazacotados de sandeces! (80)

Curses on those who, in the crafted labyrinth of society, overthrew nature and put pedantry in its place. They founded a citadel of lies atop a pile of books chock full of nonsense!

Books are associated with lies. We recall the earlier joint statement by the narrator and Amparo: "El estilo es la mentira. La verdad mira y calla" ("Style is a way of lying, whereas truth stands staring and silent") (44).[28] Books, being unable to avoid style, are by definition unable to reveal the whole truth. The narrator, through the use of darkness, is able to reveal the *presence* of elements which exceed official culture, but he cannot describe them to us—he can point out the *existence* of the *página negra*, but he cannot read it to us. When José Ido has revealed Amparo's secret in whispers to Felipe (whispers we cannot hear), the two immediately decide that neither spoken nor written language should ever express that secret:

Ido del Sagrario: Esto no se debe decir.
Aristo: No, no se debe decir.
Ido del Sagrario: Ni se debe escribir... (14)

Ido del Sagrario: This should never be said.
Aristo: No, it should never be said.
Ido del Sagrario: And it shouldn't be written, either.[29]

28. The translation is taken from Turner 15–16.
29. See Percival 154. The only voice that mars the bleached whiteness of public discourse is that of gossip, which, like realism, points out the stains on the whiteness of reputations but does not offer any constructive solutions. The narrator's information about Polo's downfall in chapter 14, for example, is drawn from local gossip: "Cuenta la mandadera . . ." ("As the errand girl tells it . . .") (50); "Cuenta la criada . . ." ("The maid recounts . . .") (51).

Because Amparo's marriage to Agustín would fly in the face of the hegemonic social norms, Amparo cannot even say to herself that he wants to marry her; she pauses and then decides that this thought is a moment of delirium (madness, again, signifies what falls outside cultural norms):

¿(P) or qué no había de auxiliarla quien aspiraba nada menos que a...? Sueño, delirio, esto no podía ser... (44)

Why shouldn't she get help from someone who aspired nothing less than to . . .? Mad fantasies; it couldn't really happen.

The other possibility, that Agustín wants her as a mistress, is equally inexpressible: "¿Quería hacerla su esposa o su...?" ("Did he want to make her his wife or his . . .?") (44). In fact, Amparo's whole existence, given her sin, exceeds the limitations of Spanish culture; it is for this reason that she cannot write Caballero or tell him verbally of her sin (44, 74); all attempts to express it remind her of Ido's *folletines*. Amparo eliminates language, wants to destroy all written words, aspires to be the "black hole" into which language would disappear (Percival 157–58). For the reader, the silence continues. We cannot hear Amparo confess to the priest; we cannot read the letters Marcelina possesses (115); we cannot hear Amparo's final confession to Agustín (122).[30] Neither Amparo nor the narrator can put into words her future relationship with Agustín, even as she prepares to leave with him for Bordeaux:

Incrédula, la joven miraba al que había sido su novio, al que por fin iba a ser su... (122)

Incredulous, the young girl stared at the man who had been her fiancé, who in the end was going to be her . . .

Rosalía finds no words to define Amparo morally:

¡Conque no puede hacerla su mujer porque es una... y la hace su querida...! (123)

So he can't make her his wife because she's a . . . , and he makes her his lover![31]

---

30. See also Urey on "the text's privileging of silence" ("Repetition" 48).

31. We recall that in *El doctor Centeno*, Alejandro Miquis's mistress cannot be named; she is referred to throughout as La Tal.

Culture, then, is a trap for the narrator as much as for the characters. Like Amparo trying to escape from Polo's apartment, the narrator can point to the door leading out of the prison but cannot go through it. The claustrophobic spaces of the novel make the protagonists, the narrator, and the reader feel like the trapped bat which represents Rosalía's secret idea:

El pensamiento revoloteaba por lo alto de la sombría pieza, chocando en las paredes y en el techo, como un murciélago aturdido que no sabe encontrar la salida. (27)

Rosalía's idea fluttered around high up in the somber room, bumping into walls and ceiling, like a bewildered bat that can't find the way out.[32]

The demystifying discourse of the narrator functions to deconstruct the kinds of writing that conform to culture, that silence nature. It reveals how the *folletín* glosses over sex, and the newspaper silences politics.[33] The narrator's discourse makes plain that crucial aspects of nature are being silenced, but he cannot fill that silence with an alternative voice. The realist novel exists to demystify already existent structures (genres, regimes), not to create a new one. Realism is thus shown in *Tormento* to depend for its existence on the status quo, and on its representative genre, the *folletín*. The white-washed, stereotyped world of the *folletín* must first be in place before realism can denounce it. Given the association of the *folletín* with the color white and realism with the color black, the very print on the pages we read (blackness stamped on whiteness) is semanticized in this novel as it often is in poetry. In this case the printed page acts as a metaphor for the novel's generic hybridization, a reminder that *both* genres are necessary to the text's existence. Nothing could illustrate more clearly than does the printed page the dependence of realism on the existing, unsatisfactory political system.

It is instructive in this context to compare the novel to the newspaper which Polo reads. First, in a delirium, Polo imagines himself

32. Charnon-Deutsch notes the labyrinthine organization of Rosalía's dwelling ("Inhabited Space" 36–37). Cluff shows how Amparo, in her final visit to Polo's apartment, must retreat into ever-smaller rooms (163).

33. Both the *folletín* and the newspaper are products of the same new printing technology that goes along with capitalism; again, we are shown that new economic strategies do not remedy the stifling aspects of culture.

reading a large newspaper *written in another language* (a language which *could* express something contrary to the existing system), a newspaper which proclaims another regime: " 'Revolution in Spain; The Monarchy Falls; Clergy Abolished, Freedom of Religion' " (58). When Celedonia brings him the real newspaper, his reading is described as follows:

Desgraciadamente para él, la Prensa, amordazada por la previa censura, no podía ya dar al público noticias alarmantes, ni hablar de las partidas de Aragón, acaudilladas por Prim, ni hacer presagios de próximos trastornos. Pero aquel periódico sabía poner entre líneas todo el ardor revolucionario que al país abrasaba, y Polo sabía leerlo y se encantaba con la idea de un cataclismo que volviera las cosas del revés. (58–59)

Unfortunately for him, the press, gagged by prior censorship, could no longer report alarming news. It couldn't speak of the bands of insurgents in Aragón, led by Prim, nor could it predict upcoming disturbances. But that newspaper had managed to say between the lines all of the revolutionary fervor that had set the country aflame, and Polo knew how to read it and was delighted at the idea of a cataclysm that would turn things upside down.

Several factors are noteworthy. First, the narrator wishes the novel to have a political function—that of filling in what the censored newspaper cannot say, namely the coming of revolution.[34] But, paradoxically, the novel is exactly *like* the newspaper in that it can point toward revolution (or toward sexual desire) but cannot represent it directly. The newspaper communicates revolutionary fervor *between the lines*, just as the novel communicates Amparo's sin in the ellipses, in the conversations we cannot hear. We are now forced to reevaluate our earlier description of the role of whiteness. If, as above, whiteness represents the *folletín* of the *Mujer Virtuosa*, it *silences* revolutionary and sexual desire. But we now see that the whiteness between the lines is necessary to grasp the meaning of the black, printed words. Without the whiteness between the lines, we would not know how to interpret the darkness, Amparo's *página negra*, the existence of desire. It is here that the utopian aspect of romance genres becomes active. Since romance is not bound to repre-

34. This gives the novel a function similar to the one it has had in Latin America—that of writing the history which the historians cannot write.

sent the real (what historically did occur), it can invent an ideal, utopian solution to the dilemma, the claustrophobia, the darkness of reality. Paradoxically, the realist novel must make use of the utopian aspect of the *folletín* in order to represent what the conservative ideology of the *folletín* has been silencing—alternative societies, nature. It is here that we can bring into play the constructive side of *Tormento*'s intertextual hybridization.

The narrator, in his critique of the established regime, has gotten into a double bind which he cannot resolve on his own. We can represent this double bind by drawing on Jameson's use of Greimas's semiotic rectangles (*Political Unconscious* 46–49, 82–83, 166–67, 254–57, 275–77). If we regard Amparo for a moment as the ultimate victim of culture (understood as the existing regime), we see that each of the two men who seeks to woo her embodies a conflicting combination of character traits and personal history. Neither combination will do as it stands. At the beginning of the text, Caballero has come from the freedom of nature but is virginal in love (34). Though he has had the freedom to satisfy his desire, he has not done so. Polo, who because of his link to the existing regime (institutionalized in the Church) does not have license to satisfy his desire, is unable to restrain it.

The two characters are thus created according to the oppositions "culture vs. nature" and "sterility vs. potency." Polo combines culture with potency, an option forbidden in the context of Spain, and one which has made him an outcast. Caballero, at the beginning of the text, combines nature with sterility, an option unsatisfactory for him. But Caballero attempts different combinations of these two oppositions over the course of the novel. He will next attempt to become a representative of the ideology of *honra*, abandoning nature for a strict adherence to cultural norms, and remaining sterile. It is now his view that the only way he will be able to be happy is through the legitimacy provided by culture: " 'Everything in an orderly fashion,' he would say. 'I'll either live by the rules, or I won't live at all' " (76). From this position, he cannot by definition provide a remedy to Amparo's predicament, since through her sexual act she has lost all claim to legitimacy within the system of *honra*. It is only at the end, when Caballero is forced to choose between legitimacy and Amparo, that the utopian, positive aspects of romance take over. Caballero realizes, first, that he does not understand the rules of "legitimate" society and therefore cannot function in it ("This world isn't for you" [113]). Next, he realizes that he wants to forgive Amparo even if this means rejecting social norms: "I feel like forgiving her, Madam Society, and I could care less what you think" (116). Finally, he becomes aware how repressive these norms are, how incompatible with desire:

Zapato de la sociedad, me aprietas y te quito de mis pies. Orden, política, religión, moral, familia, monsergas, me fastidiáis; me reviento dentro de vosotros como dentro de un vestido estrecho... Os arrojo lejos de mí... (118)

I've been shod by society, and now the shoe pinches and I'm going barefoot. Law and order, politics, religion, morality, family, what a load of crap. You drive me up the wall. If I stay in your straitjacket any longer, I'm going to explode. I'm flinging the jacket away.

Caballero's final position, then, appears to be an affirmation of nature and desire. But, as Bridget Aldaraca points out, America was not the Edenic society imagined by Polo, but rather, the anarchic and brutal reality of neocolonialist capitalist expansion. Caballero is thus seeking an ideal middle ground between an overly disordered nature (America) and a stultifying culture (Spain) (Aldaraca, "Tormento" 224–25). It is here that romance takes over the novel. Here, as Jameson puts it, Tormento abandons the indicative mood of realism and enters the subjunctive mood, the mood of what is hypothetical, what is desired (Political Unconscious 164–65). The new society is based on what is considered sin in the honra system—Agustín and Amparo will satisfy both sexual and material desires, and furthermore, they will not maintain the outward appearances dictated by religion. This society cannot, in the framework of Tormento, be portrayed directly, for this would require writing to overcome the dichotomy between black and white, between nature and culture. The demythifying discourse which dominates Tormento feeds on the discrepancy between signifier and signified, between appearance and "reality." But in the truly revolutionary society (as opposed to the real society of the Restoration), such a discrepancy would no longer be necessary; desire could be satisfied legitimately. Hence, realism cannot represent this society.[35] In such a new world, the conduct of

35. This is the reason why Rosalía and Bringas cannot accept the invitation they

Amparo would no longer be a sin, would not be a *página negra*.[36] But the use of the romance mode permits the narrator to lead us to the doorway of that new society through the novel's ending.[37]

The end of *Tormento* is laden with interpretive possibilities. Most crucially, we note that Amparo's escape with Agustín is in polemical contrast both to the conventional ending of the sentimental *folletín* and to the conventional ending of the realist novel. As Alicia Andreu has explained, the *folletín* of the *Mujer Virtuosa* ends in marriage as a reward for the chastity and abnegation of the poor heroine ("El folletín como intertexto" [59]). Amparo will enjoy Agustín's wealth and body without having been "virtuous" according to the norms of the *folletín* and without legitimizing their relationship through marriage. The realist novel, on the other hand, characteristically ends with the punishment of the individual desire that has dared to defy social norms. *Madame Bovary* (1857) ends in the heroine's suicide, *La Regenta* (1884–85) in her ignominious dishonor. In *Anna Ka-*

---

receive from Agustín and Amparo (now settled in France) in chapter 39 of Galdós's *La de Bringas;* the narrator could not represent a society which did not embody the signifier-signified contradiction which, in these novels, is coextensive with Spain.

36. Galdós's *Fortunata y Jacinta* (1886–87) will be more optimistic about the possibility of changing Spanish society. This is reflected in an inversion of the meaning of the colors black and white. By the end of *Fortunata y Jacinta,* the color black is associated with the priest who hopes to get Fortunata to repent of her revolutionary claim to be the legitimate wife of Juanito because she has borne the latter a son (974); Fortunata herself will *light up* as she declares that she is an angel. Catherine Jagoe has studied the ways in which this novel subjects the dominant paradigm of the angel in the house to radical questioning (see Jagoe, *Gender* ch. 5). I want only to point out that here, whiteness can be associated with a new and revolutionary way of thinking, which is impossible in the Old Regime prison of *Tormento.*

37. John H. Sinnigen is the only critic, to my knowledge, to have done a political reading of *Tormento.* He shows that Spain is suffering from allegiance to the precapitalist institutions of the ancien régime, with its appearance/reality dichotomy, and he points out *Tormento's* unmasking of the Restoration as being almost as stagnant as Isabelline Spain. Since Agustín, the capitalist hero, is forced to abandon Spain, this possible regenerating force is lost to the ancien régime. Sinnigen does not, however, explore the critique of capitalism which makes the latter an ambivalent force in *Tormento.* His belief in the text as a reflection of empirical reality also keeps him from appreciating the text's utopian thrust. (Of the escape to France, for example, he asks, "how much less hypocritical can society in the Bordeaux of the Second Empire be?" [29].) The main distinction between my approach and that of Sinnigen is that I attempt to link the pervasive questioning of political systems in *Tormento* to the text's formal peculiarities, to its ambiguous blend of romance and realism.

*renina* (1875-77), the heroine throws herself in front of a train—is it coincidental that Amparo's escape from repression is effected by train? *Tormento*'s ending does not preclude happiness for Amparo as would pure realism.

One can interpret the ending in at least two ways. It may appear that Galdós is steering a middle course between punishing his heroine and what would most clearly fly in the face of accepted values, namely, for Agustín to marry Amparo despite her "sin." According to this reading, Amparo's role as mistress is partially a punishment, for she must sacrifice social legitimacy if she is to get private happiness. But another interpretation is also possible. If Agustín were to marry Amparo, this would mean seeking legitimacy for their relationship from the very institutions of Isabelline Spain that have been defined as repressive and undesirable. If *Tormento* is to point the way toward a truly *new* society, it must be one which has broken with the past, which is not contaminated by its norms. Agustín appears to intuit this necessary break when he declares, "Marriage makes me nauseous" (120). In this way, *Tormento* creates a utopian compensation for what was *not* achieved in reality by the revolution of 1868 and the Restoration—that is, a clean break with the ancien régime.

It would be an exaggeration to imply that the narrator, by sending Agustín and Amparo off to an amorous escape from Spain, advocates the overturn of *all* the repressive norms operative there. It appears that the narrator endorses the bourgeois conception of the sexes as opposite and complementary in nature. Man operates in the material world, while woman as angel is a spiritual creature, indifferent to it. Thus, the narrator has little objection to Agustín's incessant buying of luxury goods (42, 68). But when Rosalía develops a desire for clothing and luxuries, she is described as "vanidosa" (87), and a hint of her coming dishonor is given:

Y esta grandiosa visión, estimulando dormidos apetitos de lujo . . . hacía de ella otra mujer, la misma señora de Bringas retocada y adulterada . . . (119)

This grandiose vision, arousing her slumbering craving for luxury, made her into another woman, the same Mrs. Bringas touched-up and adulterated.

Rejection of societal norms, too, is a very different matter for male characters than for female ones. Polo's rebellion against "las mímicas teatrales del púlpito" is praised by the narrator:

Era un hombre que no podía prolongar más tiempo la falsificación de su ser, y que corría derecho a . . . efectuar la revolución de sí mismo, y derrocar y destruir todo lo que en sí hallara de artificial y postizo. (51)

He was a man who couldn't keep falsifying his being any longer; he was heading straight to bring about an inner revolution, to overthrow and destroy everything artificial and fake he found in himself.

Caballero's final rebellion against society (his escape with Amparo) is presented as a triumph over society's outraged representatives, the Bringases. But *Amparo* is praised precisely for *conforming* to social expectations, for not wanting more than what society tells her to want. In a revealing example, Amparo explains to Agustín that social norms give her no means to feed herself, and that she may have to become a nun (32). Agustín decries the kind of society which would force such a solution on women ("That's for dead countries" [33]). But a few lines later, Amparo is praised for wanting only order and tranquility, for embracing the principles of the very society which does not enable her to earn enough to eat. The comment "Such good sense!" is shared between the narrator and Caballero. (We recall that Caballero elsewhere praises Amparo's conformity with her poor station in life [35].)

As discussed earlier, the narrator portrays strong-willed women as bossy and selfish, contrasting with the positive portrayal of Amparo, who obeys and serves men willingly. The end of *Tormento*, then, creates the paradoxical union of a man who has just done a three-day reflection on Spanish society and has been resurrected as a rebel, with a woman whose values conform, if not to the aristocratic preening of the Old Regime, at least to the separate spheres of bourgeois capitalism. The narrator can thus have his cake and eat it too; a thoroughgoing questioning of existent society can, in *Tormento*, be undertaken without necessarily changing the submissive conduct of women. (Amparo, in the train, is, as always, charmingly mute: "sin decir *esta boca es mía*" ["without making a peep"] [123]). This, truly, is Utopia!

We might conclude by recalling the one character who mars this masculine paradise. This is Refugio. Refugio is, of course, a minor character, yet her very presence in the novel suggests that she lurks as a threat somewhere at the periphery of bourgeois male consciousness. Among the women negatively portrayed in *Tormento*, Refugio is the most dangerous for the narrator. Rosalía and Marcelina, after all, are representatives of an outdated mode of production, albeit one which would persist in Spain much longer than Galdós could have foreseen. Further, they *conform* to the models of womanhood prescribed by the Old Regime; one can predict their actions and attitudes without difficulty. But Refugio's values are not so clear. She is associated initially with a bohemian youth culture that rejects bourgeois norms. Significantly, she is a model for painters, the subject of an art that might compete with texts like the narrator's, which place domestic angels at their center. Further, several aspects of her portrayal indicate that she wants to be in charge of her own destiny. On her initial appearance, she is shown as *writing herself* with a comb dipped in pomade, "like a quill in the inkwell, writing on her forehead letterlike curls of hair" (37). Amparo, of course, is defined precisely by her inability to find a language that is her own. Refugio's connection with writing, of course, already makes her morally suspect; we find a few barbs about her appearance and morals in this initial description.[38]

Yet the narrator is initially relatively well disposed toward Refugio, since he can consider her waywardness as the result of poverty. Refugio points out the intolerable situation of the woman who is penniless yet cannot be considered virtuous if she works for money. She defends her recourse to the pawnshop by pointing out that working at the Bringases' is not giving Amparo a penny to live on: "Could we survive on your leftover cake and your yard and a half of ribbon?" (39). When Amparo begins to prepare for her marriage to Agustín, Refugio has a chance to revert to the desired model of domestic conformity; now money for her to live on is guaranteed. Refugio's decision to make independence and desire her priorities, even when her living is assured, is what makes the narrator turn unequivocally against her. She is characterized ever more negatively as the text proceeds. He calls her a "streetwalker" ("andariega") (46) and blames her disagreeable qualities on her licentious habits:

Refugio . . . se transformaba rápidamente, por la ligereza de sus costumbres, en una mujer trapacera, envidiosa, chismosa. (75)

38. Catherine Jagoe has demonstrated Galdós's extremely negative attitude toward women writers; see *Gender* ch. 2.

Refugio . . . , because of her loose lifestyle, was rapidly becoming a deceitful, envious, gossipy woman.

Finally, he comments on her trajectory using the metaphors of hegemonic discourse:

Refugio se había disparado sin freno por la pendiente abajo, y ya no era posible contenerla. (86)

Refugio had taken off headlong down the slippery slope, and it was no longer possible to contain her.

Thus, Agustín may choose to adopt "el amor libre," but Refugio becomes a "bad seed" if she does so as well. What is interesting for a rethinking of women's roles in these novels is that Refugio is able to *disappear* and not be found. Amparo cannot locate her for days on end, and the narrator sheds no light as to her whereabouts. While it is of course suggested that Refugio is selling her body, such hints are vague. Nineteenth-century propriety and euphemism might preclude such matters being addressed directly. But within the context of society's relentless pursuit of those it defines as sinners—the system that made sure Amparo's secret was revealed—such vagueness may function in another way, indicating that society simply *does not know* what Refugio is doing.[39] The narrator, too, has lost control of her, and his condemnatory phrases are not heard by their target. Like Mariano of *La desheredada* in his vagabond phases, and like the Isidora who disappears into the streets at the end of that novel, Refugio is associated with a working class of threatening and uncertain aims, which cannot be controlled. It is clear that the independent-minded woman, whatever her financial state, will be lumped in with the working class by the narrator, for her revolutionary attitude overflows middle-class boundaries, and the frameworks which shape his thinking have nowhere else to put her.[40]

The ultimate effect of the interaction between the romance genre exemplified in Ido's *folletín* and the discourse of empirical observation is thus to create conditions in which each genre's dialectical nature is revealed. Both are shown to contain elements that tran-

39. Refugio has found *refuge* from the repression of the surrounding culture. For a consideration of the role of refuge in *Tormento* and *El cuarto de atrás*, see "Mass Culture and Escape," in ch. 6.

40. It is literally "no longer possible [for him] to *contain her*" (86) in his text.

scend existing social structures as well as elements that reinforce them. Realism is precisely a rich combination of generic conventions which foregrounds such contradictions and acknowledges them as its conditions of existence. Even the novel's ending, which seems to aim at a fusion of the revolutionary elements of both genres (that is, the romance capacity to imagine the new and different, and the demystifying critique of what exists), is finally shown to contain within itself two components—Agustín and Amparo—that behave according to different laws. This time it is gender which disrupts the harmonious fusion of genres.[41] In the end, different readers will have to seek the possibility of escape from repression in different places. Some will follow Agustín and leave the geographical limits of the claustrophobic kingdom. Others, with Refugio, will find the greatest freedom in hidden pockets within that kingdom, in spaces that the narrator cannot represent (or control) any more than he can portray the utopian Bordeaux where Agustín finds fulfillment.

Mass cultural discourses traverse *Tormento* in multiple ways. To include conduct manuals in a consideration of cultural production shows up the immense permeability of all literary texts, however elitist their vocation, to ideas repeated incessantly in the popular media. Many writers of the day attempted to postulate their relationship to mass culture as a simple binary opposition—mass culture was simply the opposite of their own "high" art. But texts like the ones considered in this study, by incorporating mass cultural forms and exploring the areas of overlap as well as those of disjunction, acknowledge that the picture is far more complex.

41. As Catherine Jagoe notes in relation to Galdós's early novels, "Gender seems to determine the asymmetric use of realism. . . . The treatment of the heroines obeys a different code to the representation of the male protagonists, and indeed selectively disrupts the narrative's realist or verosimilar dynamic with the discourse of the sentimental novel" (*Gender* ch. 3).

# Chapter Four

## Apocalypse Again: Mass Culture, Misogyny, and the Canon in

## Goytisolo's *Reivindicación del conde don Julián*

I have my books
And my poetry to protect me;
I am shielded in my armor,
Hiding in my room, safe within my womb,
I touch no one and no one touches me
I am a Rock, I am an island.—Simon and Garfunkel, "I Am a Rock"

The danger for artists, for geniuses . . . is woman.
—Nietzsche, *The Case of Wagner*

Los géneros menores están en las mismas condiciones que las mujeres en los países machistas, se goza de ellos pero no se les respeta.

Minor [literary] genres are in the same situation as women in macho societies—they are enjoyed, but not respected.—Manuel Puig

### Introduction

• • • **A** persistent commonplace among critics of twentieth-century Peninsular literature is that Galdós and Goytisolo represent diametrically opposed choices of literary technique and objectives.[1] This view is, no doubt, the result of an artificial separation between specialists in nineteenth-century novels and specialists in the twentieth-century postwar novel. Galdós, for the postwar specialist, has become "Don Benito el Garbancero," the faithful reproducer of colloquial street speech, unconcerned with polished style or with the autonomy of art, naively holding a mirror up to nature over four

---

"I Am a Rock," from Simon and Garfunkel's album *Sounds of Silence* (Columbia Records, 1965); words and music copyright © 1965/copyright renewed by Paul Simon, used by permission of Paul Simon Music.

1. Even Brad Epps, who refuses the bait of most critical clichés about Goytisolo, and whose argument will be central to my analysis below, hastens to dispel any confusion about this particular point: "Let me quickly add that I am not ascribing to Goytisolo some deep affinity to Galdós or a realist aesthetic . . ." ("Politics of Ventriloquism" 284).

decades.[2] Goytisolo, by contrast, is the rebel, rejecting the whole Spanish literary tradition and the norms of staid, bourgeois society. He dares to tear down the most cherished tenets of Francoism while the dictator still rules (*Reivindicación del conde don Julián* was written in 1970 and published outside of Spain); and he does so in an audacious violation of conventional literary syntax, using a language that is dense in literary allusion, yet remains playful, humorous, brimming with vitality.[3] Goytisolo represents the refreshingly new, while Galdós is the writer of old chestnuts like *Doña Perfecta*, which one left behind without regret after leaving graduate school.

My reading of *La desheredada* has already indicated the impossibility of reducing Galdós's work to this simplified idea of "realism." My more provocative enterprise in this chapter is to demonstrate that the roots of Goytisolo's *Reivindicación* are firmly planted in nineteenth-century soil. I will argue that the images and attitudes contained in *Reivindicación* can only be understood with reference to nineteenth-century cultural tropes; that the narrator's attitude toward mass culture and women reproduces nineteenth-century beliefs and obsessions; and that the text of *Reivindicación* is a response to social changes analogous to those which Galdós confronted in *La desheredada*. In thus historicizing *Reivindicación* (against the version the narrator gives of his own text as a rebellion outside of time and history), I maintain that we can best understand *La desheredada* and *Reivindicación* as rather closely placed on a continuum rather than as opposites. We can also learn more about *La desheredada* through such an analysis of *Reivindicación*, for many tendencies that were incipient in Galdós have become exacerbated in Goyti-

2. "Don Benito el Garbancero" was the sardonic epithet applied to Galdós by the modernist writer Ramón del Valle-Inclán in his 1920 *esperpento Luces de bohemia* (41). *Garbanzos* are chick-peas, both very typical of Spain and very plebeian; Valle found Galdós's style as colloquial and prosaic as this humble food.

3. Most critics of *Reivindicación* simply accept and glorify the narrator's most explicit version of his enterprise. Studies abound which praise his success in achieving sexual liberation, his destruction of "sacred Spain," his preference for chaos over order, and his linguistic breaks with tradition. There are relatively few studies which question this version, and very few which refuse the bait of the narrator's presentation of his text as "outside history." Since my arguments about mass culture and misogyny in the narrator's discourse depend precisely on historicizing, I will not attempt to be exhaustive in citing the existing scholarship on *Reivindicación*. The present chapter owes much to a few studies to which I will refer below.

solo, and their function is more easily understandable from this late twentieth-century vantage point. The principal lesson of *Reivindicación* for a reading of Galdós's text will be its development of the relationships between mass culture, misogyny, and the literary canon.[4]

This chapter will consider the misogyny of the narrator of *Reivindicación* in some detail before exploring the links between misogyny and mass culture in the novel. While the focus on misogyny may seem digressive, my argument is that the high/low opposition, whether made by narrators or by cultural critics, is most often a manifestation of a desire to keep *other* things separate, be it the sexes or social classes. Texts like *La desheredada* and *Reivindicación* establish structural homologies between sexual conduct, class relations, and the relations of high art and mass culture. To look at the high/low opposition is thus potentially to learn about misogyny or politics; to look at misogyny or class relations is often to encounter cultural distinctions.

## High/Low I: Transgression and Its Discontents

el loco va y viene, como
siempre, en ocio ensimismado

the madman, strolling back and forth
as usual, lost in his own thoughts
—Goytisolo, *Reivindicación del conde don Julián*[5]

In the ninety-year interval separating *La desheredada* from *Reivindicación del conde don Julián*, the idea of an omniscient narration which pretends to be about the lives of third persons has gone by the wayside. Whereas, with *La desheredada*, it is necessary to tease out the narrator's obsessions from the repeated metaphors on art and the metadiscursive comments he makes during a story ostensibly about

4. For an explanation of the novel's title and a plot summary, see the appendix.

5. In this and subsequent references to Goytisolo's *Reivindicación del conde don Julián*, Spanish quotations will be taken from the Seix Barral edition. Page numbers following quotations in English refer to *Count Julian*, by Juan Goytisolo, translated by Helen Lane. Copyright © 1974 by The Viking Press, Inc., English language translation. Used by permission of Viking Penguin, a division of Penguin Books USA Inc. An asterisk indicates a modified translation.

Isidora, in *Reivindicación* the reader is treated to the narrator's discourse about himself and his surroundings. And when the narrator does invent a hero (Julián) as imaginary protagonist of his story, we witness the process of that invention at work and can deduce the reasons for which the narrator invents such a character.

Both the Galdosian and the Goytisolian narrator are writing from an unevenly modern city. Because Goytisolo's nameless narrator has sought out Morocco for its underdevelopment, and because he is particularly fascinated by those aspects of Tangiers which are most foreign to European sensibility, critics have tended to forget that the Tangiers from which he speaks is *not* pure underdevelopment at all. In fact, it very likely bears many resemblances to the Madrid from which the Galdosian narrator wrote a century earlier—both are patchworks in which the latest inventions of modern technology coexist with areas untouched by modernity and capitalism. Old and new encounter each other in a chaotic hodgepodge on the city streets.

Because much of the text is devoted to the imaginary invasion of Spain by the narrator's invented, omnipotent alter ego, Julián, criticism has often ignored the distinctions between the narrator and Julián. The narrator's experiences as he walks through the city are usually considered as mere "raw material" to be ingeniously developed and rewritten during Julián's invasion of Spain. I believe that we can explain very little about *Reivindicación* without reference to the very specific circumstances of the narrator in Tangiers; the text is generated according to the peculiar needs of his psyche. That psyche, in my reading, is not simply that of an individual, but a culturally determined complex of obsessions which illuminates the predicament of modern man in general, and the Spanish, male writer in particular.

The narrator, in exile in Tangiers, is engaged in a belated reproduction of the paradigmatic exiles of the great European modernists of the early decades of the century, who wrote from major cities which were in many respects impenetrable to them.[6] The cities are diverse, teeming with different nationalities and social classes; the writer finds no stable structure into which he can integrate. The city frag-

6. See Raymond Williams, "When Was Modernism?" in *The Politics of Modernism* 34.

ments experience into disconnected, often antithetical images. The writer is isolated in the crowd: "immersed in the crowd, yet not a part of it: following a different rhythm" (28–29). Radically disconnected from the world around him, the writer turns that experience of alienation and fragmentation into the specific, fragmentary techniques of modernist narration. His emphasis is on the medium, since he is unfamiliar with the social content of what he is witnessing. His communication is with other exiled writers like himself.

Two main features distinguish our narrator from this composite described by Williams. One is that Goytisolo's writer has exiled himself to the Third World rather than to European centers of capitalist production. The other is that the alienation has become so exacerbated as to border on psychosis. The first two parts of the text, which describe the narrator's daily wandering through the city, present a pathetic figure. He is paranoid, terrified not only of the Spanish police ("their eyes that see everything, . . . their evil tongues that know everything" [7]), but of daily life in Tangiers. Each morning he must conquer his fear of leaving his apartment, comparing his mental fabulations to the stories Scheherazade told to delay her death (5). Once outside, we see his fear of getting lost in the crowd, his need for a guide, his acute sense of abandonment when a child who has been showing him the city disappears (55). We see his inability to understand the city ("an equation whose terms you are unfamiliar with" [29]), his constant temptation to seek refuge in the womblike protection of a café. He avoids human contact, fleeing from it in terror when it is forced on him. His heart beats rapidly after such encounters. Only the flute music played by the knife sharpener affords him temporary calm; it seems to erase the complex modernity of the city, enveloping it in a precapitalist folklore. Repeatedly, the narrator is racked by feelings of guilt (which, he tells us, are residue from his childhood) and overcome with shame; he imagines himself trapped in a gallery of mirrors at the fair, the onlookers laughing as he helplessly searches for the exit (73). His social relations are mediated by money or by drugs, as when he has his daily dose of hashish with a group of Arabs watching television in a café. Given his fear of human contact (both physical and emotional), he populates his inner world with imaginary characters, split-off parts of himself. So alienated is he from both the outside world and himself that he speaks of both in the second person. The text, written as the narrator's second-person

discourse to himself, becomes a circular communication which protects against the outside world and claims self-sufficiency.[7]
In order to maintain the fragile boundaries of his crumbling identity, the narrator follows a rigid routine, repeated every day of the
week. His wanderings through the city always follow the same route;
he enumerates the few belongings in his room to gain a sense of
familiarity (José-Carlos Pérez 164). He puts the best face on his isolation, claiming to live outside of history (16), to be free to go where he
wants (37). He protects himself by intellectualizing, giving literary
form to the banality of his day. He is an actor in his own drama
("silence, please, ladies and gentlemen, the curtain is about to go up"
[5]). Most importantly, he makes Góngora, the leading poet of the
Spanish baroque period, his protective muse whose poetry will enable him to find coherence in the threatening city: "transmitting its
redeeming signals to you across the centuries, guiding signs that
reach you even amid all the chaos, delivering you from the deceptive
labyrinth" (28). Góngora's poetry lies on his night table; he appeals to
the poet to help him "to live with roots: . . . my only sustenance your
nourishing language" (104). The desire of this terrified man is, in
short, to disappear into the safe realm of literature, to be exempt from
life in the world altogether.

The narrator is the first to admit, however, that the world he is so
afraid of is inside himself ("knowing that the labyrinth lies within"
[40]). It is clear that the characters he encounters in the city (some
of whom melt unexpectedly into thin air) are projections of his
obsessions. So, I would argue, is the city itself. In what follows, I
will explain the narrated city as the discourse of a late nineteenth-
century bourgeois fantasy. The reasons for the persistence of these
nineteenth-century obsessions in a late twentieth-century text will
be explored later in the chapter.

Peter Stallybrass and Allon White argue that our means of making
social and cultural divisions or classifications involves a fluidity, a
symbolic transcoding, between the body, the psyche, geography, and
the social. All four are structured in terms of a high/low opposition,
which is often described in terms of the difference between the clas-

7. This self-communication is the result of the narrator's alienation from all social
classes (he despises the bourgeoisie but cannot feel part of the working class); from any
sense of patriotism or national roots; and from capitalism and Russian communism
alike. His pathological fear of even superficial human contact completes the picture.

sical body (the Greek statue, closed, finished, graceful, high on a pedestal) and the grotesque or carnivalesque body (excessively corpulent, full of orifices and protuberances, lowly, all-inclusive). Thus, Western culture's oppositions between northern and southern countries, between high art and mass culture, between bourgeoisie and proletariat, between reason and the unconscious, are often expressed using the images of these two bodies, or as oppositions between the upper and the lower body.

Stallybrass and White cite Norbert Elias's observation that only with the rise of the middle classes does a conflict begin between socially inadmissible impulses and social demands (89–90). This creates a specific historical form of neurosis. As a result, the bourgeoisie develops an increasingly phobic relationship to the grotesque body. By the nineteenth century, the attempt to reject the "low" aspects of the self has become even more intense.[8] The lower half of the body becomes unmentionable, and instead the bourgeoisie write obsessively about the lower half of the *city*—its slums, carefully kept as separate as possible from bourgeois suburbs. In the nineteenth-century bourgeois imagination, the "low" terms of all oppositions blur into an indissociable mass; each is seen as causally linked to the others. Thus poverty, illness, dirt, disease, sexuality, animals, the working class, savages, and the prostitute are imagined as inextricably connected; reference to one of these terms commonly relies on images drawn from the others. With illness symbolically linked to this whole chain of "low" elements, the bourgeoisie lives in fear of contagion and becomes phobic about bodily contact on the city streets, where nothing separates high from low. The prostitute becomes symbolically central to bourgeois fantasy life—and to its literature—because she is one channel where everything associated with the "low" can contaminate the "high," bourgeois world. The dread of the low is accompanied by fascination; young bourgeois men go "slumming" to gaze upon the forbidden Other, whom they associate with nighttime revelry, drunkenness, and unbridled desire. Bourgeois women do not have the outlet of slumming; they often succumb to hysteria, in which terrors associated with the lower body find their expression as symptoms in the upper half.

Goytisolo's narrator has come to Tangiers in an attempt to find his

---

8. See Stallybrass and White, chs. 3–5.

own, repressed lower body. Although this is a text often associated with sexual liberation, I will argue that any liberation there might be is actually carried out by the imaginary character, Julián, and not by the narrator.[9]

The nineteenth-century complex of associations and obsessions is the legacy of the narrator's childhood in a wealthy Spanish residential area of the 1940s. As a child, he listens to the fascinated gossip of two bourgeois women about the Moorish caretaker of a nearby construction site. The sexualized Moor is said to have had an affair with a corpulent, alcoholic, flower-selling woman of the neighborhood, and to have publicly urinated on her retarded child after they quarreled (78–80). The whole nineteenth-century chain of associations is present—the lower class, sex, alcohol, the night, lower bodily functions, and so forth. The result is that the listening child-narrator finds himself "relentlessly pursued by premonitions and desires: . . . with pounding heart" (80).

The description of Tangiers in part 1 of *Reivindicación* is much like the discourse of a nineteenth-century bourgeois city dweller free-associating about his obsessions, desires, and fears. The intense repression of the narrator's own sexuality results in its projection onto everything and everyone. This begins with the sex life of a cat which has just been found dead by some neighborhood boys:

existencia rescatada, quien sabe, por furtivos momentos de amor : ardientes noches del invierno africano, propicias a todos los éxtasis, a todos los olvidos : roncos maullidos de prodigiosa densidad erótica que a menudo, en medio de tu sueño, te desvelan (18)

an existence possibly redeemed by furtive moments of love: nights of burning passion in the course of the African winter, affording every sort of ecstasy, every variety of oblivion: incredibly erotic, raucous meowing that has often kept you awake in the middle of the night (9)

We note the stereotype of Africa as perpetual aphrodisiac, and the projection of sex and the lower body onto animals; the latter is immediately repeated when the narrator observes the dead insects he has collected, some "dying in the midst of performing their digestive or

9. Even Julián's sexuality is not equivalent to sexual liberation, because of the intense hatred and fear of women that Julián shares with his inventor. See Epps, "Politics of Ventriloquism."

reproductive functions: in the euphoria of a sumptuous banquet or prolonged, languid copulation" (10).

Aside from the tourists, the cityscape is mainly populated by other incarnations of the nineteenth-century obsession with the "low." The narrator's journey through the city is punctuated by encounters with different kinds of beggars. An old woman whose gaze is like a mute reproach sits immobile by a wall, her hand held out like a starfish (12). Another beggar tells him his troubles and those of his family as he hits him up for a daily handout; the narrator tries to escape, but inevitably runs into him at every corner (13–16). Later, he is pursued by

una horda de mendigos que corren detrás de ti, te tiran de la manga, te rodean, amenazan, suplican, intentan cortarte el paso... (74)

a horde of beggars at your heels: surrounding you, tugging at your sleeve, threatening you, whining at you, attempting to block your path (60)[10]

He avoids their gaze, described as "*demanding" (74) and "viscous" (87). Aside from the class guilt evoked by the omnipresence of the beggars, encounters with them are traumatic because they insist on touching him—a bourgeois phobia—and because even their gaze is seen as contaminating, associated with the viscosity of the lower body.[11]

Lame or deformed Arabs, the rotting food and pungent smells of the market, a madman, a homosexual observed in the city—all continue the chain of associated symbols of the "low." In order not to leave out any possible qualifications to be a nineteenth-century man, our narrator also fears he has (or actually has) syphilis, stopping for a

---

10. Leopoldo Alas's *La Regenta* (1884–85) is an excellent place to study nineteenth-century anxieties about the low, as Noël Valis has done. Valis notes that Oviedo, the city where *La Regenta* takes place, was preoccupied at the time with the proliferation of beggars, and had unsuccessfully attempted to expel them from the city ("On Monstrous Birth" 202–03). *La Regenta* is a text rewritten in many ways in *Reivindicación*, both in terms of the general theme of the disastrous effects of Spain's hypocritical sexual repression and in many specific plot events.

11. Stallybrass and White point out that the stare of the poor is seen as humiliating and aggressive, while that of the rich is believed to be pure (135). This is borne out in *La Regenta*, where the wealthy Ana is troubled successively by the gazes of a toad in the fields, her maid, and working-class men who pass her on the street (*La Regenta*, ch. 9).

daily blood analysis and injection; before this daily "rebirth," he sees himself as "infested with germs, rotten to the bone" (6). He reproduces the nineteenth-century focus on epidemics (cholera, syphilis) in his plan to inoculate Spanish blood banks with a rabies which will then spread throughout the social body.

The ultimate expression of the narrator's fear of bodily contact and repulsion at the grotesque body comes when he attempts to "purify" himself by entering an Arab sauna, but must first find a niche in the mass of men already there. He advances "cautiously"; the steam has transformed the Moors into "viscous, ductile, frightening, submarine fauna: spherical visages like puff-fish, arms like octopus tentacles, empty, dead eye sockets" (69). He sighs with relief when he finds a place, having eluded "flabby, unnecessary excrescences of flesh" (70).[12]

In a key episode, the adult narrator inadvertently recreates the story he heard as a child when he begins to urinate in the urinal of a café, only to find someone is already there, invisible in the darkness below. Referring to his penis as "*your astonished guiltiness," he hastily returns it to its "*lair" and flees (47). We later learn that his preoccupation with syphilis and with the grotesque body, as well as the guilt and fascination associated with the lower body, come from the church sermons he heard as a child. They have caused in him an irreversible repression; his sexualized discourse may be considered analogous to the hysteric's displacement of lower bodily functions onto the upper body.[13] In this case, as the narrator makes abundantly clear during the invasion of Spain, the violent tongue with which he narrates the rape of Spain by the Arabs with their "snakes" is a displacement of the penis he does not dare to use.[14]

The narrator seems to have chosen Morocco in a conscious attempt to combat his repression through constant immersion in the

12. The narrator's terror at bodily contact will surface again when he takes a crowded bus home: "the vehicle is jam-packed, and bunches of people are hanging out the side door . . . : impossible to escape: . . . you are caught between the devil and the deep blue sea, *helpless, trapped between the prima donna, the peasant woman with the basket of eggs, and the acrobatic cyclist: the sweat rolls down your back . . ." (199–200).

13. See Stallybrass and White 185.

14. The narrator is also obsessed with violence but cannot stomach actually watching it when he encounters it on the street (José-Carlos Pérez 162).

elements the bourgeoisie have rejected as the "low." The result is a constant state of combined fascination and terror. Given that the scene the narrator describes is actually the contents of his own psyche, the choice of an urban setting is easily understood. For the city is the source of nineteenth-century obsessions with slums, sewers, and prostitutes. And the city is also a liminal place of constant encounters between low and high. It reflects the narrator's bourgeois self in its cafés and cosmopolitan multilingualism; and it reflects the content of his fantasy life in all its "low" ingredients.

What the narrator is trying to do is to invert the system of values associated with Franco's Spain and the European bourgeoisie—to degrade what they cherish, and exalt everything they abhor. In doing so, he inverts most, but not all, of the traditional oppositions central to Western culture:

The Narrator's Oppositions

| *"High"* | *"Low"* |
|---|---|
| Third World ("natural") | Spain and the West (commercial, "fallen") |
| sex | religion |
| proletariat, beggars | bourgeoisie |
| the irrational (violence, instinct) | the rational |
| primitive | developed |

But the narrator retains in their traditional relations with high and low three key oppositions:

| high art | mass culture |
|---|---|
| classical body | grotesque body |
| man | woman |

The associations between these three oppositions, and the man/woman opposition as the foundation of the entire text, will be discussed at length below. For it is a war between the sexes which determines the narrator's representation of the literature–mass culture relationship.[15] For the moment, I will bracket the gender question

---

15. The insights on gender gained in a reading of *Reivindicación* can be productively projected back onto *La desheredada* as well; see below.

as I explore the attempted inversion of values. It is necessary, first, to qualify my assertion that the high art/mass culture opposition is treated in a traditional manner by the narrator. For the narrator does degrade the classics he considers quintessentially Spanish (the Golden Age honor play, the Generation of 1898), lumping them together with mass culture as the "low." On the "high" side of the opposition are Spanish works written by exiles, outsiders, rebels, and homosexuals (Rojas, Cernuda, Buñuel, Blanco White, and others), and the general corpus of non-Spanish, Western high culture.

All of the "low" terms, associated with Franco's Spain, are described in terms of the grotesque body, with special emphasis on animals and excrement. The narrator satirizes the Generation of '98's fetishizing of the Gredos mountain range north of Madrid as embodying the purest essence of Spain. He associates it with a mountain goat who wanders through Gredos defecating; the turds are then sniffed in ecstasy by the stereotypical Spaniard, Don Alvaro Peranzules. Don Alvaro himself is a crustacean, with his hard shell being akin to the ossified clichés that govern the worldview of the Spaniard. Saint Teresa is compared to a hen. In another nineteenth-century conflation of "low" elements, the narrator curses the corpus of classics: "may pigs root and wallow in this pestilential sewer" (132).[16] He dismisses the whole Spanish collection of the Tangiers library as "four centuries of Castilian *rot" (133).

On the level of discourse, the Spanish classics are made grotesque by being taken off their pedestals and made to mix with the jargon of the mass media. Fragmented into bite-sized clichés, the classics are now equivalent to the disconnected items in the newspaper; the hybridization of high and mass serves to trivialize both. The most offensive sector of the mass culture industry for the narrator is tourism, clearly associated with the grotesque body in the obese "Hija de la Revolución Americana" who wears huge sunglasses and lots of makeup, adorning herself in a red fez she acquires in the Tangiers square as a souvenir (35–37). And the central symbol of Franco's Spain is of course the prostitute, representative of Spain's willingness to "sell out" its most cherished values of austerity, spirituality, and chastity in order to attract tourist dollars. Thus, the prostitute, who

16. Stallybrass and White note the idea, widespread in Victorian England, that swine roamed the sewers (147).

in traditional bourgeois discourse is meant to incarnate the *antithesis* of the bourgeoisie, becomes in *Reivindicación* that class's supreme representative.

The other side of the coin is that the conventionally "low" elements of the Tangiers cityscape are "elevated" by the narrator's highbrow classical discourse. The flute playing of the itinerant knife sharpener becomes "the shepherd's flute of one of Pan's disciples, a companion of Bacchus" (8). The utterly grotesque body of a lame, deformed beggar is rendered "beautiful" by a comparison with the ballet dancers Pavlova and Nijinsky (33); the grotesque body has been made "classical." References to classical mythology are brought in constantly to describe the most banal of objects and circumstances.[17] The narrator's most explicit statement of inversion is an exaltation of rot, which follows a description of the intense smells of various foods rotting in the sunlight of the open market. It is a declaration of opposition to Spain:

proclamándolo orgullosamente frente a tus engreídos compatriotas : todo lo que sea secreción, podredumbre, carroña será familiar para ti : caricias rudas, lecho áspero : antiguo y sabio amor de mahometano chivo : lejos de vuestras santas mujeres y sus sagrarios bien guardados (44)

proudly proclaiming to your conceited compatriots that everything that is secretion, rottenness, carrion will be your chosen realm: rude caresses, a hard bed: expert love-making in the age-old manner of the Mohammedan he-goat: far from your saintly Spanish women and their zealously guarded sanctuaries (32)

The narrator is trying to shed his bourgeois identity by conquering his aversion to smells. What is interesting in the passage above is the use of a very "nineteenth-century" slippage from rot to homosexuality. The bourgeois obsession with decay and sewage was a mechanism compensating for the repression of the lower body, and thus rot is sexualized in the nineteenth-century imaginary. We see that the narrator has chosen homosexuality for the same reasons he embraces rot—both are viscerally rejected in Spanish culture.

---

17. *Reivindicación* is a prime example of the modernist process of "decorating the city" described by Ramos (112), with the difference that what is made beautiful by style and literary trappings is not modern technology but underdevelopment. The political implications of such a move need hardly be underscored.

Jo Labanyi has insightfully demonstrated the many ways in which the narrator actually reproduces elements of Francoist ideology rather than transgressing them.[18] She emphasizes, among other things, the narrator's very Christian quest for purification, reading the praise of putrefaction in the market as a form of ascesis (201). For her, the narrator is not free, because transgression perpetuates the taboos it breaks (202). By defining himself as the photographic negative of what he was brought up to be, she argues, the narrator is putting on a mask which mirrors the crustacean mask of Francoist clichés he denounces in the Spaniards; he continues to define himself according to an external set of values (203).

To insist on the difference between the narrator and his imaginary invention, Julián, is to realize that the failure of the attempted transgression is even more total than Labanyi indicates. Despite the exaltation of rot when it is Moorish, we have seen that the narrator uses absolutely traditional images associated with the lower body and the socially low (excrement, animals, the prostitutes, and putrefaction itself) to debase Franco's Spain. This means that the narrator has not truly questioned the repugnance of the bourgeoisie for the lower body.[19] This, in turn, indicates that his own personal project of liberating his lower body must fail. And so it does. For whatever the activities carried out in imagination by Julián (and even these, as Labanyi suggests, are only a photographic negative of those of the respectable Westerner), the lifestyle of the narrator is nothing other than bourgeois. To truly embrace the low would be to live the carnival of the night, to enjoy the sensuality of the crowd on the street, to abandon the library. But the narrator incarnates rather the nineteenth-century *flâneur* who wanders the city *observing* the crowd as an *outsider* to it.[20] His life consists of weaving paths from one café to another, with a movie thrown in; drugs provide diversion. Far from

18. I refer the reader to her excellent study for the particulars. See *Myth and History* 196–214.

19. The narrator's conscious mind tries to break through his repression, but his unconscious is colonized by it, producing terror and guilt. The narrator's fantasy of killing Alvarito is merely an attempt to repress his respectable bourgeois self rather than his "lower" impulses. But the bourgeois self, like its lower counterpart, cannot be eliminated; it is simply reborn the next day, demanding its place in his psyche.

20. John Rignall, in *Realist Fiction and the Strolling Spectator*, sees the *flâneur* as a recurrent and representative figure in the realist novel.

experiencing the carnival of the night, the narrator retires home. As bourgeois writer, he uses the city as raw material which he must represent by observing it from *above*—hence his frequent recourse to *miradores* from which he can get a panoramic view of the city (30, 48, 52, 55). He appeals to Góngora to lift him above the madding crowd: "soaring falcon, noble Poet, come to my aid: bear me aloft to the realm of more luminous truths" (104). The poet soars like a bird over his material; the price is that he will never be *part* of it. The "high" modernist form of the novel can thus be read as a flight from its "low" content; as Pérez notes of Goytisolo's writing career, the more Goytisolo espouses the primitive, the more complex and intellec-tualized the narrative discourse becomes (José-Carlos Pérez 9).[21]

Critics have already reproached Goytisolo with abandoning all notions of solidarity in *Reivindicación*.[22] Given that the supposed Third World described in the novel is simply a compendium of West-ern fantasies of the "low Other," it is not surprising that no attempt is made to actually discover or engage with Moorish culture.[23] The Arab is instrumentalized, functioning merely as a signifier of trans-gression. More serious, as Schaefer-Rodríguez has indicated, is the idealization of Arab poverty and the implication that it lies *outside* Western capitalism rather than being actively generated by the latter (49–50). For me, the final reason why the goal of individual liberation must fail is that the individual is never as separate from the social as the narrator seems to believe. Killing the persistent beggar as he does at the end will not alleviate his class guilt. And he has repressed those elements of Spain which mar the picture he wants to paint of it as unequivocally corrupt. The narrator represents Spain as populated by modern technocrats, materialistic members of the petty bour-geoisie, and intellectuals of the "'98" variety who ignore progress; all of them consent to Franco's rule. He is trying very hard to create a

---

21. The use of Góngora as guide and muse contains several ironies. First, the narrator takes the most difficult poetry ever written in Spain, where metaphors of other metaphors create a labyrinth of uncertainty, and seeks in it a guide to rescue him from the labyrinth of the city (28). Secondly, he asks certainty ("luz más cierta," a more certain light) of a Baroque literature which can only offer a play of signifiers. Third, he tries to get past his repression by taking a priest as his model.

22. See especially Schaefer-Rodríguez, but also Labanyi, *Myth and History*.

23. As Allon White indicates, by the modernist period, transgression has lost its public dimension and become a private matter, rarely subversive of the social order.

Spain he can unambiguously hate. But the result is that he betrays not only his adoptive Arab culture (which he stereotypes) but the many Spaniards cruelly oppressed both economically and politically under the Franco regime. The narrator seems to stake the construction of a firm identity on these omissions. But the effort involved in repressing so much of both Arab and Spanish reality is so great that his entire day, repeated endlessly, is spent trying to achieve it.

### High/Low II: Woman, Mass Culture, and the Search for Male Purity

[O]ur contemporary culture oscillat[es] between hysteria (confusion of sexual difference) and paranoia (its reinforcement).
—Alice Jardine, *Gynesis*

tu vientre liso ignora la infamia del ombligo

(your smooth belly is untainted by the infamy of the umbilical cord).
—Goytisolo, *Reivindicación*

It is now time to examine the oppositions which the narrator does *not* invert—those between high art and mass culture, and between man and woman. It seems plausible to conjecture that these are the most basic classificatory structures for the narrator's sense of self, for they remain unquestioned despite his conscious attempt to invert all Western values. I will argue that the category of gender (and specifically the fear and hatred of women) is the fundamental organizing feature of both the form and the content of the text. It determines his attitude toward mass culture and highbrow literature and is even more crucial to his motivation for writing than the drive to destroy Franco's Spain.

The first pages of *Reivindicación* contain not only an invective against Franco's Spain (understandable since we gather the narrator has been persecuted by Franco's police) but also a less easily explained vocabulary of mothers, stepmothers, umbilical cords, and wombs. Upon waking in Tangiers, the narrator imagines himself tied by an umbilical cord to the Spanish shore he can see from his window; he is overcome by anxiety at the idea of being trapped and devoured by the mother's digestive and reproductive system (4). He goes on to explain that he must keep the shores of Spain in sight as a permanent guarantee that he is not inside, engulfed by it (5). Yet maternal imagery is not only negative; the narrator's dark room in Tangiers provides a "reassuring fetal *darkness," acting as a "soothing womb" protecting him from the cruel sunlight and the uncertainties of the outside world (6). In a shift of terminology, the narrator then redefines Spain as a bestial Madrastra crouching in wait (7). The initial description of the Spain the narrator is attacking is thus inseparable from his struggle with women, and particularly with the figure of the mother. This will continue to be the case throughout the text; the narrator will later represent Spain as a giant Vagina explored by tourists; Spanish women will be raped and tortured; and the specter of incest between mother and son will be raised in part 4, only apparently resolved by the son's suicide. Brad Epps has brilliantly diagnosed the flight from women and the hatred of women enacted in the text, denouncing its reproduction of the traditional silencing of women's voices throughout history ("Politics"). What is not clear from reading Epps or other critics who have pointed out the misogyny is where it comes from. I will attempt here to identify some of the historical determinants of this misogyny. It is a trend in modern writing which goes along with a specific kind of treatment of mass culture; it cannot be reduced to any specific circumstances pertaining to Goytisolo as an individual, nor can it even be limited to Spain.

What follows is a selective survey of misogyny which specifies those elements coined in the nineteenth century, and those which are peculiar to the modern writer. It will then be possible to explain the confluence of misogynies which determines the inner logic of *Reivindicación*.

The matrix (if I may be pardoned the maternal metaphor) of the misogyny rampant in *Reivindicación* is a traditional hatred of women passed down primarily through the Church. In medieval exempla, woman was seen as a bearer of death, via a contact poison in her sweat. The devil took the form of woman to harm virtuous man. In the many stories of cuckolded husbands, woman's sexual voracity was taken for granted (Goldberg). In medieval cathedral sculpture, the vice of unchastity is invariably represented as woman. Medieval church teachings regard woman as the daughter of Eve, responsible for man's fall; the only exception is the Virgin, whose importance is a medieval invention. She, of course, is the only woman who can attain the redeeming function of maternity without contaminating herself through sex; the ordinary woman is relegated to the category of Eve (Kraus). The female body is horrifying, impure, harmful to men.

In the nineteenth century, medical science defines woman by her lower bodily functions. Her mood, health, and functioning are seen as controlled by her reproductive organs; any "disorder" in these could produce hysteria, nymphomania, prostitution, madness. The "good," "normal" bourgeois woman supposedly had no sexual desire; any manifestation of such desire could be construed as pathological or dishonorable (Aldaraca, "El ángel del hogar" 78). The Mary/Eve, or Madonna/whore opposition thus continues strong. Man, of course, is defined by the activity of the upper body—reason.[24]

The traditional horror of the female body becomes associated with the whole chain of signifiers of the "low" studied by Stallybrass and White. The nineteenth century projects "onto the feminine body the obsessions and ills of the collective body" (Valis, "On Monstrous Birth" 207). In many nineteenth-century novels, the female body becomes the figure of bourgeois anxiety about sewers, beggars, the working class, disease, and sexuality. The nineteenth century, says Valis, fears the dissolution of the orderly surface of bourgeois life and the emergence of the formless, the decomposed, the inchoate. Such anxieties are projected onto woman.

The crowning figure of the low and of social ills is of course the prostitute; prostitution became known as "the Great Social Evil" (Walkowitz 32).[25] First, the prostitute is the main figure for the conduit which carries infection, filth, the "low" upward to the bourgeoisie, contaminating them and debilitating their genetic patrimony through syphilis. She is also symbolic of the diseased city, representative of all types of urban pathology (Corbin 212; Walkowitz 3–4, 32).[26] But the prostitute's symbolic supremacy is not only the result

24. The medical science of the day declared that menstruation left behind each month "a ragged wreck of tissue, torn glands, ruptured vessels . . ."; woman was seen as perpetually traumatized by this, unable to function consistently in public life (Laqueur 221–22).

25. As Laqueur points out, before the nineteenth century, it was only one of many social evils, including drunkenness and blasphemy (229–30).

26. It is easy to interpret, in this context, the anxiety of La desheredada's narrator about Isidora's disappearance into the streets as a prostitute; she represents the aspira-

of her becoming the most threatening emblem of the "low." She was also seen as having an organic connection to industrial capitalism. On the one hand, she was a trigger for class guilt, revealing the sexual and economic exploitation inherent in the system (Walkowitz 4). But more seriously, the exchange of sex for money seemed to reveal the impact of the market on the most intimate human relations; as Simmel pointed out, the prostitute, like money, was a mere means to an end (Simmel, *On Individuality and Social Forms* 122; see also Ramos 136). The fear was that the egotism unleashed in the market economy would result in the demise of society, as people used one another as mere means to an egotistical end and ignored the common good (Laqueur 229–33). All of these fears were displaced onto the prostitute, who was the object of obsessive discussion and writing.

The dishonor of the marketplace for women was not confined to the prostitute. The fear of woman's sexual voracity was displaced into theories of woman's innate voracity in the marketplace. The commonplace of the day was that woman and consumerism were inextricably linked; the guilt arising from the market economy thus fell only on her shoulders. As with sexual desire, the honest woman was supposed to lack material desires, to remain at home, uncontaminated by the marketplace. In the male nineteenth-century imagination, for a woman to frequent the stores was inextricably linked to possible sexual promiscuity.[27]

The other new element of the nineteenth-century city—again a by-product of industrialization—was the crowd, another object of intense anxiety on the part of the bourgeoisie. As the (male) individual began to feel lost in the mass, the threat of being devoured or swallowed up in its formlessness made the writers of the day associate the masses with the whole chain of signifiers defined as "low" or inchoate. And crowds, in the theory of the most popular crowd psychologist, Gustave LeBon, were *feminine*. Crowds were fickle, credulous, temperamental (110): "Crowds are everywhere distinguished by feminine characteristics. . . . The simplicity and exaggeration of the sentiments of crowds have for result that a throng knows neither doubt

---

tions of the disenfranchised classes ("los desheredados") and announces her intention to take vengeance on bourgeois men (1175).

27. We can see the connection elaborated, for example, in Galdós's *La de Bringas* (1884).

nor uncertainty. Like women, it goes at once to extremes" (LeBon 39, 50; see also Moscovici 110, 112).[28]

Some important observations must be made at this point—some in the form of conjectures, others as firmer conclusions. First, one may speculate on why male identity in particular seems to be constantly threatened by the "devouring feminine" beginning in the nineteenth century. One reason, as critics have pointed out, is the first major women's movement in Europe (Huyssen 47); women were threatening to enter spheres previously occupied only by men.[29] This made it more difficult for man to achieve a clear difference between himself and woman—woman being a stand-in for Mother, against whom he had to define his autonomy and separation (see Swartz 97).[30] As well, the Industrial Revolution brought the separation between workplace and home that sent men out of the home for most of the day and confined women inside it. The male child thus faced the constant presence and attention of the mother and lacked the example of a father with whom to identify. His separation from the mother was then all the more difficult.

An important conclusion must be drawn from the ascription of "feminine" characteristics to the urban masses. Georg Simmel, the turn-of-the-century sociologist, asserted that "the deepest problems of modern life flow from the attempt of the individual to maintain the independence and individuality of his existence against the sovereign powers of society, against the weight of the historical heritage and the external culture and technique of life" (On Individuality 324).

The individual, says Simmel, risks being "swallowed up in the social-technological mechanism" (324; italics mine). We notice that a shift has occurred in the traditional culture/nature dichotomy, always gendered male/female. The female was defined as nature when man was struggling against nature to establish an individualizing

28. The Spanish writer Miguel de Unamuno declared: "Las muchedumbres son femeninas. Juntad a los hombres y tened por cierto que es lo femenino de ellos, lo que tienen de sus madres, lo que los junta." ("Crowds are feminine. Put men together, and you can be sure that it is the feminine in them, what they have of their mothers, that brings them together.") (Vida de don Quijote y Sancho 234).

29. For the connection between the view of the crowd as female and feminism in France, see Barrows, ch. 2.

30. Swartz draws on the work of Carol Gilligan and Nancy Chodorow.

"civilization." But now that civilization itself has become the problem, technology threatens to devour man and deprive him of his individuality. The opposition changes accordingly; culture itself divides in two. Simmel uses the terms the *body of culture* and the *soul*. Others use the terms *mass culture* and *high culture*. Needless to say, the "devouring" aspects of culture are now gendered female. We observe here a process that remains constant over the centuries and is operative, as shown below, in the history of literary aesthetics: the male/female dichotomy remains constant, denoting the "valued" vs. "devalued" terms of an opposition. But the most contradictory kinds of content can be slotted into the two gender positions over time. In this case, woman has gone from being "closer to nature," in that durable cliché, to incarnating the excesses and perils of culture. In each case, the "female" term is connoted as undifferentiated, devouring, and "low," over against male individuality and separateness, connoted as "high."

At the end of the nineteenth century, as man risks becoming a prisoner of culture and technology, he fears losing the status of the subject who acts to impose form on the world. Alice Jardine speculates that this crisis of the "master narratives" may be related to women's new, aggressive use of discourse, their attempt to acquire the status of subjects. She asks whether it can be a coincidence that the rise of the women's movement occurs simultaneously with the crisis in Western systems of knowledge (92–93). The male response to women's discourse, in Jardine's view, is paranoia, involving a fear of loss of boundaries (98). One solution is homosexuality; to avoid becoming the *object* of woman's activity rather than a subject, the man can flee from contact with her entirely.

The general association of the masses with women has, of course, its manifestation in the realm of literature, where, beginning in the mid-nineteenth century, mass culture is constantly associated with women. Woman is connoted as the *reader* of *mass culture*, while man is the *writer* of *highbrow* texts. Woman is intrinsically inferior as a writer; mass culture is considered "feminized"; and a call for a "masculine" art is repeated. An especially graphic example of the male writer's misogyny comes in Flaubert's condemnation of George Sand's work. Flaubert, of course, takes the "high" artistic ground, dismissing Sand's work as too accessible to the masses. According to Julian Barnes, Flaubert in 1852 compared Sand's work "to leukorrhea, or vaginal discharge: 'everything oozes, and ideas trickle between words as though between slack thighs' " (Barnes 5). So Andreas Huyssen can credibly argue that misogyny is a determining circumstance of a significant current of modernist writing; Goytisolo writes at the tail end of that current. The "ominous expansion of mass culture throughout the social realm" is "the hidden subtext of the modernist project" for Huyssen (47). Modernism is a flight from the banal and the everyday, in which mass culture played a large part. And since mass culture is gendered feminine, the flight from mass culture is always also a flight from women. As man fears being engulfed and losing his ego boundaries in the (feminine) mass, so modernism "fears being devoured by mass culture through co-option, commodification, the 'wrong' kind of success" (53). Modernist art shores up its formal boundaries to distinguish itself from mass culture, always gendered feminine.[31] The gendering of the modernism/mass culture dichotomy persisted until quite recently, although its "primary historical place" is the late nineteenth century (62). The decline of the force of the mass culture = woman equation is, says Huyssen, the decline of modernism.

Catherine Jagoe ("Disinheriting") suggests that the intensity of male writers' identification of women with inferior, "mass" culture may be a tactical response precisely to women's growing prominence and respectability as writers during the nineteenth century in Spain. Women, she argues, had done much to make the novel a respectable genre in the 1850s and 1860s; previously it had been stigmatized as immoral. As women's novels, written in the "idealistic" genre, gained a large share of the literary market, male writers adopted strategies to eliminate them from competition. Early Spanish realist works attacked women writers and readers as immoral and frivolous, stigmatized idealism as inferior and "feminine," and encoded a highly educated male reader who would displace the only flimsily educated female reader. Jagoe reads *La desheredada* as an attack on the dangers of female readers and their favorite novels, shown by Galdós to cause Isidora's fall into prostitution. The incredibly successful result of such strategies on the part of Galdós and others was

---

31. Huyssen comments: "Seen in relation to this paranoid view of mass culture and the masses, the modernist aesthetic itself—at least in one of its basic registers—begins to look more and more like a reaction formation" (53).

that literary historians have erased women from the history of the nineteenth-century novel in Spain.[32] The pattern Jagoe points out, and which is repeated in *Reivindicación*, is that when women become prominent in a given mode of novel writing, male writers react by fleeing to "higher" ground, inventing a new aesthetic, and devaluing the previous one by denouncing it as feminine.

It would seem that by the early decades of the twentieth century, a vicious cycle has developed in which male fantasies of being devoured by woman are displaced onto cultural phenomena seen as threatening or devalued; contact with these phenomena in turn reinforces male hatred of women. A walk in the city, then, could threaten male ego boundaries in general (out of fear of being engulfed by the masses) and male sexuality in particular (the threatening masses are "feminine"). Interiors were thus seen as protecting man from a hostile world which fragmented and destabilized his sense of self (Ramos 174, 187).

I have shown above how our narrator is reduced to a constant state of terror in the foreign, labyrinthine city. One may speculate about how he got that way. First, he has absorbed the fear and loathing of woman passed down through the Church; he constantly associates woman with the grotesque body and is all too ready to call upon images drawn from sermons of the 1940s to project perfidy onto her. The hostile outside world is called "Pandora's box" (5). The archetypal tourist is called Mrs. Potiphar, referring to the biblical Potiphar's wife, who tried to tempt Joseph, and who upon his refusal to have sex with her, denounced him for trying to rape her and had him jailed (Gen. 39:7–21). The 1940s also did deeper damage to the narrator's masculinity, creating the devout child Alvarito, who is nothing other than a displacement of the mother. The mother and son are mirror images of one another ("*idolized by and idolizing his mother" [77]), and Alvarito is described in terms minimizing his distance from woman: "a thin, frail youngster," "not the slightest trace of a beard profaning his softly rounded cheeks" (182, 77). One of the narrator's problems is that woman, for him, is two contradictory

32. Dale Spender similarly notes that during the eighteenth century in England, the novel was a highly respected genre associated with women—the number of women writers was legion. Yet later literary histories attribute the birth of the English novel to Fielding, and erase all women from its history except Jane Austen.

types, both inherited from tradition. She is Madonna or whore, the angel in the house or the prostitute. Where he attacks one of these, the other still remains, as we will see. In particular, his separation from the mother is incomplete, as he admits from the beginning through the image of the umbilical cord. And that innocent, devout mother is inside him as Alvarito. The narrator's problem is that women are not only the deceptive outside world, the city, the crowd; they have also penetrated his very psyche. His self-hatred is explained at its deepest level by his suspicion that, inside, he is a "woman," as repressed and devout as the Spanish women he denigrates.

The narrator is reacting in *Reivindicación* to major changes in relations between the sexes during the 1960s in Spain. The 1960s had brought lightning-quick development to the country. This meant an increase in city crowds, feminine for the narrator as for his nineteenth-century predecessors. It also meant tourism and the introduction of consumerism into a Spain that had until then defined itself as a repository of "spiritual values." Industrialization created the need for women to enter the work force, from which laws and custom had previously excluded them; the laws were now abruptly changed. As women began to work, their assumptions about their purpose in life and their relations to men began to change (Scanlon 342ff.). And both sexes were profoundly affected by their exposure to the sexual mores of the tourists (Abella, ch. 15).[33] The new sexual aggressiveness of women, we may speculate, must have been frightening for our narrator, trained in childhood to think of woman as a sexually voracious, evil temptress who lures man into mortal sin and hellfire. It would also bring doubts about whether he was masculine enough to satisfy a woman unrestrained by sexual repression. So if the narrator hates the Spain of the 1940s because it is the Madonna, the Spain of the 1960s becomes, in his mental framework, the terrifying whore.

To make matters still worse, the late 1950s and 1960s saw the rise of numerous women writers not only to prominence but to canonical status. Women were stealing the show in so striking a manner that a popular almanac for 1964 featured pictures of four women novelists who had published salient works in 1962–63 (no men were pic-

---

33. There was still, needless to say, no divorce or abortion possible.

tured).[34] Very few women writers had entered the canon on a par with male writers in the early twentieth century; only during the 1950s did the total number of works by women writers rise markedly, and did women writers achieve a similar degree of success to their male contemporaries. We are again in a situation like that described by Jagoe for the mid-nineteenth century; the result for the narrator is paranoia, and flight to a country where woman is still "not veiled but gagged" (51), unable to become the subject of her own discourse.[35]

Men, of course, had been castrated by Franco, rendered unable to decide anything but the most banal of matters and unable to speak many of their innermost thoughts.[36] The writer coming of age in the 1950s had harbored illusions of being able to effect change through the *novela social*, only to find that his novels had little or no impact on the course Spain was to take. The narrator has multiple reasons for feeling impotent.

The agonizing problem of the modern man, then, is the potential loss of stable ego boundaries, on the one hand with respect to the crowd (gendered feminine), and on the other in relation to women themselves. Since the narrator feels woman all around him (as the inchoate, corporeal crowd) and also inside him (as the mother/Alvarito), it is not surprising that he is not sure whether he is inside or outside, whether he has already been devoured or not. (His nostalgia for the womb may be nostalgia for the last time he did not have to defend himself against this threat.) His response—requiring large amounts of psychological and literary energy—is to attempt to create a territory "purified" of woman in which he can be safe. By now, the traditional culture/nature opposition has been largely reversed; a feminized, mass culture threatens to devour what is left of nature. Spain is therefore equated with women and mass culture, while Morocco's underdevelopment is connoted as masculine, vital, barbaric, natural. In order to be sure that he has not been devoured by the femi-

---

34. The women were Mercedes Salisachs, Carmen Laforet, Carmen Martín Gaite, and Ana María Matute; the caption begins, "Las mujeres occupan lugar destacado en la novelística española de 1962–63" ("Women occupy a prominent place in Spain's novelistic production of 1962–63") (*Almanaque Universal: 1964* 181).

35. The narrator's fear of women writers will be discussed further below.

36. Goytisolo speaks of his own father's emasculation by the authority of Franco in *Coto vedado*.

nine, the narrator defines Spain as feminine and Tangiers as purely masculine; women in Tangiers are muzzled, so he can move without fear. He then remains within sight of Spain, sure that he is not inside her thanks to that expanse of water "separating this shore from the other and guarding your adoptive country against the painful, poisonous scar" (55). At the best of times, he can even leave his mother tongue behind, as he joins Arab *men* in a café (56).

The narrator's attempted inversion of traditional oppositions—which would render the Spanish, bourgeois culture degraded and "low," and the primitive Moorish culture "high"—is achieved, ironically enough, through the *reinforcement* of the most traditional opposition of all: man as high, woman as low. The move to debase Spain, in other words, is nothing other than to describe Spain as female and punish her for being so. The supposedly austere, organized, vertical, virile Fascist state is shown to be woman, the grotesque body, the inchoate crowd, the spineless acquiescence to Franco, the materialistic sellout.

Woman is that grotesque mass of viscous organs described in the narrator's tour of the Coño (Vagina), metaphor for Spain:

a través de los tortuosos cuellos del útero y los esponjosos sacos vaginales cubiertos de una extraña, parasitaria foliación de algas glaucas que, irresistiblemente, evoca la imagen delirante de la Discordia y su envenenada cabellera de víboras . . . la masa de horror, de ponzoña y de asco entre paredes de tejido muscular ornadas de una fauna submarina dúctil e inquietante . . . horrible mundo, rezumante y viscoso, de canales, vesículas, glándulas, nervios, arterias, secreciones, membranas y vasos, proteico reino de lo blando e informe, de la flora rastrera e inmunda, de la obscena ebullición de lo inorgánico (169–71)

through the narrow, winding neck of the uterus and the spongy vaginal sacs covered with a strange, parasitic growth of blue-green algae, which irresistibly remind you of the hallucinatory image of Discord with her poisonous snake locks . . . these hideous, poisonous, nauseating surfaces, hemmed in by walls of muscle tissue covered with disturbing, sinuous, submarine fauna . . . a *horrible, oozing, viscous world of canals, vesicles, glands, nerves, arteries, secretions, membranes and sacs, the proteiform realm of the flaccid and formless, of nasty creeping flora, of the obscene bubbling of the inorganic (142–44)

Woman is the material body; any woman who claims to be devout is a hypocrite, for in reality she is just dying for a chance to be raped by the phallic Arab (Epps, "Politics of Ventriloquism" 289–90). Spain is a "*maternal, swollen womb" and the Spaniards "its countless progeny" (105). Thus far, the degradation is easy. But Spanish men must be proven feminine as well. This is done insistently, as men and their organizations are described as *maternal*—the professor shelters students under his maternal wing (74), the Francoist "vertical union" is a brooding hen with the Spanish masses under its wing (159). Spanish men have been castrated, boasting only a "feeble idea, as limp as a lettuce leaf" instead of the "robust cobra" of the Arabs (106). They can't penetrate a woman but spend all their time "drooling outside the inaccessible cavern or the gratuitously well-rounded excrescences" (105). Since they are impotent themselves, they play pimp to Spain's prostitute, introducing her to foreigners. Séneca—who in Francoist propaganda is known as a "Spanish" writer—offers the narrator women (131); the tourist guide gives a sales pitch which leads foreigners into the Coño (140–41). With Spanish men completely "feminized," unable to make use of the phallus, the vast female body of Spain waits anxiously for the "virility" of the Arab snakes (114). And to top it off, even the Spanish god is feminine—the baby Jesus in the church has a hairdo like Shirley Temple's! (197).

So Spain is the grotesque Vagina which so often in the nineteenth century acted as a synecdoche for woman. (The Arab is the classical body, well formed, brandishing his sword and his phallus, flying gracefully on his winged stallion over the lowly peninsula.) The modernization of Spain, its transformation into a consumer society, is figured as the opening of the Madonna's sacred vagina, transforming her instantly into a prostitute.[37] Thus, just as in the nineteenth century, consumerism is connoted as feminine, and the prostitute repre-

---

37. Goytisolo uses the image of prostitution repeatedly when describing the new Spain in other works. An example: "Poco a poco, mediante la doble corriente de forasteros y emigrantes expatriados y turistas, el español ha aprendido, por primera vez en la historia, a . . . explotar comercialmente sus virtudes y defectos, asimilar los criterios de productividad de las sociedades industriales, mercantilizarse, prostituirse y todo eso . . . bajo un sistema originariamente creado para impedirlo." ("Little by little, through the double current of foreigners and expatriates and tourists, the Spaniard has learned, for the first time in history, to . . . exploit his virtues and faults commercially, to internalize the criteria of productivity of industrialized countries, to commercialize himself and prostitute himself. And all of this, . . . under a system originally established to prevent it") (*España y los españoles* 196; translation mine).

sents the ills of modern society. (To those who argue Goytisolo's innovativeness, one would have to respond: "Plus ça change, plus c'est la même chose.") Spain has prostituted itself by accepting the betterment of its standard of living from the dictator who continues to deprive the country of liberty. This only serves to accentuate the grotesqueness of her body; she is "the Spain which may be *getting fat, but is still mute" (32). Of course Spain is mute; speech is a masculine prerogative, issuing from the upper body, while the narrator's Spain is nothing but a feminine, formless mass of flesh.[38]

The narrator has projected onto the castrated Spanish male his own anxiety about being "feminine" and has identified himself with the Moors and their constantly mentioned "serpents." He has created the ultramasculine Julián so that the reader will forget the "real" narrator's fear of women and sex. Homosexuality functions here in several ways. It seems to be a way for the narrator to acquire virility by contact with men like his mentor Tariq, and it conveniently eliminates the need for contact with the dreaded, formless, viscous, devouring Woman. (Other functions of homosexuality will become clear below.) We should note, however, that we never witness homosexual acts on the part of the narrator; it seems to be mainly a theoretical construct through which to strengthen his identity boundaries against women: "expert love-making in the age-old manner of the Mohammedan he-goat: far from your saintly Spanish women and their zealously guarded sanctuaries" (32).

The narrator is nothing if not consistent in his paranoia. It is not just geographical space that must be purified of the contaminating presence of woman, but language and culture as well. Predictably, the Spanish literary word is the prostitute with the grotesque body, linked to disease:

en la vieja e inhóspita biblioteca . . . has comprobado pacientemente los abusos del verbo : cuánta proliferación cancerosa e inútil, cuánta excrecencia parasitaria y rastrera : palabras, moldes vacíos, recipientes sonoros y huecos : qué microbio os secó la pulpa y la apuró hasta la cáscara? . . . el servilismo y docilidad de que dais muestra acredita la tesis de vuestra infamia : sois al-

38. We may conjecture that the narrator even associates feminism with Francoism, for women, in the 1960s, had dared to regain from the dictator a few of the rights which they had possessed under the Republic, and of which he had deprived them upon winning the war.

cahuetas taimadas, honorables rameras, dispuestas siempre a venderse al último y más sucio postor : . . . voraces, tentaculares, madrepóricas, crecéis y os multiplicáis sobre el papel ahogando la verdad sobre la máscara (156–57)

in the old, inhospitable library . . . you have patiently compiled evidence of the abuses of the Word: what a cancerous, useless proliferation, what creeping, parasitic excrescences!: words, hollow molds, receptacles that echo emptily: what microbe has sucked out your pulp and left only the skin?: . . . your obvious servility and docility support the theory that you are an infamous race: sly pimps, *respectable prostitutes, ever ready to sell yourselves to the highest, most dirty-handed bidder: . . . voracious, tentacular, jellyfish-like, you increase and multiply there on the paper, stifling the truth behind the mask (132)

Suleiman reminds us that the Sadic hero controls language; the victim is silenced ("Reading Robbe-Grillet" 57–58). And woman is silenced throughout *Reivindicación*, emitting almost no discourse at all (Epps, "Politics" 285). The narrator's ability to silence woman is crucial, if we are to believe Jardine that the accession of woman to discourse is a major cause of male paranoia. In the narrator's scheme of things, he must not only silence woman, but demonstrate that *his* language is *male*, different from hers. His language is a "sharp-pointed . . . weapon" used by renegades and apostates (56), a scimitar (104). Its traitorous activity is described in the following terms:

ciñendo la palabra, quebrando la raíz, forzando la sintaxis, violentándolo todo (85)

to *streamline language, to snap off roots, to violate syntax, to *break and enter everywhere (70)

The verb *ceñir* (perhaps best translated here as "to streamline") appropriates the classical body for the narrator's language; by streamlining, he purifies words of that feminine, grotesque, diseased proliferation. Of the four verbs quoted above, three are (male) acts carried out on a passive, feminine (direct) object. And all, of course, are violent.[39]

Language is inseparable from sex in the narrator's discourse (not

39. The verb *ceñir* was used in medieval times in the phrase "ceñir espada"—to put on one's sword. It retains the phallic traces of that usage and the association with violence. *Violentar* means to enter by force; both it and the preceding verb *forzar* carry connotations of rape.

surprising since, as we have seen, his discourse is a substitute for sex); linguistic expression can be figured as either rape or orgasm (the latter often homosexual). Language is the expression of "forbidden desires, illicit emotions, blinding betrayal" (105). Treason can be "macho treason" or "gay treason" (never, of course, "female treason") (112). Descriptions of the Moorish *sierpe* fade into descriptions of literary language at many points throughout the text (e.g., 43); and the serpent's activity is *matricide:* "the evil serpent that rips its mother's entrails to shreds at birth" (105).[40]

The different cultural artifacts produced through Spanish discourse are of course feminized as well, whether they be "high" or "mass." The only woman author directly named in the text is Corín Tellado, Spain's most popular writer of romance novels. Her readers, also women, must necessarily be Franco supporters, in the narrator's version:

la prima donna assoluta permanece suspendida ante la alcázar-toledana defensa del virgo de la heroína de Corín Tellado (36)

the *prima donna assoluta* . . . sits there ecstatically devouring the story of how the heroine of the latest *romance novel by Corín Tellado has managed to defend her virginity as stubbornly as the warriors defending the Alcázar in Toledo (25)

The reference to the Nationalist defense of the Alcázar fortress in Toledo, under siege by the Republicans during the Civil War, makes clear that women who won't have sex are Francoists; but then, so are women who will.[41] One of the women who will is an anchorwoman on the Spanish program the narrator watches on television; she is a "a

40. In Goytisolo's autobiographical text, *Coto vedado* (1985), language is linked to orgasm (82) and masturbation (116); creative inspiration is associated with sperm (276). Reading forbidden books is declared more sexually exciting than reading books freely chosen, in a comparison that once again makes women the victims (by force or by consent) of male sexuality: "no es lo mismo introducirse a escondidas en un harén religioso o profano con la excitante idea de una intriga plagada de peligros que escoger sin ninguna clase de apremio entre las docenas de pupilas consintientes de una casa de trato" (155) ("It's not the same to stealthily sneak into a harem (be it religious or secular) with the titillating expectation of an adventure fraught with dangers, as it is to choose, with no pressure at all, among dozens of consenting prostitutes at a brothel") (trans. mine).

41. The woman reading Corín Tellado is later referred to as a "flabby fat woman," associating mass culture with the grotesque body as well.

blond Sybil with jutting breasts" (74) from whom the narrator maintains a purificatory distance via the reference to the Sybil of classical mythology (to "literaturize" is to rise above). Female discourse
is nothing other than mass culture, or so the narrator would like
us to believe. American mass culture, of course, plays a role in
the transformation of Spain from Madonna to whore, for it is when
Isabel la Católica listens to the Rolling Stones that she becomes ripe
for Moorish penetration. The narrator's fear of being devoured by
woman is displaced onto mass culture several times. First he is "*suddenly* *surrounded by* the flood of sound pouring out of a jukebox
playing one of the Rolling Stones' top-ten records" (29). Later, he
hallucinates that he is engulfed by Spanish television, projected on
the screen he is watching: "on the screen of the little box, beneath the
reproachful stare of myriad pairs of Peninsular eyes" (89).

While mass culture is woman, the Spanish literary canon is her
counterpart, the castrated male. The literary tradition is the impotent male "standing there drooling outside the inaccessible cavern . . . the *kneeling slave proclaims at her feet that native Spanish,
academic art of 'polishing-fixing-and-giving-splendor'" (105).[42] Don
Alvaro Peranzules recites old honor plays from inside his crustacean
shell, but when attacked with insects, "his voice sounds more and
more feminine" (152). If older writers are castrated males (male Madonnas), contemporary ones are whores who have sold their political principles and their literary standards in return for fame within
Franco's Spain.[43] The narrator exclaims: "how many Parnassuses *up
for auction, and Academies for sale!" (132). These young writers simply imitate the Generation of 1898 rather than being original; they
are its "great-great-grandsons" (125). They are nothing but big, dia-
pered babies "wrapped in swaddling clothes" (23), associated in this
metaphor with excrement and with mothers.

The narrator's most devastating move is to assimilate the Spanish
canon to mass culture. The new writers are called "the monopolists
and bankers of today's vigorous prose" (117), making clear their status as intellectuals *organic* to the system. Séneca tells the narrator he

42. The motto of the Royal Academy of the Spanish Language is "Limpia, fija y da
esplendor."
43. Their mutual back scratching, with the end result of admission to the Royal
Academy and numerous prizes, is described in detail on 24–25 and 125 of *Reivindicación* in the Lane translation.

is a celebrity now that he has been admitted to the Academy and won the Al Capone Foundation prize: "listen to this: I pocketed half a million pesetas . . . and then there's the prestige, the popularity!: television, press conferences, the whole bit!" (130). The writer is juxtaposed to the bullfighter (a staple of popular entertainment under Franco) in the narrator's satire of Spanish culture. The bullring is the "navel of the Hispanic nation" (168) (evoking its link to the mother), and the different moves the bullfighter makes with his cape are satirically called "orteguinas and zunzabiriguetas" (169) in a reference to the philosophers and novelists Ortega y Gasset, Zubiri, Zunzunegui, and Zaragueta.[44] The stoical Séneca ends up appearing on television, his life and work essentialized and used to buttress Francoist ideology for the Spanish television audience. The Spanish canon is fragmented, reduced to clichés, and assimilated into mass culture; it is cut up by that narratorial phallic sword in a procedure analogous to the rape of the female characters on the level of plot (Epps 292). Conveniently, *all* Spanish culture has thus been rendered "low"; the narrator's own countercanon can then occupy the field of the "high," the "pure."

The narrator is able to destroy the feminine, "afeitada civilización hispana" and its "anémica, relamida escritura" by virtue of his association with the masculinity of the Moors; by his encyclopedic use of classical mythology and foreign authors; and by his self-proclaimed filiation with a lineage of male, "outlaw" Spanish writers which does not coincide at all with the official Francoist canon. His creation of a countercanon is a strategy of self-definition and of purification; his aim is to exclude all the "contamination" of woman/Spain/mass culture/the market. As with *La desheredada*, the drive to purification necessitates the invention of a family romance. *Reivindicación*'s narrator invents two, one literary, one personal (the latter is discussed in the next section of this chapter). The literary one involves rejecting the "low" fathers of the Generation of 1898, denying any similarity with them.[45] Any filiation with "Catholic Spain" is

44. See *Reivindicación*, ed. Linda Gould Levine, 267 n. 249.
45. The similarities with the Generation of 1898 are in fact many: (1) idealization of preindustrial life; (2) impassioned critique of the state of Spain and attempt to find its "authentic" roots (see Labanyi, *Myth and History* 198; José-Carlos Pérez, *La trayectoria* 8); (3) marked similarities with Unamuno, including deliberate courting of controversy, and an exile within sight of Spain which results in the writing of a self-

also rejected; the narrator claims descent from the Moorish and Jewish cultures which populated Spain along with the Christians in the Middle Ages (Ibn Hazam and Fernando de Rojas are representative of the two cultures which would be expelled from Spain in 1492; their texts are positive influences for the narrator). The venerable medieval tradition that begins with Count Julian and the Arab invasion of Spain is emphasized in order to legitimize the narrator's text: "*Julian's ancient treason is not a sad story, nor is it one unworthy of being celebrated in prose and verse: the most beautiful, the most splendid resources of your language will fail to do it justice" (181). This "counterheritage" is passed down through later writers who were exiled, persecuted within Spain, and/or gay. These include Cervantes (jailed and poor); the romantics Blanco White (exiled) and Larra; and the contemporary Cernuda (gay, exiled) and Buñuel (exiled), among others.[46] The baroque poet Góngora acts as syntactical rebel and serves the narrator as male muse who gives him orientation and guidance.[47]

The narrator has rejected the lure of fame and the market ("*without claiming your place at this feast that is not eucharistic by any stretch of the imagination" [17]) and the temptation of a mass readership ("set before the common herd as objects of their admiration" [23]). His text's self-sufficiency and graceful proportions (its similarity to the classical body) will mark his success in the enterprise of purification. Through its symmetry, the text proclaims its triumph over the inchoate, the crowd, woman, Franco.[48] And the symmetry and self-contained character of the text is extreme. Levine has pointed out "the perfect geometric structure of this work" (Levine 52) and its use of the three unities of time, place, and action (the latter insofar as it all occurs in the mind of a single character), borrowed from Joyce's *Ulysses*. The self-referentiality of the constant

---

generating, semiautobiographical novel—in Unamuno's case, *Cómo se hace una novela* (1927). For a consideration of the version of Unamuno that is attacked in *Reivindicación*, see Braun.

46. Mariano José de Larra was a bitter critic of Spanish backwardness; he qualifies for the list by taking his own life at age twenty-eight, partly out of desperation at the state of Spain.

47. Quevedo casts aspersions on Góngora's sexuality, calling him "sirena de los rabos" (*Reivindicación*, ed. Levine, 128, n. 88).

48. "Art for art's sake" is gay, pure; literature produced for the market is feminine in this scheme.

use of the second person, and the circularity of the text, which ends up anticipating the repetition of the invasion the next day, contribute to the impression of self-sufficiency, completion, isolation from market forces. The structure of the text is meticulously patterned, as numerous critics have shown;[49] I would add only that its resemblance to the classical body is most striking in the streamlined symmetry of the length of the four parts, very close to eighty, forty, eighty, and forty pages respectively in the Seix Barral edition. As Huyssen indicates, textual form is here a means of warding off the modern world—the inchoate, the unpredictable, the vicissitudes of everyday life, mass culture, woman; it is not for nothing that the narrator compares himself to Scheherazade (13). Like the protagonist of "I Am a Rock," the narrator "build[s] walls / A fortress deep and mighty / that none may penetrate . . ."

Reivindicación's narrator, like that of La desheredada, has developed strategies which give authority to his work by discrediting the competition. By defining purity as lack of contact with "woman" (not just women, but mass culture, Spain, the market, and such), he has effectively established two prerequisites for being a "pure" writer in Spanish—homosexuality and exile. (In his scheme in which the feminine is projected onto Spain and Morocco is purely masculine, exile is practically synonymous with homosexuality.) These exclusionary filters effectively exempt him from having to acknowledge several Spanish writers who cannot so easily be accused of acquiescence with traditional Spanish values. Were he to acknowledge their existence, he would complicate the gender picture by admitting that "real men wrote in Spain." This explains the elimination of a number of authors clearly important to the literary crucible of Reivindicación from the list of sources at the end. I am thinking of such writers as Clarín, Valle-Inclán, and most especially Luis Martín-Santos, whose Tiempo de silencio was the first Spanish novel to make use of the narrative techniques of Joyce. Tiempo de silencio was written inside Spain in 1962. Such writers cannot with any credibility be accused of prostituting themselves to the Spanish system; therefore they must be quietly left out.[50]

49. See, for example, José Ortega and Genaro Pérez. For analysis of the intertextual patterning of the novel, see Ugarte, Trilogy of Treason, ch. 4, and Linda Gould Levine, Juan Goytisolo.

50. All postwar fiction is also eliminated, much as Galdós excluded the Spanish

Recalling Catherine Jagoe's argument about Galdós's move to associate the women writers of the 1850s and 1860s with mass culture, or to repress their existence altogether, we can now look at the issue of women writers. If Jardine is correct about the effects of female discourse, women writers should be particularly threatening to the narrator's ego boundaries, for their existence means that literature is no longer a safe haven from the "femininity" of everyday life. Brad Epps has already expertly shown that *Reivindicación* operates to silence women and to flee from them, and that it punishes in particular women prominent in history, such as Isabel la Católica and Santa Teresa. He has also noted that the long list of source authors is entirely male, with the exception of Santa Teresa ("Politics"). Now it is time to look specifically at the narrator's treatment of women *writers*. I have noted above that the 1950s and 1960s saw the influx of Spanish women writers into the literary canon. What has become of these writers in *Reivindicación?* The only female character whose words are reproduced for us in the novel is none other than a "novelista de provincias" interviewed on television in the program on the referendum of 1966.[51] The passage is as follows:

cómo es usted realmente? . . .
soy femenina, sensible, apasionada, sincera : distraída también : hasta el punto de que en la calle tropiezo con todo : una vez un señor me dijo un piropo y yo me volví y le pregunté: qué decía usted? . . .
votará?
naturalmente : adoro a Séneca : es un hombre divino, divino (121–22)

what are you really like? . . .
I am feminine, sensitive, passionate, sincere: and also very absent-minded: to the point that I don't even watch where I'm going when I walk down the street and keep stumbling over things: once a man whispered a flattering remark as I passed by, and I turned around and went back and asked him: what was that you said, sir? . . .
are you going to vote?
certainly: I adore Seneca: he's a divine man, simply divine (101–02)

novels of the 1870s from the frame of *La desheredada;* we are to believe that our narrator is the only existing author of original work.

51. All other women characters are mute, except (we presume) the television announcer, whose words are not reproduced for us. The referendum of 1966 was a staged event in which Spaniards could vote "yes" or "no" for Franco.

The female novelist is a minor writer "from the provinces" (in opposition to the narrator's "high," cosmopolitan, urban status). She is associated with mass culture by being presented through the filter of Spanish television. What we know about her is that she describes herself as a female stereotype; that she is too clumsy even to handle a *piropo* gracefully; and that she adores Franco. The women social novelists of the 1950s and 1960s, clearly opposed to the regime, have been cleverly subsumed under this one supposed representative—a strategy much more effective than leaving women writers out altogether.

All other women authors (excepting Santa Teresa; see below) must be repressed, most especially those who actually influenced the text we read; were we to become aware of a woman's contribution to it, the text would no longer be "purely masculine." Although the narrator reworks a story by the seventeenth-century writer María de Zayas, she cannot be included in his list of contributors. The list closes the text and, as part of the novelistic frame, must help to seal it off from "woman."[52]

Santa Teresa is the only woman writer included. Possibly the narrator feels safe enough to include her because she is not available as a sex partner; her body is reserved for union with Christ. She is briefly quoted ("I die because I do not die" [96]) for the purpose of parody. Nevertheless, as Epps points out, she is also the object of cruel torture and rape in the person of her textual double, Isabel la Católica. The narrator would like us to believe that Santa Teresa represents his opposite. I believe that she is the object of particularly intense violence in the text because she is actually more *similar* to him than he can admit. First, she is threatening because of her self-sufficiency. If one recalls the sensual discourse of the *Vida*, it becomes clear that Santa Teresa does not need a man to reach orgasm. This calls into question the narrator's representation of women as universally dying to be raped by large phalluses. Further, like the narrator's discourse, Santa Teresa's is granted authenticity and prestige precisely in virtue of its self-sufficiency, its isolation from the contaminating world (the narrator says to Góngora, "bear me aloft to the realm of *a more true light" [104]). Most importantly, since the nineteenth century, commentary on Santa Teresa has indicated that her mystical rapture is a

---

52. See Lotman on the importance of the frame in the artistic text.

sublimation of sexual desire. She has displaced bodily desire into a discourse charged with sensuality, exactly as the narrator has done. Her artistic creativity in describing ineffable spiritual experiences challenges all the narrator's debasing associations of women with materialism and mass culture. Finally, both Santa Teresa and the narrator seek completion, unity; she will find it with God in a way that he, a tragically modern man, can never achieve by imagining Julián united in a necrophilic embrace with the dead Alvarito ("you yourself at last, become one and indivisible, in the very depths of your tortured animality" [195]). This is the case despite the narrator's clear nostalgia for the sacred, evident as Alvarito/the baby Jesus is reborn in conversion to Islam at the end of the novel. Santa Teresa has achieved the desired union with God. The narrator, for his part, asks Góngora to elevate him to a "luz más cierta"—a phrase with clear religious underpinnings. And Góngora *can* remove him from the reality he fears; Pedro Salinas has shown how in Góngora's poetry the referent disappears as it is transformed into a "sea of images" (Salinas 168). But Góngora cannot give him any certainty, only a "higher" sort of labyrinth to replace the real one. So Santa Teresa must be attacked, raped, discredited, because she represents his competition and because, in fact, she has beaten him at his own game.

The attempt to exclude women writers, then, is not an unqualified success. It is important, however, to note the narrator's insistence on making literature a men's club. This is done not only through the long list of male writers at the end, but also in a move to exclude women *readers*. Jagoe shows how *La desheredada* belittles the female reader and courts a cultivated, masculine one. By 1970, we are faced with texts like Robbe-Grillet's *Projet pour une révolution à New York* and Goytisolo's *Reivindicación*, in which the female reader must undergo the torture of watching female bodies be "willingly" tortured and raped.[53] Lest we imagine that *Reivindicación*'s rage against women is peculiar to Goytisolo or to Spain, it is important to note the almost uncanny similarities with this Robbe-Grillet novel, written in the same year. Both texts "self-generate," with single words giving rise to entire segments in Robbe-Grillet, and sights in Tangiers triggering memories and textual quotations in Goytisolo. Robbe-Grillet substitutes Harlem's blacks for Morocco's

53. See Suleiman, "Reading Robbe-Grillet."

Arabs. The Sadic rape and torture of women are omnipresent in both, and both throw a twist into the Sadic fantasies—the woman *enjoys* the torture (Suleiman). It is tempting to imagine (and whether it happened or not is immaterial) an encounter between Robbe-Grillet and Goytisolo in a Parisian café in which the two of them brainstorm about the new misogynistic literary techniques that will keep women out of the literary game.

## Mother Trouble, Gender Trouble, Mass Culture Trouble

Stallybrass and White observe that classical writing can only be produced by "a labour of suppression, a perpetual work of exclusion upon the grotesque body" (105). This labor troubles the identity of the classical body, because "what is denied is also desired" (105–06), and because the classical body always rediscovers the grotesque *within* itself (113). Thus our male, highbrow narrator is doomed forever to discover woman and mass culture within himself, his surroundings, and his text. The hard work he performs to eradicate them must be repeated daily, for they sprout up again as soon as he leaves off the work of killing them.

As Suleiman illustrates for Robbe-Grillet, the fantasy of the extreme misogynist is to self-generate, to not have to be born of woman. Writing is one means to this male self-creation.[54] Our narrator wants to recreate Count Julian without the other characters in the legend ("without Rodrigo, or Frandina, or Cava" [7]), attempting perhaps to eliminate the nuclear family. He tries to eliminate Franco's Spain (woman) by turning it into a huge Vagina and raping it. He then kills off the woman in himself (Alvarito): "probe your innermost heart / *stifle . . . every impulse to be kind and forgiving" (180). He will be "reborn" through sodomy with the phallic, male Arab, and hopefully achieve self-generation. It turns out that the *sierpe* functions as the ideal animal for the narrator not only because of its phallic properties but also because its uninterrupted smoothness represents self-

---

54. The violation of the maternal organs in Robbe-Grillet's text, argues Suleiman, is a metaphor of the modern writer's activity; it negates the world of flesh and blood generated by mothers. To write is not only to dominate (language/the mother's body) but to self-create (62): "Woman, the irreducible Other, is eliminated to make way for the engenderment of the same by the same" (60).

generation: "your smooth belly is untainted by the infamy of the umbilical cord" (105).

But as Suleiman indicates, the woman killed or tortured in the Sadic text is not always a stand-in through whom the mother is killed. She may also be a displacement, a way of venting rage or incestuous desire while preserving the mother's purity (59–61). And this is in fact the ultimate reason for the failure of the narrator's quest for liberation from woman and from his many fears about the world and his own body. In the whole enraged attack on the text's different women and on Alvarito, the narrator has built in meticulous safeguards so as to exempt the mother. Women, as we noted, divide into Madonnas (or *beatas*, in 1940s Spain) and whores. But all *beatas* in the novel must be proven really to be whores before they can be symbolically eliminated by the degradation of torture and rape. This is true of Alvarito as well, who must lose his innocence, beauty, and faith before he can be forced to end it all. The mother is the only woman in the text who is never transformed, never raped. Her face is "pure, immaculate, *soothing" (187)—and we remember that "soothing" was the word applied to the womb at the beginning of the text (6). She is necessarily unaware of what is happening to her son, for that knowledge (a biblical kind of knowledge) is sexual and would contaminate her: "the child's innocent, unsuspecting mother *remains absorbed in her devotions" (193).

The narrator's lack of separation from, and incestuous desire for, the mother is made explicit when Julián demands that Alvarito bring his mother to him as a sexual partner. We realize that Alvarito's ensuing suicide is not, in fact, about liberating the narrator from his bourgeois complexes or his Spanish upbringing. It is nothing other than a self-sacrifice for the sake of saving the mother's purity. In this context, we can reinterpret the narrator's homosexuality. It is not only the result of his loathing of the female sexual body but also a way to remain loyal to the mother by never replacing her with another female love object. Self-generation itself is a wish that signifies adoration of woman as well as repulsion. While on the one hand it means that the man does not have to be gestated in that horrible world of viscous organs, on the other it means that he can retroactively remove the sexual sin the mother must have committed to bring him into the world. Self-generation is yet another ploy to keep the mother pure.

The care to save the mother is also evident in discourse on Spain. The initial references to the umbilical cord uniting the narrator to Spain are quickly displaced by repeated references to Spain as a *Madrastra* (7). As (wicked) stepmother, she can be violated and degraded; as mother, she could not.

The narrator's incomplete separation from the mother, then, creates a vicious cycle. The narrator hates the "woman" in himself that remains tied to the mother. In his rage, he goes on a rampage against other women. But this never moves him forward, since he has carefully preserved the mother from harm and thus has deified her even more. The text ends by referring to the music played in the street as designed to "*lull to sleep, to rock the cradle" (238); the narrator will return to his room/womb, where he does not have to worry about "acting like a man."

Other women are the objects of the rage the narrator cannot direct at the mother. But by debasing them *through* the lower body and representing them *as* the low, grotesque body in order to "save" the mother as "elevated," he completely ruins his own chances for personal liberation. For if the lower body is woman and degradation (as in the traditional bourgeois dichotomies), the narrator will remain unable to own his own lower body, to have sex, to urinate, or to defecate without guilt. The narrator has fallen into this trap by not inverting *all* bourgeois oppositions at once. By maintaining the "classical body" and man as "high," the grotesque body and woman as "low," he has condemned himself both to perpetual bodily repression and to the fear of the (feminine) crowd. (The anger will presumably escalate. Since it is the devaluation of woman that has spoiled the narrator's chances for liberation, he will become even more furious at her the longer he is unable to overcome his repression.)

There is a sense, then, in which the narrator accepts the Francoist ideology that "matter, the corporeal, physical bodies in general, obey, or ought to obey, the dictates of the spirit" (98). Since sex is still regarded as contaminating, the narrator can be purer than the Spaniards by sublimating sex into writing, displacing it into the upper body. The truth of the Spaniards, he claims, is in the lower, grotesque body; his literary authority comes from his claim to transcend that body. But so do his perpetual rage and fear.

The gender opposition the narrator sets up between Spain as "female" and Tangiers as male/rough/natural cannot, of course, survive reality testing. Our nameless writer needs Góngora as his male guide to keep him safe in the "formless, spongy matter" (28) of the crowd. Sometimes the muse fails in his task, and that fear of being devoured by flesh comes true, as when the narrator loses his boundaries on the crowded bus: "fused into a single, tentacular, vociferous mass" (199). But worst of all is that woman and mass culture, which the narrator imagines exclusive to the developed world, have invaded underdevelopment, blurring his nicely set up gender boundaries. And the Spanish culture industry doesn't just invade, it *penetrates*—a masculine verb if there ever was one—destabilizing the gendering of mass culture as feminine:

el oráculo de cuello almidonado . . . emite informaciones que atraviesan el hercúleo Estrecho, ganan la africana orilla, penetran por medio del artefacto en el moruno café (90)

the oracle in starched collar . . . broadcasts cryptic news reports that cross the Straits of Hercules, reach the shores of Africa, and *penetrate the Moorish café by way of the little magic box (74)

What the narrator seems to hate most of all about mass culture in the broader sense is tourism, which has turned Spain into a prostitute. So his indignation is great when it turns up in Tangiers. He calls the tourists "Martians" to underscore their utter foreignness to his cherished territory. They are the grotesque body; their bus lets off its "cargo of fat, sweating passengers" (34). The narrator conducts an intense labor of projection onto the tourists of everything he most dislikes. "Mrs. Putifar" is chosen as their representative. She is called "the Daughter of the American Revolution"; by implication, all tourists are ultraconservative. She is the female, grotesque body *par excellence*, with her peeling nose, excessive makeup, huge bust, and large painted toenails (35–37). She is the ultimate consumer, piling up souvenirs. The hint that there is an agenda behind this scathing portrayal comes when the narrator satirizes her as being "in the half alcoholic, half sentimental euphoria of a person recently freed of petty complexes and inhibitions" (36). We realize we are being taken in; the narrator is working so hard to make the tourist look bad to conceal the deep similarity between himself and her. For both of them—and the tourists in Spain as well—have left their countries in search of a sun-filled escape from modernity and sexual repression (she uses alcohol; he uses kif). They have all sought this escape in an underdevelopment that they decorate with stereotypes and projections of their own fantasies. And all are exempt from the repressive rules that govern the citizens of the countries they visit.[55] The main difference between the narrator and Mrs. Putifar is that she "decorates" her underdeveloped paradise with phrases from mass culture, while he does it with tropes from classical mythology.

But there is still one difference between the narrator and the tourist; he is producing a text. He can claim to "redeem himself" by producing as well as consuming. This factor brings us to his other alter ego in this passage: the tour guide.[56] In *La desheredada*, the character who provoked anxiety and competitiveness in the narrator was Juan Bou. As an "organic intellectual" of the new technological world, he turned ballads reproduced by machine into a business venture. In *Reivindicación*, the "organic intellectual" who is the narrator's "mass culture" counterpart is the tour guide; and we the readers are the "high" counterparts of his "herd" of tourists (46). The guide is compared to the great nineteenth-century Spanish orator Castelar; the narrator refers to "the meaty, fluent commentary of the *cultivated guide," with its "beautifully rounded periods, sonorous phrases, with a patina of erudition both elegant and delightfully witty" (34)—a clear *mise en abîme* of the text we are reading. The narrator is our "cultivated guide" in Tangiers, who sprinkles references to Homer, Quevedo, and the ballet throughout his description of the open-air market. Both he and the guide exoticize Arab music by attributing mysterious power to it (8, 35). Thus, as the narrator of *La desheredada* projects onto Isidora and Juan Bou the characteristics he does not wish to confront in himself, *Reivindicación*'s narrator does so with Santa Teresa, Mrs. Putifar, and the tour guide.

Although the narrator's text is emphatically highbrow, mass culture—that "feminine" entity—turns out to be both its raw material and its connective tissue. As the narrator saunters through Tangiers in part 1, he is accosted by signs (DONNEZ VOTRE SANG, SAUVEZ UNE VIE); graffiti (CON LOS NIÑOS EL LATIGO ES NEC-

---

55. The narrator has also, in imagination, been a tourist in Spain's Coño, notwithstanding his presentation of himself as an intrepid epic hero, a latter-day Aeneas.

56. One tip-off of this equivalence comes when we discover that the child who guides the narrator through the city is an imaginary double of the narrator himself (55).

ESARIO); the newspaper with its advertisements and Spanish television schedule; the omnipresent billboard JAMES BOND, OPERA-
CION TRUENO, última semana; and the hits of the Rolling Stones
on the radio. Part 2 takes place entirely in the café in front of the
television, as the narrator hallucinates, inspired by its program on
Seneca. Bond and the Rolling Stones will be indispensable allies in
the "destruction of sacred Spain" in part 3, and the graffiti about the
whip informs part 4. Even the narrator's fabulation about Julián's
torture of Alvarito in part 4 is like a film; he refers to the "sound-
track" (177). Levine has referred to the mass cultural texts as "claves
que unen la novela" (59); it would appear that the male, highbrow
text has woman at its very core.

The Bond film (like the use of the word *penetrar* for the television)
questions the femaleness that the narrator would like to ascribe to
mass culture. In *Thunderball* (1965), gender signals are mixed, as
both the cinema itself and the underwater scenes of the film are
womblike, while the plot and script duplicate much of the misogyny
we find in *Reivindicación*. Woman is an object to be taken and tossed
aside at will (the opening song affirms "Any woman he wants he'll
get / He'll break any heart without regret"). Bond tells one of his sex
partners, "You should be locked up in a cage"; when another woman
dares to double-cross him, he coldly assures her he felt no pleasure
during sex with her. Mass culture, as Huyssen points out, has always been an industry controlled by men, through which women are
harmed more than men (62); the ascription of femininity to it will
not hold up. The problem for the narrator is that if mass culture isn't
clearly the female, grotesque body, his own highbrow writing isn't
necessarily virile either.

## Spain 1940–1970: The Arrival of Consumer Culture

In preparation for a comparison of the projects undertaken in *La
desheredada* and *Reivindicación del conde don Julián*, we must consider why a narrator of 1970 is giving voice to nineteenth-century
obsessions and what changes occurred from the 1940s to the late
1960s to provoke the composition of a text like *Reivindicación*. The
Francoist postwar period was one of material privation and political
repression of an intensity perhaps unique to Spanish history. Fran-

coism itself was a complex ideological mix strongly marked by fascism and making use of a modern totalitarian state apparatus. Yet some of the ideology disseminated under Franco took shape among nineteenth-century Spanish ultraconservatives reacting against liberalism and secularization. This was the case of the Carlists, one important faction that backed Franco in the Civil War. The Spanish Church was also mired in pre-twentieth-century ideas. It now regained control of education, and its textbooks contained diatribes against the so-called "modern errors" originally enumerated by Pius IX in the mid-nineteenth century (Abella 76). Women were very deliberately brought back to the nineteenth century by the derogation of Republican legislation which had begun to better their lot. In most respects, they were again ruled by the Civil Code of 1889 (Scanlon 321), according to which men made all decisions governing their wives' property and right to work (Scanlon 347). New laws were made specifically to ensure that women would stop working once they married (Scanlon 321); women who did work were paid substantially less than men (*Anuario estadístico de España 1945–46*, 1184ff.).[57] Scanlon comments: "The books and pamphlets on the role of women which were published in the forties and fifties are almost indistinguishable from those of the nineteenth century. All the old myths were revived" (329).

The discourse on prostitutes, epidemics, and beggars, which Stallybrass and White associate with the nineteenth century, return in the narrator's discourse partly because such phenomena recurred in the 1940s in the much bleaker context of rationing, homelessness, and terror. Epidemics, prostitution, syphilis, mendicity took on alarming proportions. Statistics for 1943 show 63,000 syphilis cases and 41,000 other venereal disease cases treated in Madrid alone.[58]

Prostitution and mendicity were rampant among the widows and orphans of Republican soldiers killed in battle. They were not entitled to a pension and had no other means of support (Abella 32, 54). Undoubtedly the problem of prostitution generated a lot of rhetoric from Church and State authorities during the 1940s as the narrator passed through school. But given the reasons for it and the political

57. The *Anuario* will henceforth be abbreviated as *AEE*.
58. *AEE 1945–46*, 1324–25.

affiliation of those who were forced to exercise it, it is highly ironic that our now-adult narrator should use the prostitute as the emblem of the Spain of the *1960s*, precisely the moment when working-class women were actively encouraged to work and would no longer be forced into such a life. The uncritical adoption of the symbol of the prostitute in a narrator so critical of the capitalist exploitation of children, Arabs, and working men forced to emigrate from Spain to make a living only illustrates that misogyny knows no political affiliation.

The changes in Spanish life from the privation of the 1940s through the economic boom of the 1960s could not have been more dramatic. Spanish life stagnated until the late 1950s, when Franco brought in technocrats to save the country from economic collapse. Then the transformation was rapid. Spain developed industrially. Tourism boomed:

*Foreigners entering Spain*

| | |
|------|------------|
| 1953 | 1,710,273 |
| 1955 | 2,522,402 |
| 1958 | 3,593,867 |
| 1964 | 14,102,888 |
| 1968 | 19,183,973[59] |

The corresponding development of the hotel industry can be easily imagined. The country's national revenue doubled between 1950 and 1962 (after adjustment for inflation). The income per capita increased from under $300 in 1960 to $900 in 1970 (Fusi 132). Where in 1950 only 34 percent of dwellings had running water, by the early 1960s it was 67 percent.[60] In 1960, 42 percent of the population worked in agriculture; by 1970, only 25 percent did (Fusi 162). In 1960, only 4 percent of households had a refrigerator or a car; by 1969, the figures were 63 percent and 24 percent respectively (Fusi 163). Where only 400,000 telephones were in service in 1944, by 1968, there were 3,700,000.[61]

Cultural life showed similarly impressive developments:

59. *AEE 1956*, 806; *AEE 1965*, 355; *AEE 1969*, 339.
60. Fusi 132; Furustad 5.
61. *AEE 1945–46*, 936; *AEE 1969*, 175.

| Year | Number of radio stations | Hours of daily transmission |
|------|------|------|
| 1947 | 56 | 6 |
| 1955 | 102 | 9.5 |
| 1964 | 165 | 12[62] |

In the late 1950s, only 140,000 televisions were to be found in Spain (*Almanaque* 232); by 1962, there were 750,000 (Furustad 5). Fusi notes that only 1 percent of households had a television in 1960; by 1969, 62 percent had one (163). In 1959, Spanish television only broadcast an average of 5.5 hours a day. By 1964, it had climbed to 10.25, and by 1968 to 15.75 hours.[63] Finally, the number of book titles published in Spain rose from 4,504 in 1944 to 20,008 in 1968, with the increase occurring after 1954.[64]

The university population remained small, though it more than doubled in twenty-five years (1943–44: 41,764 students; 1966–67: 105,370).[65] But the proportion of female university students had increased during those years from 13 percent to almost one third. In the Facultad de Filosofía y Letras, women made up about two thirds of the student body in the mid- and late 1960s.

We thus see, in the 1960s, an increase in the size of the crowd, an enthusiasm for capitalist development and consumer goods, the advent of a new mass cultural medium, and important changes in the role of women. These transformations are roughly analogous to the changes of the mid-nineteenth century to which *La desheredada* responds. It is now time to locate Galdós and Goytisolo on the continuum of responses to uneven modernity in Spain.

## Coda: Galdós and Goytisolo—"Uneven Modernism" from Dawn to Dusk

The reader will already have noted many of the similarities in the ways Galdós, in *La desheredada*, and Goytisolo, in *Reivindicación*, respond to their unevenly modern situation. I will point up a few of the major procedures and metaphors they share and then indicate

62. *AEE 1956*, 791; *AEE 1965*, 368.
63. *AEE 1965*, 369; *AEE 1969*, 368.
64. *AEE 1945–46*, 522; *AEE 1969*, 332.
65. *AEE 1945–46*, 429; *AEE 1969*, 327.

some *differences* between the two—differences which indicate the evolution of the predicament of the modern writer from 1880 to 1970.

Most fundamentally, both writers are seeking to produce a literature that is "pure," sheltered from the market and from women. They dream of such purity through the spaces of the novels, postulating the Aransis palace and Morocco as territories not governed by the "fallen" market and public sphere. They also actively seek out literature which is not connected to the present, contradictory mixing of Old Regime with New. Galdós seeks models in the writers of the pre-industrial Golden Age, attacking only the honor play, whose norms are still causing trouble in the present. Goytisolo, from a later vantage point, considers most Spanish literature to be part of the problem rather than the solution. He requires more stringent tests of purity for his authors: exile; *converso* or renegade status; or extreme disregard for a sizable readership. This latter criterion makes the impenetrable Góngora his model. Each writer sees a greater potential for "purity" in foreign art (Beethoven, Genet, Lautréamont), thus reproducing Spain's national inferiority complex. Finally, though somewhat less explicitly, both writers are seeking "higher" ground in flight from both the "feminine" masses and the female writers whose prominence threatens them.

In order to convince their audience of their difference from, and opposition to, the market, both narrators portray art produced for the market as prostitution and claim noble literary parentage (Cervantes, Góngora) that sets them "above" other authors. Most remarkably, both portray themselves as outsiders to a system run by "organic intellectuals" and based on connections and favor swapping. By emphasizing that they will not stoop to such tactics to become famous, both narrators make their success seem doubly miraculous—achieved without "pull," despite the establishment, *their* fame alone can be "pure."

But the search for purity is a failure in 1970, just as it is in 1880. The spaces sought out for their separateness turn out to be invaded by "impure" forces—the palace has been profaned by Miquis and Bou, Tangiers by "woman," tourists, and mass culture. The "cult" value of these spaces even turns out to have been *produced* by the market itself; the palace has the "cachet" of nobility, and the underdevelopment of Tangiers is perpetuated by colonialism and then the tourist industry. And all the problems of a would-be pure art examined in relation to *La desheredada* (irresponsibility, narcissism, co-opting) apply to Goytisolo's narrator as well; after all, where does he get the money to write and wander the streets of Tangiers?

Both writers articulate the problem of the purity of art by linking it to questions of sexual purity and class mobility. Strikingly, both have recourse to the metaphor of the family to represent the crisis of the country. In both texts, the bourgeois family is deeply dysfunctional because of its equation of sexuality with sin. Parenting is also problematic, and defective parenting is the central metaphor for political and artistic crisis in both texts. *La desheredada* and *Reivindicación* are written from the viewpoint of the child who denounces the failure of its parents, both biological and political. Ambivalence about parents pervades the novels; the crisis of the nation seems to come both from the forgetting of one's authentic parents/origins and from the inadequate parenting provided by those parents/rulers.

Both narrators are tortured by the problem of sexuality, and divide their characters, in Manichaean fashion, into the chaste and pure (the *marquesa*'s grandson, Alvarito) and the unremittingly sexual (Joaquín Pez, Julián). Unable to admit their own conflicts about sex, both narrators project them onto women. The promiscuity of a woman supposed to be virginal (Virginia, Spain as Coño) creates the crisis at the root of both texts. Woman incarnates both male dreams and male fears in relation to modernity. As *beata*, she represents the hope of a terrain (like the Aransis palace) untouched by modernity. As prostitute, she represents the most dreaded yet desired effects of that same modernity. But the dilemma of sexual purity is not resolved in the novels any more satisfactorily than the homologous question of the purity of art.

The ambivalence about class palpable in *La desheredada* is also present in more muted tones in *Reivindicación*. Like the gender question, the treatment of class is inseparable from the problem of art's role in the modern world. Our narrators are both slippery and contradictory about the class struggle. Both condemn the system which forces children into perpetual slavery in a factory from which they will never escape. Galdós documents the horrible conditions of Mariano's work in the rope factory; Goytisolo, the horrible apprenticeship of the Arab children caught in the web of the silk industry (50–51). Yet neither applauds the upward mobility of the petty bour-

geoisie, and neither wants the poor to look like the rich. The Galdosian narrator waxes indignant about how everybody wears a hat these
days; Goytisolo's narrator is relieved that "the marvelous benefits of
the consumer society have not yet reached these parts, and fashion
has not yet made the members of *the various [social] levels all resemble peas in a pod" (12). Both seem to prefer that the poor remain
picturesque in their poverty rather than climb the social ladder. Yet
the narrators themselves both desire a kind of "noble" status—the
right to enter the palace, or the prominence of *Count* Julian.

One explanation for this ambivalence about changing social relationships and the rights of the poor may be the fact that the central,
narcissistic concern of each text is the problem of the status of art.
Neither narrator seems able to imagine any good coming to art from
the democratization of culture. Both represent the world of the rising
petty bourgeoisie as a fallen world full of cheap imitations of older
works. These writers are caught in the trap of what Raymond Williams calls "cultural pessimism."[66] The growth of capitalist mass
communications means to them the gradual demise of minority
"high culture." Yet the privileged economic position held by these
writers is what permits them to produce their art, so they cannot
espouse a genuinely alternative social and cultural order either.
Therefore "there is nothing most of them want to win but the past,
and an alternative future is precisely and obviously the final loss of
their privileges" (Williams, *Politics of Modernism* 125). Caught between their deep allegiance to a "high culture," which they have to
admit is elitist, and the insistent problem of poverty, these narrators
withdraw from the social struggle. But they are constantly racked by
the ensuing guilt, which compels them to represent in their highbrow texts the plight of the people they have abandoned.[67]

The important coincidences in the response to modernity of the
two writers should not lead us to conclude that ninety years have
passed without impact. Goytisolo's narrator can be imagined as the
Galdosian narrator a century later. What is still incipient in *La desheredada*'s narrator—isolation from all social classes, anxiety at the

66. "Culture and Technology," in *The Politics of Modernism* 120.
67. Galdós will become a socialist later in life; Goytisolo has already flirted with
Spanish and European communism and has been thoroughly disillusioned. But the
sense of having abdicated their social responsibilities tinges each narrator's discourse.

teeming modern city, doubts about reaching an audience, unease about female sexuality—has become exacerbated in the narrator of *Reivindicación* to the point of driving him mad. If society seemed irrevocably fragmented into antagonistic sectors in Galdós, it is the ego which has by 1970 shattered into parts at war with one another. The contradictions in the Galdosian narrator's stance toward his material (sometimes seeming to believe his own omniscience, others acknowledging doubts about what he can know about the modern world) are the beginnings of cracks in the unity of the ego. By *Reivindicación*, we witness the extreme measures the narrator must take to keep himself together at all (self-reassurance, enumeration of his belongings, drug use, flight from uncomfortable situations). The isolation already perceptible in both narrator and protagonist in Galdós has become total for the Goytisolian narrator. Isidora dreamed of a complete world of whole families, friends, and social connections, but she progressively lost over the course of the novel even the few of those things she initially had. Galdós's narrator was unsure to whom he should dedicate the text, but he still made a stab at it, still wished for the novel to have an impact on the outside world. Goytisolo's narrator is trapped in the world of his own obsessions, unable to see beyond them to make contact with others. In his text, the dedication has been replaced by epigraphs which allude to the inside of the text rather than to the outside world. The use of the "tú," as already noted, enables him to communicate with himself in a show of self-sufficiency. Given the narrator's rejection of bourgeois society, he condemns himself (at least on the level of plot) to having no readers at all. For he identifies with the simplicity of underdevelopment and its inhabitants, but writes in a convoluted language the latter cannot read. While Galdós's narrator takes the Spaniards to task for not taking seriously social critiques like his ("Society, familiar with its leprosy, doesn't even scratch itself anymore, because it no longer stings" [1055]), Goytisolo's writer is no longer prepared to admit that he cares about having any readers at all.

The other area where the evolution of the writer's stance is evident is the question of how best to respond to the crisis of Spanish values. Galdós seems to be uncertain whether to go forward or back: does Spain need a return to older, more authentic values, or does it need additional modernization? Is the problem the persistence of "uncivilized," barbarian sectors alongside the modern state, or is the modern state itself the problem? *La desheredada*'s narrator vaguely postulates that what is needed is a more harmonious integration of the new with the old, the reestablishing of a link with the past. He uses metaphors of resurrection and recognition to convey this utopian dream. Goytisolo's narrator has no such illusions. Both the old and the new are irrevocably contaminated; both must be destroyed, and an entirely different society created. (He calls himself the "recreator of the world" [124].)[68] Where Galdós thinks of civilizing the barbarian, Goytisolo wants to "barbarize" civilization. This wholesale rejection of civilization translates in Goytisolo's text into a celebration of violence which the Galdosian narrator could never condone. For better or for worse, however, by 1970, the only violence the writer has the power to carry out is the breaking of the rules of grammar and syntax.

68. The only return to the old which he would consider helpful would be a return to the Moorish invasion of 711.

# Chapter Five

## Beyond High and Low:

## Carmen Martín Gaite's *El cuarto de atrás*

Culture can seem like a substitute for politics, a way of posing only imaginary solutions to real problems, but under other circumstances culture can become a rehearsal for politics, trying out values and beliefs permissible in art but forbidden in social life.
—George Lipsitz, *Time Passages*

Yo pensaba que también podía ser heroico escaparse por gusto, sin más, por amor a la libertad y a la alegría.

I thought it might also be heroic to escape simply because one felt like it, out of love of freedom and of happiness.
—Martín Gaite, *El cuarto de atrás*

• • • **C**armen Martín Gaite's *El cuarto de atrás* (1978) places mass cultural texts such as romance novels, radio songs, and mystery stories at the core of its complex structure. While canonical writers such as Cervantes, Machado, and Darío are also quoted in the novel, their works take a back seat to the mass cultural genres, and no effort is made to distinguish canon from pulp, high from low. With mass culture the star of the show, the richness and variety of its potential uses can be explored in *El cuarto* with a depth not possible in our other novels, which have a stake in limiting its power. This chapter contains two sections. The first explores the many roles mass culture plays in the novel—for the middle-aged protagonist trying to recapture her childhood; for herself as a child during the Spanish Civil War and the harsh postwar period; and for the novel's narrator, who endeavors to convey the past as a lived experience to the reader. The second section briefly reflects on the claims the novel makes for the centrality of mass culture to the writing of history. In the following chapter, I explore the ways *El cuarto* answers and amplifies questions raised in the novels already analyzed—questions about the role of art and mass culture in modern society, about what is required to create new fiction, about the complex relationship of fiction and escape, and about the role of gender in the mass cultural novel.[1]

## Preserving a Precious Past: Mass Culture, Memory, and Collective Identity in *El cuarto de atrás*

The opening pages of *El cuarto de atrás* are a record of frustration and failure. The narrator-protagonist C., alone in her apartment and plagued by insomnia, strives to recreate the sensations she experienced as a child in bed awaiting sleep.[2] But the experience is not the same:

> Pero miento, igual no, era otro el matiz de la expectativa. He dicho "anhelo y temor" por decir algo, tanteando a ciegas, y cuando se dispara así, nunca se da en el blanco; las palabras son para la luz, de noche se fugan . . . Daría lo que fuera por revivir aquella sensación, mi alma al diablo, sólo volviéndola a probar, siquiera unos minutos, podría entender las diferencias con esta desazón desde la que ahora intento convocarla . . . (*El cuarto* 10–11)

> But that's not true, it wasn't just the same, the exact feel of the waiting was different. I have said "eagerly and fearfully," just to hear myself talk, groping my way along blindly, and when one takes a shot at random that way, one never hits the bull's-eye. Words are for the light. At night they run away, . . . I'd give anything to relive that sensation, sell my soul to the Devil just to experience it again, if only for a few minutes; I might understand the ways in which it differs from this irritation out of the midst of which I am trying to summon it now . . . (*Back Room* 2–3)

Because of the protagonist's inability to recover her childhood feelings, the many objects in her bedroom which allude to the past become oppressive and forbidding; they call out to her but enable her to recall only "dates, rotten fruits" (9). The frustration grows as C. dis-

---

1. For a plot summary, see appendix.

2. I will refer to the narrator-protagonist as C. and to the author as Martín Gaite in order to counteract the temptation the text offers to equate them. To conflate the two is to ignore both the question of why key aspects of the author's life are left out of the text, and the fact that the novel's other character is also intimately related to the author who generated him. On the author's relationship to the characters, see Epps, "Space of Sexual History."

covers an old love letter written to her by a man on a beach; she dreams of being able to talk to him but cannot remember who he is. She ends the chapter with the wish to communicate: "I have just enough time to say: 'I want to see you, I want to see you,' with my eyes closed. But I have no idea who it is I'm saying that to" (18).

The first chapter thus introduces the two principal aims of the book we are about to read: to recapture the past as a full experience with all its original nuances of feeling; and to communicate that experience to an interlocutor. As we learn later in the novel, the personal quest to recapture the experience of the inner child is complemented by an equally difficult quest for an adequate literary form with which to convey that experience. Our middle-aged protagonist is an author suffering from writer's block, wanting to write the inner history of the Franco era but fearing that such a text would become either a dry collection of dates and facts or the memoir of an individual life of no interest to anyone else. Throughout the novel, she discusses with the man in black the possible form the book could take. So initially, the path to both content (past experience) and form is blocked for the female protagonist. It will be mass cultural texts (romance novels, mysteries, songs, etc.) which act as the magical agents that permit these aims, seemingly unattainable in the first chapter, to be fully realized.

Like the magic pills that the mysterious man in black gives C. to enhance her memory, popular texts serve in the novel as triggers that bring back the past along with all its sensations.[3] Already in the first chapter, C. introduces us to her childhood dreams of being an independent woman by remembering her imitation of the heroines of the short novels of Elisabeth Mulder in the magazine *Lecturas* (6–7). The memory of a romance novel read in adolescence, *El amor catedrá-tico*, gives rise to an explanation of the difference between the feminist woman idealized during the Republic and the self-sacrificing, active, yet domestic woman set up as a model by the Falange's Sección Femenina (87ff.). The chance rediscovery of a picture of Conchita Piquer (113) triggers memories of doing homework while listening to *boleros* on the radio and being jolted into attention by the bitter songs of this unique singer (149–52). The image of Deanna

---

3. Popular texts function here in a way identical to Proust's famous *madeleine* in *The Remembrance of Things Past*.

Durbin skating to school while eating a lemon ice cream brings back the memory of C.'s own comical attempts at roller skating (58–59), and of the lemon ice cream which was a valued treat during the poverty of the postwar period (64). For the middle-aged narrator, then, mass culture is a mediator between the present and the distant past. Through the popular texts of her youth, C. is able to recall the past not as the lifeless series of facts and dates which she so longs to avoid, but as the network of everyday activities, dreams, and associations which she originally experienced. Fredric Jameson has described the way popular songs become impregnated with each listener's own history and individual circumstance:

The passionate attachment one can form to this or that pop single, the rich personal investment of all kinds of private associations and existential symbolism which is the feature of such attachment, are fully as much a function of our own familiarity as of the work itself: the pop single, by means of repetition, insensibly becomes part of the existential fabric of our own lives, so that what we listen to is ourselves, our own previous auditions. ("Reification" 138)

Thus the *boleros* and love stories of the forties make C.'s adolescence come alive in much the same way that hearing a song by Simon and Garfunkel or Bob Dylan returns a younger generation to its own roots in the sixties.

If the popular culture of the postwar period is for the middle-aged narrator-protagonist a means of return to her childhood, it played an equally crucial but very different role for the child who first experienced it. The memories narrated in *El cuarto de atrás* focus predominantly on the war and postwar periods—that is, on the hardest years of the Franco era. In the model of the world presented in *El cuarto de atrás*, the coming of dictatorship means the superimposition of a false, denatured world upon the "real," varied, unpredictable world of the Republican period. A bogus but intense *normality* is imposed, in which everything is flattened, muted:

Franco . . . había conseguido infiltrarse en todas las casas, escuelas, cines y cafés, allanar la sorpresa y la variedad, despertar un temor religioso y uniforme, amortiguar las conversaciones y las risas para que ninguna se oyera más alta que otra. (132)

Franco . . . had managed to insinuate himself into all the houses, schools, movie theaters, and cafés, do away with spontaneity and variety, arouse a religious, uniform fear, stifle conversations and laughter so that no one's voice rang out any louder than anyone else's. (128)

It is a "muffled atmosphere" (150–51) in which suffering cannot be expressed at all.[4] And happiness, too, is fake, imposed by the regime, attributed to Isabel la Católica and to all the creators of Franco's "new Spain," although as the young C. observes, none of them *look* happy (89). In this context, mass culture divides into two categories: texts which attempt to buttress Francoist ideology, and texts which allude to *real* emotions, dreams, or situations that belie the false, anaesthetized world of the postwar period.[5] Some texts, then, reinforce the norm; others suggest the exception, the deviation from the norm. C.'s visit to a *balneario* (which served as inspiration for her first novel) is described as a boring and predictable experience:

era todo tan normal, un mundo inmerso en la costumbre, rodeado de seguridades, habitado por personas acquiescentes y educadas que se dirigían sonrisas y saludos, inmediatamente dispuestas a acogernos en su círculo, a cambiar con nosotros tarjetas de visita de cuyo intercambio nacerían amistades perennes y obligatorias . . . (48)

[E]verything at the spa was so normal, a world steeped in tradition, surrounded by every sort of security, frequented by affable, well-bred people who smiled and politely greeted each other and were immediately disposed to welcome us within their circle, to exchange calling cards with us, an exchange that would give rise to enduring and obligatory friendships . . . (42)

But one night the collective singing of a *bolero* provides a propitious atmosphere for the young C. to stare passionately into the eyes of a young man for whom she has conceived a literary love. The text of the song bears reproducing:

Ven, que te espero en el Cairo,
junto a la orilla del Nilo;

4. "Pain was an insignificant and ridiculous cockroach. One needed only to keep all the corners of the house clean for it to flee in mortification, put to shame by its trivial existence" (88).

5. The narrator contrasts "that official, circumspect happiness imposed by fiat" with "that hearty laughter and that song that come pouring forth from a spring whose waters no one channels" (121).

la noche africana,
sensual y pagana,
será testigo mudo de nuestro amor... (51)

Come, I'm waiting for you in Cairo,                    ·
on the shore of the Nile;
the African night,
sensual and pagan,
will be the silent witness of our love. (45)

The song negates and erases the narrow, mediocre world of the postwar period by proposing an exotic escape similar to that which occurs in Woody Allen's *The Purple Rose of Cairo*.[6] Under the influence
of the song and the gaze it inspires, C. dares to write a love letter
which she plans to give to the object of her passion. She notes that
such behavior is totally antithetical to the prescribed manners of the
"decent and decorous young lady" (47) of the forties. The mass cultural text, then, does not simply offer an escape from the closed
reality of postwar Spain; it also provides an impetus (an "incitación"
in the words of Américo Castro) to break with the norms of that
reality.[7] However, the dream associated with the *bolero* is shattered
as news of an attempt to assassinate Hitler brings reality to the fore
once again; C. tears the letter to pieces and renounces the dream.

The pattern is repeated in the claustrophobic world of C.'s grandparents' house in Madrid, where two maids from Burgos ensure that
nothing ever is "out of place" and where all visits are announced and
predictable. C. escapes from this prisonlike world by reading, playing, or listening to popular songs and ads on the radio. The texts of
the radio songs (70–71, 72–73) again refer to a dream world of afflu-
ence and beckon the listener to escape to imaginary places such as
Cúnigan. The young C. promises herself to let disorder reign in her

6. Could Goytisolo's narrator have gotten his ideas about the Arab world from
songs like this?

7. The idea of the mass cultural text as impetus to rebellious action runs counter
to Horkheimer and Adorno's version—produced during the forties—which sees mass
culture as precluding rebellion (see *Dialectic of Enlightenment*). Once again, the importance of context proves critical; under extreme poverty and repressive conditions,
mass culture can be a call to action, where it might have opposite effects under conditions of relative prosperity.

own future home, and dreams of escaping from the house on the Calle Mayor to find adventure on the mysterious streets of Madrid.[8]

Mass cultural texts, in these two childhood experiences, act as vehicles of feeling. They do so in each case by opening up a *space* not previously present. The text of the *bolero* about Cairo is described as a "forbidden, secret place" "within which . . . our eyes spoke to each other" (45). The radio ad for Cúnigan brings to the fore the child's intense desire to explore unknown territory in the city rather than always adhering to the predictable, prepared plans of her parents and being imprisoned in her grandparents' house. The space opened by mass cultural texts in a context of repression and powerlessness, then, becomes impregnated with deep yearnings, dreams, secret associations, thoughts of rebellion. Its function is identical to that of the theater, which enthralls the child C. as a spectator and, later, as an actress—the imaginary space provides the freedom to invent oneself, to be someone else, however temporarily.[9] We note that the most precious function of fiction, in the view of this narrator, is carried out equally well by "highbrow" literature and by mass cultural texts; no such distinction is ever made in *El cuarto de atrás*, where other kinds of distinctions are more important. Consuming fiction not only creates new spaces in the imagination but stimulates in turn the creation of other fictions that spawn still more imaginary worlds. This is the case of the island Bergai, created by the young C. and her classmate under the influence of *Robinson Crusoe* and their favorite romance novels. The marvelous occurs within the cracks in the system, in the "brechas en la costumbre" (76) ("breaches of habit" [70]) which the narrator sees as essential to literature:

. . . los cuentos bonitos siempre hacen perder la noción del tiempo . . . gracias a ellos, nos salvamos del agobio de lo práctico . . . (91)[10]

8. The same escape to another world is present in C.'s trip to a Portugal which fairly resonates with echoes of the novels of chivalry and the *fado;* this time the norm which the protagonist evades is the obligatory Servicio Social (42–44).

9. George Lipsitz: "Theater attendance enabled individuals to play out fictive scenarios of changed identities, to escape from the surveillance and supervision of moral authorities and institutions" (8).

10. And of course one of these cracks is nothing other than the back room, described as "a kingdom where nothing was forbidden" (187). The back room existed first as a physical space, later as a mental one, a treasure-box for all the dreams, hopes, and invented narratives evoked by fiction.

. . . good stories always make a person lose all sense of time . . . thanks to them we keep ourselves from being overwhelmed by practical tasks . . . (85)

Thus far, we have assessed the impact of "positive" texts, those which evoke real emotions, erase the falsified world of the Franco era, and become vehicles for rebellion, self-creation, secret lives. But other texts support the system. By showing that even within a given genre, texts may support diametrically opposed political creeds, *El cuarto de atrás* offers a salutary corrective to those who assert that all mass cultural texts are ultimately alike. The association made by many critics—both conservative and Marxist—of highbrow texts with norm breaking and lowbrow texts with the reinforcement of the status quo, is here shown to be generalization. C. distinguishes texts not in terms of the high/low opposition or in terms of genre or mode of production, but by *content*. For example, two very disparate kinds of romance novels influence C.'s upbringing. The first is the love story of the Republican era; its protagonists are described in detail:

. . . mujeres de mirada soñadora, pelo a lo *garçon* y piernas estilizadas, que hablaban por teléfono, sostenían entre los dedos un vaso largo o fumaban cigarrillos turcos sobre la cama turca . . . ; otras veces aparecían en pijama, con perneras de amplio vuelo, pero aunque fuera de noche, siempre estaban despiertas, esperando algo, probablemente una llamada telefónica, y detrás de los labios amargos y de los ojos entornados se escondía la historia secreta que estaban recordando en soledad. (13)

. . . women with dreamy eyes, hair cut in a "boyish bob," and stylized legs, who had conversations on the telephone, held a tall glass between their fingers, or smoked Turkish cigarettes on the "Turkish bed" . . . At other times they appeared in lounge pajamas with wide floppy legs, but even though it was nighttime they were always awake, waiting for something, most likely a telephone call, and behind their bitter lips and their half-closed eyes lay hidden the secret story that they were recollecting in solitude. (6)

The Franco regime brings renown to conservative authors whose works serve as propaganda for a very different kind of woman. The most famous of the conservative romance writers is Carmen de Icaza:

sus heroínas eran activas y prácticas, se sorbían las lágrimas, afrontaban cualquier calamidad sin una queja, mirando hacia un futuro orlado de nubes rosadas, inasequibles al pernicioso desaliento que sólo puede colarse por las rendijas de la inactividad. (94)

Her heroines were active and practical. They choked back their tears, confronted any and every calamity without a word of complaint, looking toward a future edged in pink clouds, invulnerable to the pernicious dejection that could seep in only through the cracks of indolence. (88)

The "official story" is also conveyed through the women's magazine *Y*, published by the Sección Femenina of the Falange.

Another way in which *El cuarto* breaks down critical clichés about mass culture lies in its exploration of the role of the radio song in a context characterized by hunger, deprivation, and repression. We are used to thinking of radio songs as inciting consumption—either the public will buy the recorded songs themselves or they will buy the goods advertised between songs. In the 1940s in Spain, however, the vast majority of Spaniards had to devote their scarce resources to mere physical survival. And yet, in this context, the radio song took on immense importance. Martín Gaite explains:

"En tiempos de escasez hay que hacer durar lo que se tiene, y de la misma manera que nadie tira un juguete ni deja a medio comer un pastel, a nadie se le ocurre tampoco consumir deprisa una canción, porque no es un lujo que se renueva cada día, sino un enser fundamental para la supervivencia, la cuida, la rumia, le saca todo su jugo..." (179)

"In times of scarcity one must make what one has last, and just as no one throws a toy away or leaves a cake half eaten, so it would not occur to anyone to consume a song quickly, because a song is not a luxury that comes one's way every day, but a fundamental item necessary for survival. One takes good care of it, thinks about it, extracts all its juice . . ." (179)

As with the romance novels, the popular song could serve either as a type of "anaesthesia" (149) or as a disturbing reminder of problems that official discourse prefers to ignore. Manuel Vázquez Montalbán, in his *Crónica sentimental de España*, describes the two kinds of song and the role played by popular texts in the postwar period in terms similar to those of Martín Gaite. For Vázquez Montalbán, the main concerns of Spaniards in the 1940s were to survive (food was rationed throughout the decade) and to find a way of living with each other after the outpouring of hatred and the atrocities of the Civil War. Since Franco imposed a total silence regarding politics, mass culture—in the form of movies, songs, fashion—was seized upon as something everyone could share. Most songs spoke of hope, love, and happiness and were used by the people as a means of survival. These sweet *boleros* were reassuring and encouraged conformity with the new regime; in the words of Vázquez Montalbán, mass culture served to "depoliticize social consciousness" (35). But for both Vázquez Montalbán and Martín Gaite, the songs of Conchita Piquer contained a protest against the dictatorship. Her songs told stories of prostitutes, marginalized and condemned by a society which could not assimilate them or even explicitly acknowledge their existence.[11] The innocent love and happy marriages of the *boleros* give way to betrayal, unrequited love, and exploitation in the bitter songs of Conchita Piquer. Once again, these songs acted as vehicles for the real, for the pain that lay underneath the muffled emotions and official triumphalism of the postwar period. Martín Gaite has this to say about the protest latent in the songs of Conchita Piquer:

Aquellas mujeres que andaban por la vida a bandazos y no se despedían de un novio a las nueve y media en el portal de su casa intranquilizaban por estar aludiendo a un mundo donde no campeaba lo leal ni lo perenne, eran escombros de la guerra, dejaban al descubierto aquel vacío en torno, tan difícil de disimular, aquel clima de sordina, parecido al que preside las convalecencias, cuando se mueve uno entre prohibiciones, con cautela y extrañeza. Nadie quería hablar del cataclismo que acababa de desgarrar al país, pero las heridas vendadas seguían latiendo, aunque no se oyeran gemidos ni disparos: era un silencio artificial, un hueco a llenar urgentemente de lo que fuera. (152–53)

Those women who staggered through life and did not bid their intended goodnight at their front door at 9:30 on the dot made people uneasy, because they hinted at the existence of a world where fidelity and eternal values had not won the day. They were the rubble left by the war. They exposed to view that emptiness that lay all about, so hard to hide, that muffled atmosphere, like the one that presides over sickbeds, when one's every move is made amid prohibitions, cautiously, and with a feeling of being entirely out of

11. Rafael Abella notes that widows and orphans of Republican soldiers were not entitled to a pension, and were forced to exist by begging, or in the case of younger women, "the solution imposed by the circumstances was prostitution, which grew exponentially" (32–33). Thus the songs of Conchita Piquer which expressed the point of view of the prostitute had a special political charge.

place. Nobody wanted to speak of the cataclysm that had just torn the country apart, but the bandaged wounds still throbbed, though no moans or shots could be heard. It was an artificial silence, an emptiness that there was an urgent need to fill with anything whatsoever. (150–51)

For Vázquez Montalbán, these songs—sung by the women of the forties "with all their heart"—were a form of unconscious protest against the poverty, mediocrity and repression of the postwar period (43). Since open political protest was impossible, Vázquez Montalbán suggests that one must look for more subtle signs of protest like a bitter tone of voice or an aggressive line of a song.[12] The song, then, was essential in the postwar period as an outlet for feelings that could not be expressed in any other way.[13]

The popular texts of the postwar period, as represented in *El cuarto de atrás*, are thus part of a struggle for hegemony.[14] The "new Spain" seeks to convince the populace of its version of reality through school texts, the magazines of the Sección Femenina, and romance novels featuring active yet domestic women. The texts which question the official version fall into three categories. They may be Spanish texts produced before the dictatorship, like the romances of Elisabeth Mulder; they may be texts produced during the dictatorship which manage to break through the "anaesthetic," as in the case of Conchita Piquer's *coplas;* or they may be texts from other countries which

12. Vázquez Montalbán 35–36. Martín Gaite's emotional investment in the songs of Conchita Piquer is apparent in an angry attack on an inaccurate collection of these lyrics which appeared in 1972, edited by none other than Vázquez Montalbán. See Martín Gaite, "Cuarto a espadas sobre las coplas de posguerra," in *La búsqueda de interlocutor* 167–80.

13. T. J. Clark's analysis of the political charge of performances in the Parisian *café-concert* of the 1860s confirms the risk of inviting a public of both the bourgeoisie and the lower classes to identify with lower-class figures: "In producing the popular, bourgeois society produces its opposite; and for the most part it manages to make that opposite into an image—one withdrawn or provided at opportune moments. Yet the image itself . . . is inimical to everything the bourgeoisie believes in, and its effects cannot be calculated as accurately as the class would wish. There is always a chance that a line or phrase will be used by the singer to enforce fleetingly the kind of attention—the kind of collective vehemence—that . . . the censor fear[s]" (236). Such functions of the popular song suggest new methodologies for the historians of repressive regimes, as well as for the mass cultural theorist. In contexts where newspapers and history books are censored, one may expect the tensions, dreams, and protests of ordinary people to take refuge in the lines of popular songs.

14. On the notion of hegemony, see Gramsci, *Prison Notebooks* 326–27, 333.

present models of conduct that contradict Francoist norms and expose them as arbitrary, as in the films of Deanna Durbin.

Thus far I have focused mainly on two periods in the life of the narrator-protagonist: the post-Franco present in which she talks with the mysterious stranger, and the Franco era which began for her in 1936 in Salamanca. But in the first chapter of *El cuarto*, C. is trying to recapture the feelings of an even more distant time—her childhood during the Republic. Time in *El cuarto de atrás* thus divides into three distinct periods. The middle period (the Franco era) was experienced by C. as a single block of time: "All the years of his reign came tumbling down on top of me. To me they felt like a homogenous block. . . . I am simply not capable of discerning the passage of time all during that period, or differentiating the war years from the postwar ones. The thought came to me that Franco had paralyzed time . . ." (129–30). In the first chapter, C. is trying to leap over the block of time that represents the Franco regime, to recover the sensations of childhood untarnished by later developments.[15] To understand what C. wants to communicate through the text of *El cuarto de atrás*, we must look at how the Republic and the Franco era are represented in the novel as a series of oppositions.[16]

The years of the Republic are associated by the child C. with games and freedom.[17] She describes the outdoor games played in the street when there was only one car in town to interrupt them (109); indoor games were brought as presents by her uncle Joaquín, whom C. also remembers making "risqué remarks . . . that were not fit for children's ears" (111). Through her uncle Joaquín, C. even sees politics as a kind of exciting game. He teaches her a tongue twister containing the names of politicians such as Lerroux, who are guilty precisely of introducing a game into Spain, a kind of roulette called "el estraperlo" (127). The child C. is fascinated by the variety of options available in the "game" of politics:

15. The coming of the war and the dictatorship had prematurely hastened C.'s adolescence and, later, made it impossible for her to fully grow up. The narrator-protagonist is trying to get past that long adolescent block in her encounter with the man in black.

16. For the idea of the model of the world in a literary text, see Lotman, ch. 8.

17. Kathleen Glenn has explored self-reflexivity in *El cuarto de atrás* as a kind of game, noting the link established in the space of *el cuarto* between reading and games. See "Literature as Juego."

. . . a mí, hasta los nueve años, la política me parecía . . . un juego para entretenerse las personas mayores. Pero notaba que se divertían con aquel juego; . . . no daba la impresión de monótono sino de variado, siempre estaban apareciendo cromos con personajes nuevos, y cada jugador proclamaba sus preferencias por uno determinado . . . (130)

. . . up until I was nine years old, politics seemed to me to be a . . . game for the amusement of the big people. But I noticed that they had fun playing that game . . . it didn't appear to be a monotonous game, but rather one with lots of variety. Colored cards with new figures kept appearing all the time, and each player announced his preference for this one or that . . . (126–27)

The space most representative of this festive view of the Republic is of course *el cuarto de atrás*, "where I learned to play and read" (84). This room is the space where all the rules can be broken, the antidote to the grandparents' house on the calle Mayor:

[El cuarto] era muy grande y en él reinaban el desorden y la libertad, se permitía cantar a voz en cuello, cambiar de sitio los muebles, saltar encima de un sofá desvencijado . . . , tumbarse en la alfombra, mancharla de tinta, era un reino donde nada estaba prohibido. (187)

The back room was very large, and in it disorder and freedom reigned. We were allowed to sing at the top of our lungs, move the furniture around as we pleased, jump on top of a rickety old sofa . . . , to lie on the rug, to get ink stains on it—it was a kingdom where nothing was forbidden. (187)

The *cuarto de atrás* functions as the realm of the exceptional, the space where behavior that is usually repressed can find an outlet. During the Republic, this space offers the young C. freedom from the rules imposed by adults.

With the war, however, the function of the *cuarto de atrás* changes. The large sideboard no longer houses games, but serves as a pantry to hoard food; the back room is invaded by stuffed partridges and sausages "until we ceased to have a room to play in because the articles of prime necessity had shoved our childhood aside and driven it into a corner" (189). Just as play and freedom give way to simple survival in the space of the back room, so everything that the Republic represents is erased by the Franco regime. The oppositions in table 1, presented through C.'s memories, illustrate the change.[18]

18. The oppositions are translations of words used by Martín Gaite herself.

Table 1

| Republic | Franco | Post-Franco |
|---|---|---|
| childhood | adolescence/adulthood | |
| freedom | rules, imprisonment[1] | |
| impulse, the unexpected | routine, keeping accounts | |
| disorder | order | |
| individuality | conformity, uniformity | |
| variety | omnipresence of Franco[2] | |
| communication, laughter, singing at the top of one's lungs | keeping quiet[3] | |
| night (mystery, doubt, adventure) | day (cheerfulness, certainty, faith) | |
| reading, escape, madness | activity, sanity[4] | |
| Elisabeth Mulder | Carmen de Icaza | |
| the back room | the novelistic spaces outside the room (school, grandparents' house, Carmencita Franco's palace, etc.) | |

In the Post-Franco column: a large **?**

1. See the description of the Sección Femenina's rigidly domestic image of women (96); the images of women from the Republican era are the heroines of Elisabeth Mulder's novels, who are awake late at night and free to go out alone (13–14); and the nude photographs in the magazine *Crónica* (115). The representatives of freedom and imprisonment are Deanna Durbin ("the very image of freedom" [65]) and Carmencita Franco ("a creature trapped in a prison . . . amid the tapestries lining her gilded cage" [58–59]).

2. The child C. viewed the politicians of the Republic as "figures in a deck of cards that you could use to make all sorts of combinations" (128). Franco, by contrast, "was the one and only . . . his power was indisputable and omnipresent . . ." (129).

3. Under the Republic, "[p]eople talked about whatever they liked" (129), but with the new regime, C. and her sister are admonished: " 'don't breathe a word about this,' . . . 'don't tell anybody they've killed Uncle Joaquín' " (51).

4. During the Franco era, "staying put, conforming, and making the best of things were good; skipping out, escaping, running away were bad" (121).

The advent of the Franco regime eliminates the first term of each of the above oppositions, beginning with the *cuarto de atrás* itself. By the present moment of narration, after Franco's death, other important elements of C.'s past have also ceased to exist. The entire house in Salamanca has been demolished (169); the friend with whom C. invented Bergai and a *novela rosa* is now dead (179); and those childhood writings themselves were burned by C. in a moment of pyromania (38, 196). Fortunately, for C. and for the reader, the *cuarto de atrás* is not only a physical space which has disappeared; it is also a part of the mind. This form of the back room—memory, or the subconscious—survives the Franco era precisely because it is *"atrás"* (behind), marginal, unseen by the system:

me lo imagino también como un desván del cerebro, una especie de recinto secreto lleno de trastos borrosos, separado de las antesalas más limpias y ordenadas de la mente por una cortina que sólo se descorre de vez en cuando; los recuerdos que pueden darnos alguna sorpresa viven agazapados en el cuarto de atrás, siempre salen de allí, y sólo cuando quieren, no sirve hostigarlos. (91)

I also imagine it as the attic of one's brain, a sort of secret place full of a vague jumble of all sorts of miscellaneous junk, separated from the cleaner and more orderly anterooms of the mind by a curtain that is only occasionally pulled back. The memories that may come to us as something of a surprise live in hiding in the back room. They always emerge from there, and only when they want to. It's no use trying to flush them out. (85)

Now that the physical space of freedom has disappeared, mass cultural texts (*boleros, coplas,* etc.) provide a mental space for all deviations from the norm. The mental *cuarto de atrás* is "furnished" with the trappings of popular culture. The novel thus offers an unusually graphic representation of how unconscious desires and fears find their expression in apparently trivial forms of mass culture.

The writing of *El cuarto de atrás* begins at the moment of the dictator's death. The political project of the novel is to effect a miracle—to make present once again all the characteristics of the Republic (liberty, individuality, variety, etc.) which during the Franco era existed only in the hidden regions of the mental *cuarto de atrás*. C. also wishes to communicate to a younger generation (represented by her daughter) the spirit of resistance to the Franco regime that was kept alive for her by forms of popular culture during the long, monotonous years of the postwar period. Thus, the novel, published while the future of Spain was still unclear, resurrects the characteristics of the Republic in order to make them available for use in the creation of a new system out of the fossilized apparatus of the Franco regime.

C.'s problems in writing her book, discussed at length with the man in black, derive from the ambitious nature of her aims, which may be summarized as follows: (1) to recapture the feelings of childhood erased by the Franco regime; (2) to reinstitute true communication after the decades in which silence and uniformity were the norm;[19] (3) to make the past present, to recover all that was lost during the Franco years; (4) to communicate the past to those who never knew it, not as a series of dates and dry words, but as the full experience it originally was; and (5) to transmit not only the past of an individual, but the dreams, hopes and customs of a whole generation.

As we have seen, the first objective is achieved through the forms of mass culture which, like the pills of the man in black, open the metaphorical curtain which had imprisoned C.'s childhood memories in the mental *cuarto de atrás*. The second objective, to reestablish true communication, must be attained by overturning the omnipresent and powerful norms of the dictatorship, operative for four decades. This overturning is implicit already in the book's title, where the "cuartos de adelante" are denied importance and displaced by the *cuarto de atrás*. The norm-breaking function of the book becomes explicit in the first epigraph:

Para Lewis Carroll, que todavía nos consuela de tanta cordura y nos acoge en su mundo al revés. (7)

For Lewis Carroll, who still consoles us *about all that sanity and welcomes us into his world turned upside down.[20]

This epigraph announces the intention of the book in a variety of ways. First of all, the repetition of the direct object pronoun "nos" emphasizes that the book has a collective rather than an individual focus. Second, the "world turned upside down," which is later re-

---

19. For a discussion of the theme of communication in Martín Gaite's work, see Kathleen Glenn, "Communication."

20. I have modified Helen Lane's translation here, as indicated by an asterisk.

flected in the picture with the same title (22), again indicates a reversal of the world "right side up," which until the time of writing was the Franco regime.[21] The phrase "who still consoles us about all that sanity" is explained over the course of the novel. During the dictatorship, those who did not follow the regime's norms of conduct received the denomination "loco"; for example, forward women are condemned: " '¿Esa? Esa es una loca' " (125) (" 'That one? She's a madwoman' ") (120). *El cuarto de atrás*, by contrast, includes a *mise en abîme* of its own intentions in the mention of Erasmus's *In Praise of Folly* (149). Thus the *cordura* of the epigraph is clearly equivalent to the norm of the Franco regime; the words "still" and "*all that* sanity" recall how long and how intensely that norm was enforced.[22]

The third objective, that of making the past present in order to recover what was lost, is attained by narrating the frame story through the conventions of the fantastic. Martín Gaite's use of Todorov's prescriptions for the fantastic mode have been amply studied; for my purposes, it suffices to recall C's summary of Todorov: "It *talks about . . . breaking through the boundaries between time and space" (11–12)—and her later quotation: "The time and space of supernatural life are not the time and space of daily life" (142).[23] As a

21. Blas Matamoro interprets *El cuarto de atrás* as a critical revision of the social realism of the 1950s, reading the *cuartos de adelante* as the visible, ordered world which the "generación de medio siglo" documented at the expense of what was invisible and unconscious. He notes that the popular genres which Martín Gaite resuscitates in *El cuarto de atrás* were also left out by the neorealists, "perhaps because they thought they were inappropriate, 'unreal' sources, or because they were, in a more obvious way, the surface scabs of official mass culture" (600). I argue that Martín Gaite shows part of the mass culture of the postwar period to be an antidote to official culture rather than its representative.

Linda Gould Levine explores another aspect of the "world upside down" created in *El cuarto de atrás:* that the artist is a woman, guided by a male muse, inverting the classic European tradition of Dante and Petrarch. I will explore the more active, guiding function of the man in black in the next chapter, as I discuss the question of mass culture and refuge.

22. The young C. is aware that she will never openly break the rules of the regime; rather she will escape through her imagination, an endeavor which she explains as almost a contradiction in terms, a *locura:* "Escaping without venturing outside, more difficult still, a mad undertaking" (122). Ruth El Saffar shows how *El cuarto de atrás* represents the culmination of Martín Gaite's earlier work by putting "an end to the association of that fervent dreaming with taboo, madness, and danger" ("Redeeming Loss" 11). See the discussion below of the ambivalent role of the refuge in *El cuarto*.

23. See Brown, "A Fantastic Memoir"; and Durán.

result, the child C. and the mature C., C.'s current house and the childhood one that has long ceased to exist, can all be present at once:

Mi imagen se desmenuza y se refracta en infinitos reflejos: estoy volando sobre los tejados de la mano de una amiga que ya murió y, al mismo tiempo, avanzo por un pasadizo junto a la hermana del hombre de negro. (167)

My image shatters and is refracted in infinite reflections. I am flying above the rooftops hand in hand with a friend who is dead now, and at the same time I am walking along a passageway alongside the sister of the man in black. (167)

C. has succeeded in saving the past from oblivion; speaking of a room described in her novel *Ritmo lento*, she declares:

mientras yo viva, existe la habitación . . . , aunque sea producto de mi fantasía, . . . qué más da, también el cuarto de atrás sigue existiendo y se ha salvado de la muerte, aunque hayan tirado la casa de la Plaza de los Bandos . . . (169)

As I long as I live, that room continues to exist . . . even though it's a product of my imagination . . . What difference does that make—the back room also continues to exist and has been rescued from death, even though they've torn down the building on the Plaza de los Bandos. (169)[24]

But how can one communicate all that has been "saved from death" in writing, when C. tells us that writing converts the most urgent ideas into "dissected butterflies"?[25] Martín Gaite solves the problem through the use of metafictional techniques that obscure the borders between book and reality, speech and writing, present and past, product and process.[26] From the beginning of the novel, we

24. In this context, we may recall that the *Diary* of Anne Frank was originally published in Dutch under the title *Het Achterhuis*—"the house in back." (The English translation renders this phrase as "the Secret Annex.") The parallels with *El cuarto de atrás* are both moving and illuminating. Each "back room/house" contains a reality which is not tolerated by the "*cuartos de adelante*," which in each case are under a dictatorial regime. And although the world of the two "back rooms" has long been physically lost, in each case there remains a text which bears witness to the past and saves it from oblivion.

25. As Ruth El Saffar puts it, "The task . . . is to recover true experience from its entrapment in fiction and to liberate, at the same time, the word from its deep complicity with death" ("Liberation and the Labyrinth" 187).

26. The terms *product* and *process* are those of Robert Spires. See *Beyond the Metafictional Mode*, ch. 7. I refer the reader to Ruth El Saffar's illuminating medita-

are treated to constant mirror images in which fiction and "reality,"
past and present, allude to one another in a way that muddles their
borders, refusing stasis. First we pass from the adult narrator's room
in Madrid to her childhood room in Salamanca; we then find out that
the creation of the childhood room was inspired by the magazine
*Lecturas*. This magazine also contained romance novels featuring
women in pyjamas, unable to sleep, waiting for a phone call. This
piece of information catapults us once again into the present of narration in Madrid; we realize that our adult narrator is created out of the
materials of a forty-year-old fiction, out of the dreams of her childhood self of being an independent woman. Later, the adult narrator
declares that the engraving of Luther and the devil on her bedroom
wall often seems to be a mirror reflecting her situation in "reality."
She also stops the action of her conversation with the man in black to
specify how he is modeled on the male protagonists of the *novela
rosa*:

Enciende dos [pitillos] en su boca y me pasa uno. Muy de novela rosa este
detalle. (180)

He puts two [cigarettes] in his mouth, lights them, and hands me one of
them. A touch straight out of a romance novel. (190)[27]

Such devices make it impossible to separate a level of the "real" out
from fiction. The limits of what can be represented, of what might
occur, are thus stretched; fiction animates "the real," the past comes
to life in the present, the present is but an enactment of a past fiction.
The moments of indecision about the form this very text should take
are recorded in it—should it be an essay entitled "Usos amorosos de la
postguerra" ("Amorous customs of the postwar"), a memoir, or a
fantastic novel? C. also explains the problem of putting experiences
in print; the man in black advises C., "you should learn to write the

---

tion on the crossing of the carefully guarded border between fiction and reality in *Don
Quijote* and *El cuarto de atrás* (see "Redeeming Loss").

The success of the techniques merging book and reality, product and process is
attested by the title of Debra Castillo's article: "Never-Ending Story: Carmen Martín
Gaite's *The Back Room*." She states that the novel remains "open-ended instead of
permitting it to shut itself up between (or behind) the covers of a book, or a pile of
folios" (815).

27. This gesture may be modeled on the 1942 film *Now, Voyager*, in which Paul
Henreid repeatedly lights two cigarettes in his mouth and passes one to Bette Davis.

way you talk" (136).[28] At the end of the book, C. herself reads the manuscript we have just read—inside the book itself.[29] And to further confuse the borders between reality and literature, Martín Gaite includes within the fiction a commentary on her previous work, which is attributed to C. The mention of titles such as *El balneario, Entre visillos, Ritmo lento,* and *Usos amorosos del dieciocho en España* tend to make the reader forget that C. is (at least in part) a fictional character, and that *both* C. and the man in black are creations of Carmen Martín Gaite. The text seems to expand to include not only itself and the author's past texts, but a future one as well—*Usos amorosos de la postguerra española,* published in 1987, nine years after *El cuarto de atrás.*

Perhaps the most fundamental problem facing C. is how to convey her experience to a reader unfamiliar with the war and postwar periods. The epigraph by Georges Bataille alludes to the methods that will be necessary to achieve this:

La experiencia no puede ser comunicada sin lazos de silencio, de ocultamiento, de distancia. (8)

Experience cannot be communicated without bonds of silence, concealment, distance.

The "bonds of silence, concealment, distance" refer to the fictionalization which keeps the text from being one more boring memoir of the kind that C. herself detests. In order to recount a collective experience as much as an individual one, Martín Gaite leaves out of the novelistic world certain key events in her life, notably her marriage to and separation from Rafael Sánchez Ferlosio.[30] Having rendered her protagonist slightly less autobiographical, she uses mass culture as a bridge once again—this time between her protagonist and her reader. Though several popular genres are discussed by the characters

---

28. I owe to Renée Sieburth the insight that the man in black functions much like Cervantes's friend in the prologue to part 1 of the *Quijote.* Each is an imaginary friend who gives advice that enables the fictive author to overcome the obstacles to writing the very text we hold in our hands.

29. See Robert Spires, "Intertextuality." Marcia L. Welles calls the structure of *El cuarto de atrás* a "playful game of mirrors," comparing its blurring of process and product to Velázquez's *Las meninas* (202).

30. Kathleen Glenn notes the distinction between the extratextual author and the narrator-protagonist ("From Social Realism").

(the mystery novel and suspense film are but two examples), I will focus on the genre which most closely molds the novel's narrative conventions—the *novela rosa*.[31]

I have illustrated above how the young C. experienced childhood and adolescence through the filter of the dreams and ideals contained in popular texts. If the reader of *El cuarto de atrás* is to replicate her experience even approximately, he or she must also experience her memories through the filter of the same popular literature which the young C. once devoured. But popular texts such as romance novels are written according to a formula which varies according to the culture and period within which they are produced; the Harlequin romances of today are quite different from the sentimental novels read by C.[32] Even during C.'s own youth, she read romance novels written during the Republic and was then forced to absorb a new series of conventions when the Republic gave way to the Franco regime. The only way for C. to convey her experience to a younger reader, therefore, is to write her text using the same conventions that shaped the romances of her youth—and simultaneously to teach that reader how those conventions worked.

C. does this through a multileveled *mise en abîme*, a reflection of the *novela rosa* on three narrative levels.[33] The child C. *reads* romance novels; the middle-aged C. tries to *live one out* with the man in black; and the narrator *writes* one (*El cuarto*), albeit with modifications. Over the course of the novel, through C.'s memories and through digressive commentary during her conversations with the man in black, the reader receives instruction about the typical plots and governing conventions of her childhood romances.

The reader of *El cuarto de atrás* is taught the conventions of the *novelas rosa* of the Republic, with their women in pyjamas, already in the first chapter of the novel. Other plot coincidences follow, as the mature C. feels afraid of the storm outside yet protected by the man in black; she thinks of a line from a *novela rosa:* " 'Oh, Raimundo,' Esperanza exclaimed, . . . 'I'm never afraid when I'm with you. Never go away' " (31). In the climactic scene in which C. expects

31. Elizabeth J. Ordóñez has studied Martín Gaite's absorption and transformation of the *novela rosa* and her mixing of different popular genres. See also Linda Gould Levine; Roger; and Castillo, "Never-Ending Story."

32. For a discussion of formula in popular texts, see Cawelti, "Concept."

33. For the mechanics of the *mise en abîme*, see Dällenbach, Paterson, and Borges.

a declaration of love or revelation of identity by the stranger in black, C. describes for us how this scene is similar to the climaxes of the *novelas rosa*. She even makes explicit the stylistic similarities:

el corazón se me echa a latir como un caballo desbocado, esto del caballo desbocado lo decían también con frecuencia aquellos libros . . . (141)

My heart began to race like a runaway steed. That phrase about the runaway steed also turned up frequently in those books . . . (138)

And C. emphasizes that she cannot help shaping the present work according to these conventions:

es difícil escapar a los esquemas literarios de la primera juventud, por mucho que más tarde se reniegue de ellos. (141)

It is difficult to escape the literary stereotypes of one's earliest years, however hard one tries to renounce them. (138)

It would appear that for the young C., the *novelas rosa* of the Republic provided models to be imitated, while the protagonists of the novels of the Falangist Carmen de Icaza were to be mistrusted. But C. has not been able to escape their influence completely, as is made evident by another *mise en abîme*. The mature C. reads the beginning of one of her own recent articles on Conchita Piquer: " 'The advantage of ⁺having gray hair, apart from its dubious aesthetic value . . .' I read to myself" (137). On the following page she explains how Carmen de Icaza changed the conventions of the *novela rosa*: "The heroine might not be all that young, she might even have gray hair" (138). The mature C., then, is constructed using elements from both strains of the *novela rosa*.

The mature C. is now able to question the conventions of the romance novels, even as she realizes that she cannot escape their influence. A similar doubleness is present in the reader. On the one hand, we are drawn into the story of C.'s encounter with the man in black and wonder whether it will lead to romance. On the other, we recognize the playful metafictional techniques which Martín Gaite uses to tell her story and the many ways in which the text departs from the conventions of C.'s childhood readings.

The multileveled reflection of romance, therefore, makes use of the conventions of the popular genres to create the kind of implied reader of which C. dreams—one who can situate the events of the past within the framework of hopes and expectations created by the narrative formulas of that same past. A final question remains: why such emphasis on mass cultural texts? Readers of Martín Gaite's essays know her to be profoundly influenced by Flaubert, Clarín, Santa Teresa, and Unamuno, to name but a few of her favorite authors. Yet these canonical authors are left out of the frame of the novelistic world of *El cuarto* or are included through indirect allusions rather than explicit mention.[34] The few "classic" texts which are mentioned receive a specific kind of treatment: they are quoted directly, and the quotation is often one that most Spanish readers would recognize. For example, the poem by Rubén Darío:

La princesa está triste,
¿qué tendrá la princesa? (64)

The princess is sad
What can be troubling the princess? (58)

Quotations from Machado and from Cervantes's "La Gitanilla" are also found (30–31, 39–40). Though mass cultural texts are also quoted frequently in the pages of *El cuarto de atrás*, they are much more integrated into the textual structure than their canonical counterparts, and they are explicitly acknowledged as generic models for the plot of the novel. (*Don Quijote*, another subtext for the plot, is *not* mentioned.) Why, then, does Martín Gaite downplay her canonical readings and foreground the popular ones in creating the protagonist C.? I believe the answer is twofold. First, as shown above, Martín Gaite's purpose in writing *El cuarto de atrás* is to recapture a collective past rather than individual memories. This collective experience, which transcends political difference, is emphasized by C.'s comments upon seeing Carmencita Franco on the television screen during Franco's funeral:

hemos crecido y vivido en los mismos años, . . . hemos sido víctimas de las mismas modas y costumbres, hemos leído las mismas revistas y visto el mismo cine, nuestros hijos puede que sean distintos, pero nuestros sueños seguro que han sido semejantes . . . (136–37).

34. An example of indirect allusion to highbrow literature is the use of the cockroach at the beginning and end of the story; as Joan Lipman Brown and others have noted, the cockroach alludes to Kafka's *Metamorphosis*, a canonical text of the fantastic tradition ("A Fantastic Memoir" 14).

We've grown up and lived in the same years . . . We've been the victims of the same manners and mores, we've read the same magazines and seen the same movies. Our children may be different, but our dreams have surely been much the same . . . (133)

Martín Gaite thus wishes to convey her postwar memories in a way that will strike a chord of recognition in her contemporaries, of whatever political stripe. The allusions to the mass cultural genres of the 1930s and 1940s help to create this bridge between her own experience and that of other Spaniards who remember the war. And for those younger readers who do not share her memories, Martín Gaite shapes her story through the ephemeral popular formulas of the 1930s and 1940s. The "classics" which she read in her youth were not produced during those years and thus cannot serve to transmit the time-bound worldview which she wishes to save from oblivion.

A final reason why popular genres are an appropriate vehicle for transmitting the precious heritage of the physical and mental *cuarto de atrás* lies in their marginal status in relation to the "valores eternos" ("eternal values") which formed the cornerstone of official culture during the Franco years. The novel presents to us a woman, writing from her marginal position inside the home, writing of an even more marginal space (a back room), and using as literary models the marginal mass culture of an era long gone. It is the lesson of *El cuarto de atrás* that precisely from those areas considered marginal by the centers of power may come the magic necessary to overturn official hierarchies, and the means to resuscitate what the "official story" claimed to have eliminated—the festive, free, and fanciful spirit of a "mundo al revés."

## Fiction, Memory, Mass Culture: Martín Gaite's Theory of History

Perhaps the most important facts about people and about societies have always been encoded in the ordinary and the commonplace.
—George Lipsitz, *Time Passages*

Among the many fascinating possibilities which lie hidden in the back room is a blueprint for the writing of a new kind of history, using methods that, at the time of the text's appearance, were just beginning to gain currency among historians. Mass culture occupies a central place in this new historiography. Both Goytisolo and Martín Gaite dismiss the official Francoist versions of history they learned in childhood, but the alternatives they propose are almost opposites. Goytisolo's narrator attempts to replace official myths about Spanish history with an inverted myth that reads the Moors as "good guys" and their civilization as crucial to Spanish culture. He tries in his imaginary invasion to free himself and Spain from the country's recent history, never realizing how historically specific his own obsessions are. Martín Gaite's protagonist presents the writing of history as a problem within *El cuarto de atrás*, as one of her longstanding motivations for writing the novel: "All of this goes back to my initial perplexities in the face of the concept of history, there in the back room . . ." (98–99). She tells us that very early on, she distrusted history books: "neither glorious exploits nor exemplary conduct struck me as trustworthy" (91). These doubts crystallize around Isabel la Católica,

en la falaz versión que, de su conducta, nos ofrecían aquellos libros y discursos, donde no se daba cabida al azar, donde cada paso, viaje o decisión de la reina parecían marcados por un destino superior e inquebrantable. (103–04)

*in the deceptive version of her conduct put before us in those textbooks and those speeches, where no room was left for chance, where each step, journey, or decision of the queen appeared to bear the mark of a superior and inevitable destiny. (98)

Martín Gaite's own text aims to do something quite different: "[to tie] together the march of history and the rhythm of dreams" (98). The debates within the text about how to present the material, then, are more than mere metafictional play; they call our attention to the problems with conventional ways of writing history or memoirs. Three main defects of such works are emphasized: they focus on a few heroes, made to look exemplary; they present individual lives or historical events as if everything were determined by a totally intelligible causality; and they project onto a given period interpretations that come only with hindsight; these imposed interpretations create obstacles to memory (63–64).

Martín Gaite's brand of history is a story of the many rather than a narrative of a few leaders imposed on the many as if it represented their experience. It is the story of how identities are created through deep engagement with the discourses circulating in the mass media of the day. Mass cultural texts play contradictory roles which coexist in tension. On the one hand, they condition the dreams individuals have of their future. On the other, they create fictional opportunities to dream of being something completely different from who we are, something that escapes the suffocating circumstances into which we are born. And mass cultural texts become impregnated with personal associations peculiar to each individual. Finally, in authoritarian regimes, they often act as coded expressions of the tensions of the day. Because mass cultural texts are timebound, then, they offer privileged windows into given eras for historians concerned with everyday life.

It is important to contrast this idea of history with Unamuno's *intrahistoria*, which also focused on the common people rather than on political leaders. Unamuno likens *intrahistoria* to the tranquil ocean bottom, where the waves on the surface represent the vicissitudes of political life (*En torno* 27). *Intrahistoria* focuses on "the silent life of those millions of men without a history" (27–28). The differences with Martín Gaite are illuminating. What fascinates Unamuno is that the everyday lives of peasants have changed so little over hundreds of years. He is also charmed by their *silence*. And they are presumed to be *men*; Unamuno's women would be long-suffering mothers existing in a mode even more remote from the passage of time than their spouses. Martín Gaite focuses rather on individual lives, showing their relationship to mass cultural discourses which can sometimes—as in the transition from the Republic to Franco— offer them mutually contradictory role models over the space of a few years. She looks at the ephemeral—fashions, vocabulary, films— whereas Unamuno prefers the timeless. And she writes her story, ostensibly, as one of the common people, from inside a house rather than from a public position among the elite. Unlike Unamuno, she opens up for analysis her own historical observations, recognizing her assumptions as conditioned by the mass culture of her youth. Thus, paradoxically, to focus on mass culture in writing history does not mean evading "serious" problems but bringing them to the fore; Martín Gaite must ask herself how she has been conditioned by the same cultural products she seeks to write about. Perhaps most suggestively, she writes her history as fiction. The Bataille epigraph indicates that experience cannot be communicated without "bonds of . . . concealment, distance." Having done more conventional historical research and published it, Martín Gaite realizes that, in this case, "what I was trying to recapture was something far more difficult to grasp" (135).[35] Thus she opens the question of the relationship between history and fiction in a way that intersects with the concerns of poststructuralist historians. Fiction here claims for itself the authority of history; and when that fiction is written by a woman, such a claim can be considered radical indeed.

35. Louis Begley, the author of the novel *Wartime Lies*, which draws substantially on his own experience as a Jewish child in wartime Poland, comments on the memoir/novel distinction in terms very similar to those of Martín Gaite: "The answer to the question about form—memoir or novel—is that there are some doors one cannot open just by turning the doorknob; their opening must be conjured. I would not have been able to open the door of 'Wartime Lies' without the intercession of its form, which is that of a novel, and the distance that the form of the novel permits the writer to take from his subject" (22).

# Chapter Six

## Martín Gaite, Galdós, Goytisolo: Dialogues on the Role of Culture

• • • *El cuarto de atrás* overturns several precedents established by the other texts analyzed in this volume. Most notably, it is the only text written by a woman, and it is the only one where a female character can speak of her own experience without the filter of a male narrator. It is also the only text to express the viewpoint of an inhabitant of a provincial town rather than a large city; her experience of the city thus rests on assumptions very different from those of Galdós and Goytisolo.[1] *El cuarto* could also be said to be the first stolidly middle-class text we encounter. Both Galdós and Goytisolo grew up in families which once were financially prominent; Martín Gaite seems to have grown up without the burden of a once-important family name. This lack of a social position to maintain undoubtedly contributes to rendering the high/low opposition almost completely inoperative in *El cuarto*, although the author's gender is probably even more crucial in this context. We have seen through reading *Reivindicación* that the high/low opposition is of-

---

1. The middle-aged narrator of *El cuarto* lives in Madrid; but the view of the city she presents is that of her childhood self, who would make periodic visits to Madrid from the provincial capital of Salamanca.

ten emphasized as a way for the male writer to shore up his ego boundaries against women and the masses. Given that mass culture is not considered in *El cuarto* as the "low" category which corresponds to and degrades "high" culture, mass culture here does not have to bear the symbolic weight of nostalgia for sexual purity or different class relations. This means that we are presented with a much more detailed vision of how mass cultural texts can interact with their audiences than in the other works studied. Finally, Martín Gaite's is the only text of the four to be written during a period of democratization and hope. Galdós's texts were written during the Restoration, which had dashed the hopes of those who had believed in the Revolution of 1868 as the beginning of true democracy in Spain. Goytisolo's text was written when Franco had been in power over thirty years, and Spaniards were enjoying long-awaited material progress rather than dreaming of revolution. The tone of festivity rather than apocalypse in *El cuarto*, then, must be explained with reference to the historical moment of its writing and publication (it began as a project on the day of Franco's death), as well as to the gender of its author. Given these departures from the patterns of the novels examined earlier, we can learn much from juxtaposing each of them with *El cuarto*, letting the continuities and contrasts which appear bring into question some of the more established myths about mass culture, and also revealing the price Martín Gaite's narrator has had to pay in order to write her text of miraculous renewal.

### *La desheredada* and *El cuarto de atrás*: Two Aesthetic Theories

Nothing could be more different than the respective versions of mass culture presented in *La desheredada* and *El cuarto de atrás*. Yet the two texts also exhibit areas of overlap that make *El cuarto*, in its own way, a realization of the artistic utopia that *La desheredada*'s narrator was unable to achieve. Both texts postulate an "authentic" past that has been adulterated or falsified in the present. In *La desheredada*, mass culture and consumerism are the agents of falsification. The real is inaccessible; it has been obliterated by fake reproductions and shiny signifiers without a referent. Mass culture, by obscuring or eradicating the real, is responsible for loss of identity. Cut off from their past, Spaniards, like their representative, Isidora, no longer know who they are. For Martín Gaite, the agent of falsification is the Franco regime, which has denatured social customs, education, everyday life, and above all emotion—a codified cheerfulness has replaced the spontaneous, hearty guffaw. While some mass cultural products reinforce the false, imposed state of affairs, other forms of mass culture have the priceless function of stimulating self-knowledge, the recovery of true identity. They provide ways to access real emotions; they catalyze dreams of a different world; they even stimulate original creation rather than making it impossible, as it was in *La desheredada*.

As might be expected, the myths of what the modern city represents are also widely divergent in the two novels. For *La desheredada*'s narrator, the city is a place of fakery, corruption, and perdition—the seat of a display of falsified identities. The city is also enormously threatening; it fragments everything, including the self, menacing the fragile ego with madness. As modernization obliterates the past, the city is the site of orphaning. The narrator longs for a refuge, a womb, where identity will become clear again. For the provincial child of *El cuarto*, however, the city represents adventure and mystery. Coming from a small town where identities are only too well known, the child C. longs for the freedom that anonymity would provide. Imprisoned in her grandparents' apartment (where she feels "swallowed up by a whale" [71]), she desires the openness and freedom of the streets, glorying precisely in the possibility of *not* knowing exactly where she is. Where the city is for *La desheredada*'s narrator the principal site of the falsification of art, the provincial viewpoint presents the city as the space where art reaches its potential, where the theater can achieve the marvelous in a way that is impossible in the rare performances in Salamanca.

Both *La desheredada* and *El cuarto* locate the main headquarters of art in a space associated with the past—the Aransis palace and the back room. The differences are instructive. The Aransis palace is associated with death, cut off from modern life, irreverently invaded by the masses; it is therefore unable to pass down its lessons and is no longer available for the creation of a new art. True art is thus located in a past from which we are cut off. The *cuarto de atrás*, though it disappeared as a *physical* space for art with the advent of the Franco regime, has been preserved *mentally*. Now that the dictator is dead, its contents can be recovered and reconnected to the present. The

Franco era was like a frozen block of time; now that he is dead: "Time unfroze. The man responsible for checking its flow and presiding over it had disappeared" (134). The pre-Franco past, associated with literature and play, is now accessible, providing new generations with the identity they had lost for so long. *El cuarto de atrás* presents itself, then, as the artistic utopia desired by the narrator of *La desheredada*—it is the piece of literature that brings the old world back to life and reconnects it to the present. Where the economic changes wrought by consumer capitalism are seen as irreversible and apocalyptic for art in *La desheredada*, the political falsifications of the Franco regime are seen as reversible, making true art possible again. There is a key difference, however, between the utopia desired in *La desheredada* and the one presented as coming true in *El cuarto de atrás*. The utopian recuperation of true art, for Galdós, entailed the separation of high art from the fake reproductions of mass culture. Martín Gaite is concerned with a *political* purity, but has no stake in a cultural one; rather, the mixture of highbrow and mass cultural texts in *El cuarto* seems to be a source of artistic vitality and energy.

In keeping with their different definitions of what constitutes art, the two texts offer diametrically opposed theories of what is required to produce it. *La desheredada* postulates a lot of prerequisites—a space separate from the market, European connections, education, money, a certain pedigree, a palace. By the time of *El cuarto*, the idea of the palace has come full circle. The palace in question in *El cuarto* is Franco's dwelling and headquarters in Salamanca during the Civil War. Like the Aransis palace, it is a sad place; but it has no association with art, only with politics. It represents the source of the dour Francoist ideology that imprisons everyone, including (in the child's imagination) the dictator's daughter, Carmencita Franco, who is confined there. Where the Aransis palace functioned as a *refuge* from the laws of the fallen, public sphere, the palace in Salamanca is the place where the falsifying laws are made. In Martín Gaite's text, the space of authentic art is the back room, which, because of its marginal, hidden nature, does provide a refuge from such laws. It is a space associated with literature, games, mass culture, the freedom to "sing at the top of [one's] lungs" (187). But even such a physical space is not strictly necessary in Martín Gaite's theory of art. For the back room, if it is lacking physically, can be invented in the mind. The narrator goes even further in her theory of art: deprivation is what stimulates the imagination to produce new art: "Necessity is the mother of invention" (179). Material riches are shown as obstacles to art; if the child C. could have bought the prefabricated miniature china set she desired, she would never have invented the island of Bergai. Where Galdós's representative artist is the *marquesa*'s grandson, practicing on his fine piano in the palace, Martín Gaite's is a penniless classmate of C.'s whose parents are political prisoners. It is she who, inspired by *Robinson Crusoe*, suggests the invention of the island. In the world of *El cuarto de atrás*, the most important thing of all is the capacity of the imagination (stimulated by literature/theater/mass culture) to transform the mediocre into the marvelous:

todo podía convertirse en otra cosa, dependía de la imaginación. Mi amiga me lo había enseñado, me había descubierto el placer de la evasión solitaria, esa capacidad de invención que nos hace sentirnos a salvo de la muerte. (195)

Everything could be converted into something else, it depended on a person's powers of imagination. My friend had taught me that, she had revealed to me the pleasure of escaping all by oneself, that ability to invent things that makes us feel safe from death. (195–96)[2]

A final inversion occurs from *La desheredada* to *El cuarto*. In *La desheredada*, art is the opposite of the contents of the "fallen" public sphere, and the artist must remain separate, above its inhabitants. Where Galdós's narrator invents a literary family romance that will authorize this superior status, Martín Gaite's presents herself as a representative of the masses. For her, the work of art is the voice of the real hopes and dreams, embedded in the products of mass culture, that lie beneath the programmed gestures, the imposed behavior, of public life in the Franco era.

We may want to question Martín Gaite's presentation of herself as representative of an ample segment of Spanish society. After all, she was one of only 41,764 students entering university in 1943; only 5,504 of these were women.[3] She was one of even fewer to undertake a doctorate. Pierre Bourdieu would surely provide a whole catalogue

2. The male-authored texts studied here had projected materialism onto their female characters (Isidora, Rosalía, the national Coño). Ironically, this female-authored text puts the accent much more on the inner world of the imagination.

3. *AEE 1945–46*, 429.

of ways in which the specifics of her economic and cultural background enabled her to produce a text like *El cuarto de atrás*.[4] While recognizing the partial inauthenticity of the narrator's identification with the majority, we should nevertheless be open to some of the liberating possibilities this identification can suggest. First, Jonathan Rose has established that people sorely lacking in both economic and cultural capital have had their lives transformed through literature and have gone on to write their own texts.[5] Second, whereas in *La desheredada* the production of great art by the grandson-pianist is presented as a kind of hard labor and penance, for Martín Gaite's narrator the invention of fictions is not classified according to quality; it is inextricably linked to *play*. She thus offers her readers—not all of whom have university degrees—a chance to try their own hand at playful fabulation. In this way, she gets art out of the elitist cul-de-sac in which it had found itself in *La desheredada*—too dependent on material support, too inaccessible to readers, too many qualifications necessary to produce it.

## Mass Culture and Escape:
### The Dialectics of Refuge in *Tormento* and *El cuarto de atrás*

One of the most important dilemmas for the protagonist of *El cuarto de atrás* is contained in the opposition *refugiarse* (to take refuge) vs. *vivir al raso* (to live unprotected, on the edge). The word *refugio* in Spanish means not only a refuge but also a bomb shelter; both meanings are important in *El cuarto*. In *Tormento*, the theme of refuge is shown as crucial in the names of Sánchez Emperador's two penniless daughters—Amparo and Refugio. In each text, the refuge is shown to function potentially as either a liberation or an imprisonment, and mass culture plays a crucial role in both functions.

We may begin with the dialectic of refuge for Amparo and Refugio. It seems at first that the names of these two characters are almost synonymous—"shelter," "refuge"—and both sisters are seeking shelter because of the unprotected position in which they were left upon being orphaned. But a look at the conduct of each character reveals

4. See *Distinction.*
5. See "Rereading the English Common Reader."

some opposite tendencies present in the two names. Amparo attempts to ingratiate herself with representatives of the repressive regime which has created the stifling world of *Tormento*. She tries to gain help and shelter by limiting her being to a stereotype derived from the serial novel of the *Mujer Virtuosa*. The word *amparo* implies a social relationship—one person helps, gives protection and shelter (the verb is *amparar*), the other receives it. But such shelter within the system exacts a high price, given that Amparo's being contains ingredients—illicit sex—not found in the *Mujer Virtuosa*. The system ferrets out the prohibited contents and ceases to protect her. In the end, however, Amparo is "protected" again—this time by Agustín—and again *limits* her being to the stereotype by being silent ("sin decir *esta boca es mía*" [123]).

If Amparo "snuggles up" to the system by obeying its conduct manuals, Refugio *takes flight from* the system, revealing the relationship between *refugiarse* and *fugarse* (to flee, to run away).[6] Where *amparo* requires the action of another person who protects, *refugiarse* is a reflexive verb, an act one does for oneself. Amparo is passive, Refugio active. Refugio frustrates *Tormento*'s narrator by her ability to disappear and not be found. Undoubtedly, her success at achieving this "disappearing act" is due to the fact that her self-definition differs entirely from the model of the virtuous domestic woman endorsed by the narrator. Refugio's trajectory has taken her off the charts, outside the guidelines provided in the mass media to keep women in the desired economic role. The narrator is annoyed at Refugio's ability to hide in the cracks in the system, to reveal the incompleteness of the picture he has created. Refugio's very physical appearance features a jarring incompleteness which bothers the narrator. She is missing one of her front teeth; he refers to her as "the one with the missing tooth." In the scheme governing the representation of women in *Tormento*, this physical lack connotes a moral one; Refugio's inability to produce a toothpaste smile prefigures her divergence from the narrator's domestic ideal. But we may want to read this gap another way. When Refugio escapes from the system into an invisible gap within it, she is renouncing the money offered by Am-

6. A refuge is "a place one 'flees' in order to get away from danger." The word comes from the Latin noun *refugium* and the verb *refugere*, composed of the prefix *re* (away) and *fugere* (flee) (Ayto 436).

paro in return for domesticity. By renouncing the rewards of the system, she is revealing that what the system defines *only* as a lack (lack of security, lack of morals) has positive features, like independence and freedom, which can outweigh what the system has to offer. Her missing tooth connotes her ability to do what is so crucial for the narrator of *El cuarto de atrás*—to turn a lack into a surfeit of riches that cannot be measured in material terms.

In the novels studied in this volume, male characters escape from the system in different ways than female ones. Male characters leave the country (Agustín, Goytisolo's narrator). Female characters remain in the country but hide in the cracks in the system. We turn now to the dilemma of Martín Gaite's narrator—*refugiarse* vs. *vivir al raso*. For Refugio, the two terms turned out to be synonymous: only by living *without* "protection" can one escape the norms of the authoritarian regime. The protagonist C. can never entirely endorse this equivalence because of her childhood during the Spanish Civil War. One family, she remembers, had refused to take refuge in the bomb shelter in Salamanca; they were all killed when a bomb fell on their house. There are times when fear is essential, when living unprotected won't work. This principle prevents the young C. from imitating the open defiance of social norms on the part of lovers who eloped during the war. However, they fascinate her:

suponía una furtiva tentación imaginar cómo se tranformarían, libres del alcance de las miradas ajenas, las voces, los rostros y los cuerpos de aquellos enamorados audaces que habían provocado, con su fuga, la condena unánime de toda la sociedad, los imaginaba en mis sueños y admiraba su valor . . . (125–26)

*It was a furtive temptation to imagine how the voices, the faces, and the bodies of those bold lovers who had provoked, by their escape, the unanimous condemnation of all of society would be transformed once they were beyond the sight of others' eyes. I imagined them in my dreams and admired their courage . . . (121–22)

So C. cannot imitate Refugio. Yet her healthy self-esteem and her intellectual creativity make it equally impossible for her to pose as a model "woman of the new Spain" in the style of Amparo. Precisely because these extremes are out of bounds, the protagonist has, over her lifetime, experienced all the nuances of the concept of the *refugio; El cuarto de atrás* is a reflection on its rewards and its perils.

During the harsh postwar period, when hunger and fear were part of everyday life, the young C. used the reading and writing of literature—and this term, for her, includes mass culture—as a refuge.[7] We have already seen some of the positive functions of such a refuge. Literature—and those forms of mass culture which offer models of conduct impossible within the regime—create cracks in the system where authentic emotions and alternative standards of behavior can hide. For the young C., the existence of such crevices meant nothing less than survival: "[In the postwar era] it would not occur to anyone to consume a song quickly, because a song is not a luxury that comes one's way every day, but *a fundamental item necessary for survival*" (178–79; italics mine). This mental refuge permeated with texts has a progressive function under such repressive conditions; the ability to imagine a better life is a prerequisite for creating that life in reality when political circumstances are more favorable. This function of culture as refuge suggests the need to qualify Herbert Marcuse's condemnation of "affirmative culture," examined earlier in relation to *La desheredada*. For Marcuse, culture acts as a cop-out for the bourgeoisie by providing the temporary satisfaction of human longings that cannot be realized in modern capitalist society; culture thereby helps to preserve the status quo. Martín Gaite points up the positive side of such a function under dictatorship conditions. Literature and mass culture keep alive human longings, provide fictive identities which temporarily make the impossible possible, and as such act, in Lipsitz's words, as a "rehearsal for politics" (16). Martín Gaite's literary refuge also offers a reply to Galdós's suspicion of imagination in *La desheredada*. At the most explicit level of that novel, Isidora's escape into a world of wealth, prominence, and family makes her unable to function in the real world; her distraction and her belief that she deserves riches make her ripe for victimization. To escape into the imagination, in *La desheredada*, is to begin to slide down the slippery slope toward prostitution—surely a cautionary tale for female readers. Martín Gaite shows how the capacity to escape can actually *prevent* victimization: if one has a rich inner life, one is

7. "Do you think I take literature as a refuge?" . . .
  "Yes, of course, but it's of no avail to you" (49–50).
  "How old were you when you began to write?" the man in black asks me . . .
  "Do you mean how old was I when I began to take refuge?" . . .
  "Yes, that's what I meant" (52).

partially immune to both material hardship and ideological pressure to conform. The final positive function of the refuge is that, in *El cuarto de atrás,* it acts as a magical warehouse which preserves the authentic, the carefree, and the marvelous through the forty years of the Franco dictatorship. As such, the refuge is priceless, having saved from oblivion all that is worth living for so that it can later form the cornerstone of a new political order.

But the act of taking refuge also brings with it a risk, a tempting trap, into which the middle-aged protagonist of *El cuarto* has partially fallen. It is the temptation not to leave the *refugio* even after the danger is past. If one does not leave the refuge soon enough, one may never do so. The refuge then changes in function. It becomes a place that guarantees a sense of safety in return for restricting one's conduct to the tried and true behavior that worked in times of danger. Politically, it represents the negative side of "affirmative culture": taking refuge in literature can create a protective cocoon that precludes both individual self-realization and political change. The sorts of mass culture that reproduce the regime's ideology—including the Sección Femenina's magazine *Y* and the romance novels of Carmen de Icaza—encourage a conduct kept within strict limits. The adult protagonist recognizes their continuing influence on her as she finds herself unable to take romantic risks with the man in black. First, she is tempted to rest her head on his shoulder but is immediately "besieged by an army of reasons charged with safeguarding normality and warding off danger" (32). Later, she would like to move closer to him and quiz him about the love letters he has in his suitcase at home, but she does not dare. The source of the hesitation is finally revealed as her eye falls on some notes she has taken about the 1940s: "'Cautious, circumspect literature. Models of conduct characterized by the refusal to take the initiative. Fear of scandal . . .'" (198). The fear of being taken for "una fresca"—the ultimate stigma of the 1940s—continues to determine C.'s conduct long after sexual norms have changed. It prevents C. from relating comfortably to men. The result: "I learned to turn this defeat into *literature" (182).

Sexual reticence is not the only effect of remaining too long "encastillada" in the literary refuge. At the beginning of the novel, C. feels she is stagnating, unable to recapture the adventurous feelings of childhood. Literarily, she seems to be on the wrong track as well. It is here that we see the most crucial function of the man in black.[8] He is a guide for C.—like Virgil for Dante—both personally and literarily. But he inverts the traditional function of guides in literature, including guides we have seen in the other novels here studied. Traditionally, the guide keeps the protagonist safe in a dangerous, confusing world, often described as a labyrinth. In *La desheredada*, Doctor Miquis attempts to guide Isidora through the perils and mirages of modern mass culture and into the safe territory of angelic domesticity. Goytisolo's narrator finds Góngora an orienting beacon, "rescuing" him from the city he calls a labyrinth. Both of these guides ultimately fail in their mission. In *La desheredada*, Isidora ignores Miquis's advice, as all of Spain does with the narrator's. In *Reivindicación*, Góngora provides temporary relief but cannot give his follower an enduring sense of safety. The male narrators invoke the figure of the guide to express their desire for greater control over their circumstances (and, sometimes, over their women as well). The guide is a promise of a refuge from a hostile world. Martín Gaite's protagonist, by contrast, needs a guide to get her *out* of the refuge and into the world again, now that Franco is dead and the danger is past. She needs to learn from him not how to be safe but how to take risks, how to "vivir al raso." He diagnoses her problem: "you've spent your life without leaving your refuge" (197). The literature she writes will have to change accordingly; as he rebukes her, " 'Literature is a defiance of logic, . . . not a refuge against uncertainty' " (49).[9] The man in black gives her a lesson in what is required. He recalls the story of Tom Thumb, who had left a trail of breadcrumbs in order to retrace his steps, but found they had been eaten by birds. On his next walk, he left white pebbles in order not to get lost. For the man in black,

---

8. My interpretation here adds a new function to those considered by other critics, who "have tended to focus on the role or identity of the interlocutor as critic, interpreter, potential lover, and even creative midwife" (Epps, "Space" 77).

9. Before the arrival of the man in black, C. had already recognized the problematic nature of her need to know exactly where she is, on what ground she stands. She comments: " 'Signs orient us, help us to escape from abysses and labyrinths, but the nostalgia of the perdition that was imminent nonetheless lingers on" (10–11). She also notes that her historical research was a "safe" road, but not her true vocation: "I was aware that I was going astray, deserting dreams in order to come to a compromise with history, forcing myself to put things in order, to understand them one by one, out of fear of being shipwrecked" (49).

this is an error. C. must learn rather to lose her way, to walk on the border between fiction and reality, madness and sanity, to not be sure what side she is on.

Since the man in black must induce C. to take risks not only literarily but personally, he cannot inspire confidence and security. His anonymity is functional, making him hospitable to all kinds of projections. His presence is sometimes jarring and uncomfortable, yet it is inspiring:

no es confianza lo que ofrece, es algo de signo incluso opuesto a la confianza, inquietante y sugestivo . . . (97)

What he offers isn't confidence, on the contrary, it's something quite the opposite of confidence, something disturbing and provocative . . . (91)

The final product of C.'s encounter with the man in black is *El cuarto de atrás*, suggesting that his guidance has had some results. C. is far from cured of the intense, irrational fears that derive from the war, or of her timidity with men. But the little golden box of pills left to her by the man in black suggest that she will have other chances to lose her path in creative ways in the future.

### Goytisolo and Martín Gaite: Ruses of the Underdog

We may conclude with some reflections occasioned by juxtaposing our two texts of the 1970s. Looking beyond the two novels' striking divergences (best explored by Epps, "Space"), I will be interested in the common features of the psychological makeup which characterizes the two narrators. Precisely because the two texts are so different, this rare common ground can give us insight into the function of the imagination, and of literature/mass culture, under extreme repressive conditions.

Both narrators were children during the Civil War, and both, as adults, remain subject to overwhelming attacks of fear, triggered at the most unsuspected moments. The sheer force and persistence of this emotion makes it a likely root cause of the compensatory imaginative activity which, for both, creates a second, private world paralleling the "real" one. When fear, repression, and poverty imposed limitations, the imaginary existence became correspondingly richer. A secondary fear was added, once Franco was established, to the fears of bombs and firing squads which remained as residue from the Civil War. This was the fear of sexuality, conveyed through the Church and through the propaganda of the Falange in magazines and teenage gatherings. Both adult narrators have remained incapable of overcoming both the fear of sex itself and the ancillary fear of the social condemnation of sexual relations. But the opposite sex becomes a key component of the imaginative and literary life of each narrator. Each nurtures fantasies and fears of the opposite sex derived from mass culture—the clichés of the devouring female or the mysterious yet protective masculine stranger. Literature, which may have begun for each narrator as a shield against bombs, becomes a cocoon which buffers the protagonists against the dangers of the opposite sex. But the images of femininity and masculinity they absorbed as children from the mass culture of the 1940s were flat stereotypes; their own existence as full human beings by definition exceeded these limited prescriptions. Given the institutional insistence on conformity to gender roles, the experience of feelings or character traits which departed from those roles could be expected to produce confusion about gender identity in our protagonists. And so it is. Goytisolo's narrator hovers between homo- and heterosexuality, identifies with the female Scheherazade, transforms Caperucita Roja into Caperucito Rojo. Martín Gaite's protagonist initially plays down the importance of gender difference. As she compares an engraving of Luther and the devil on her wall to her own encounter with the man in black, she describes the difference between the two scenes as "una leve transformación." This "slight transformation" is that Luther's role is acted out by a woman in *El cuarto de atrás*. Despite this minimizing of the differences between men and women, C. is still affected by the legacy of her mother's era, when reading was associated with playing boys' games, and women did not even think of going to university (85–86). She is attracted by the man in black, yet made uncomfortable by the question of whether she once was a lesbian (192).

Given the ample psychological common ground, it is especially ironic that *Reivindicación* and *El cuarto* should have to serve as a two-sided testimony to the mutual misunderstanding between the two sexes. Goytisolo's narrator is too terrified to question his view of woman as degraded materiality. Martín Gaite's protagonist realizes her male interlocutor may not be real, but she seems to want no truck with men of flesh and blood. Even their wishes are mirror images that do not overlap, with Goytisolo's narrator desiring the protection of the womb, and Martín Gaite's longing for release from that womb into the freedom of the streets.

It is important, however, to read Martín Gaite's text also as an answer to those of both Galdós and Goytisolo, on the enmeshed terrains of gender and culture. *El cuarto de atrás* vindicates the "low" terms of the very same traditional oppositions that Goytisolo had preferred not to invert:

| *"High"* | *"Low"* |
|---|---|
| man | woman |
| literature | mass culture |
| chaste, devout woman | prostitute |

These oppositions are sacred to the nineteenth-century imagination which is still running full tilt in Goytisolo; the low terms seem to blur in the female characters of all three of our male-authored novels. But where the Goytisolian narrator had tried violently to invert many other oppositions sacred to Western culture, C. is interested not in inverting but in *leveling*, creating a middle ground. The middle implies a *mixture* that is healthy, vital, that goes beyond the artificial dichotomies of high and low which the male narrators postulate in order to feel in control of a chaotic world. The truth about women, says Martín Gaite, is neither the saintly woman nor the prostitute, but something in between, something much more real than the stereotypes. And so it is with the other oppositions as well. Andreas Huyssen's predictions come true in *El cuarto:* woman's claim to equality brings with it a call for the abolition of the pretended distinction between literature and mass culture. And given the continued force of some nineteenth-century stereotypes, *El cuarto* finds it necessary to vindicate the prostitute as well, since she has been for so long one of the few ways in which men portrayed women. This occurs in the radio songs of Conchita Piquer and in C.'s reaction to them; the prostitute is humanized, becoming representative not of a corrupt state, but of its victims, which in the 1940s meant the majority of Spaniards, who had not desired Franco's rule.

*El cuarto* is a powerful contribution to the very necessary agenda of looking at mass culture without the artificial divisions of high and low, and without the pretense that women are somehow more closely linked to mass culture than men. It would be misleading, however, to conclude that Martín Gaite's protagonist has pulled off this new representation of woman and mass culture without being affected by the long tradition that excluded women from the practice of literature, or by the stigma traditionally attached to the literary woman.[10] Martín Gaite's text is marked by what Josefina Ludmer calls "tretas del débil"—the ruses of the weakling. These are stratagems that appear to pander to traditional stereotypes of woman as weak or incompetent, in order to lure the (male) reader into a text that intends to subvert those same ideas. Goytisolo's male narrator uses his literary erudition and linguistic brilliance to make his intense vulnerability and isolation appear as strengths. He does it so successfully that many critics have believed his claims of liberation. Martín Gaite's female narrator uses the opposite strategy of making female strength appear to be weakness. She creates her female protagonist (a writer) as bumbling, insecure, needing reassurance. This is especially the case just after the man in black's surprise midnight appearance:

—¿Por qué no viene a sentarse?—me pregunta el hombre de negro, señalándome un sitio a su lado en el sofá, como si fuera él el dueño de la casa y yo la visitante. Obedezco maquinalmente . . . (33)

"Why don't you come over here and sit down?" the man in black asks me, pointing to the place at his side on the sofa, as though he were the master of the house and I the visitor. I obey mechanically . . . (26)

The female author, who has created both the man in black and the female protagonist, gives the male character the upper hand, makes him the literary and sexual authority. The female writer even gives the illusion of not being in control of the text she produces; it appears magically on the desk, under the hat of the man in black, over the course of their conversation.

While such tactics can be regarded as playful, there is a more serious kind of damage apparent in the text which comes from traditional male portrayals of women. In characters like Refugio and, to a lesser extent, Isidora, the woman with a will of her own, who wants

10. The stigma can be summed up in this line from Alas's *La Regenta* (1884–85): "No he conocido ninguna literata que fuese mujer de bien" ("I've never known a woman writer who was respectable") (1:232).

to write her own story, is associated with promiscuity and moral degradation.[11] The narrator of *El cuarto de atrás* was brought up in a world where such nineteenth-century ideas still held sway: " 'Mujer que sabe latín no puede tener buen fin' " (93) (" 'A woman who knows Latin can come to no good end" [87]), said one woman disapprovingly during C.'s adolescence. The narrator seems to feel the need to prove that female writing is not tied to promiscuity, as it is in that persistent version of things. Nancy Armstrong cites Mary Wollstonecraft's program for women: they "were to make themselves as knowledgeable and independent as men by renouncing their sexual pleasure, a price men did not have to pay" (*Ideology* 13). Over a century and a half later, Martín Gaite represents her protagonist as having done just that, by eliminating from her story even all vestiges of her life with her husband, let alone extramarital encounters. The next step for the female-authored mass cultural novel will be to represent female sexuality and literary production as compatible.

11. As discussed earlier, Refugio is described as *writing* her own appearance.

# Conclusion

## Uneven Modernization and the Conditions of Emergence

## of the Spanish Mass Cultural Novel

• • • The situations faced by Galdós in 1881 and Goytisolo in 1970 shared many common features. Raymond Williams has already made clear that the rather arbitrary limitation of the term *modernism* to the art of the opening decades of the twentieth century is ideological. In particular, he notes that the great realists had "devised and organized a whole vocabulary and its structure of figures of speech with which to grasp the unprecedented social forms of the industrial city" (*Politics* 32). This was all the more true for Spain, where realism developed late. If we loosely associate modernism with the idea of rescuing art from the commodity structure of everyday modern life, it becomes clear that Galdós and Goytisolo share a similar project. In the case of Spain, because modernization came in fits and starts, alternating with periods of stagnation, it makes sense that modernism would arrive piecemeal as well. Though I have here argued its beginnings in *La desheredada*, modernism is conventionally associated with the opening decades of the twentieth century, with the poetry of Rubén Darío and the early prose of Valle-Inclán. Modernist principles inform the work of the poetic Generation of 1927.[1] And

---

1. This "generation" of poets is so called because in 1927 they paid homage to the work of Góngora, on the anniversary of his death, and put out a new edition of his *Soledades*.

modernist techniques emerge fully in the novel with the industrial-ization of the 1960s, in the work of Luis Martín-Santos and his suc-cessors. But during the twentieth century, there were also strong currents in Spanish literature which gave primacy to rural, prein-dustrial life, either as an evasion of modernity (as one senses in the work of the Generation of 1898),[2] or simply in reaction to long peri-ods of economic stagnation in which modernization and the city are not at issue, as in the novels of the 1940s and 1950s.

But it is extremely important in the case of Spain—and this is what makes much of its literature so complex and intriguing—that modernization is not, until after Franco's death, accompanied by the full democratization of the political system.[3] For me the determining factor that makes possible contradictory and richly textured works like *La desheredada* and *Reivindicación* is the extreme tension at certain periods between sweeping changes in the material and cul-tural life of the nation on the one hand, and the persistence of oligar-chic political, economic, and social structures on the other. The writer in Spain cannot aspire to the purity of literature and its auton-omy from public life, for his function as an Enlightenment intellec-tual—that of denouncing authoritarian structures where the press and the politicans cannot do so—has not yet been superseded. Both Galdós and Goytisolo begin their writing careers with novels that denounce the backwardness, egotism, and authoritarianism of the Spain of the day (the 1870s and 1950s respectively). But then these writers are forced to confront the immense changes that accompany the modernization they had thought they were seeking. Moderniza-tion has brought the masses (especially the petty bourgeoisie) much greater material comfort and greater access to cultural products (se-

2. See Litvak.

3. During the nineteenth century, a liberal state apparatus had been created, which combined uneasily with oligarchic tendencies. The Spaniard of the late nineteenth and early twentieth centuries was obviously much freer to express his ideas, to read, to organize politically, than the Spanish citizen under Fernando VII. But the citizen still had little say in the running of the country. During the Restoration period, representa-tives to Parliament were determined by local bosses (*caciques*) who rigged elections; the king often took decisive actions over the objections of that Parliament. (This was especially true of Alfonso XIII.) Under Franco, of course, the political parties of the Republic were abolished. What interests me here is that Spaniards had to gain access to consumer goods that radically altered their standard of living under a regime which denied them many basic rights and freedoms.

rial novels, film, television, etc.). But political rights and responsibilities have not accompanied the changes in either case. The Restoration of 1876 brought in rigged elections; Franco cynically created
a puppet parliament and orchestrated occasional farcical referen-
dums. The writers feel that their countrymen are guilty of happily
squandering their most precious birthright—freedom—in exchange
for the proverbial mess of pottage. The writers are now in the uncomfortable position of condemning the modernization and material
progress they had formerly defended in the face of postfeudalism.

In both centuries, there are good reasons for intellectuals to question their role. They had had a chance to govern (during the revolutionary period of 1868–74 and during the Republic of 1931–36)
but had lacked the effective power to change the old structures.
Later, they lacked even a role in the universities, which were taken
over after both revolutionary periods by Catholic conservatives (the
"neos" and the Opus Dei respectively). They still felt the need to
criticize the sempiternal authoritarian power structure of their country, but as *modern* writers, they also reacted to the dangers of modernization, just as their European counterparts did. Such modern
problems included the rationalization and mercantilization of human relations, the marginalization of spiritual values, and the lack of
identification of the writer with any social class. And in Spain, modernization, always late and hasty, means *cursilería*—that uncomfortable in-betweenness of being neither here nor there, neither developed nor underdeveloped, neither traditional nor modern. The sense
of being a cheap copy of Europe haunts both writers. For both, an
identity crisis has occurred in which tradition is no longer viable, but
new values to replace it are nowhere to be found. Goytisolo, in *España y los españoles*, comments on Spain's lightning-quick modernization of the 1960s in terms that could well have been written about
*La desheredada:*

[L]a improvisación, el mimetismo, la falta de autenticidad se manifiestan
hoy en todos los órdenes de la vida española. El español quiere comportarse
como el europeo que le visita sin tener aún los medios ni, sobre todo, el
entreno social necesarios. De ahí que, copiando los modales extranjeros en su
aspecto más aparente y superficial, su imitación degenere a menudo en car-
icatura. (196)

En los últimos quince años, el país ha perdido la mayor parte de las carac-

terísticas de la sociedad preindustrial, sin alcanzar por eso las ventajas mate-
riales y técnicas de las sociedades más ricas... Lo viejo se sobrepone a lo
nuevo sin continuidad ni equilibrio. En lugar de una evolución progresiva
asistimos a un trastorno brusco de todos los hábitos sociales y mentales.
En lo moral, como en lo económico, pretendemos quemar las etapas sin tener
en cuenta que ni las estructuras ni las costumbres pueden cambiarse de la
mañana a la noche. Nuestro comportamiento deja de ser auténtico y se con-
vierte en una copia triste y un tanto forzada. Los españoles de hoy hemos
perdido nuestra identidad secular sin habernos forjado todavía una persona-
lidad definida y nueva. (205)

[I]mprovisation, imitation, and inauthenticity are apparent in all spheres of
Spanish life today. The Spaniard wants to behave like the Europeans that
visit him without yet having either the means, or above all, the necessary
social training. So he copies the foreign manners in their most obvious and
superficial features, and his imitation often degenerates into caricature.

In the last fifteen years, Spain has lost most of the characteristics of a
preindustrial society, without having attained the material and technological advantages of wealthier countries. The old and the new form a hodgepodge lacking continuity and balance. Instead of a gradual evolution, we're
experiencing a sudden upheaval in all our social and mental habits. In the
moral sphere, as in the economic one, we're trying to skip stages without
taking into account that neither structures nor customs can change over-
night. Our behavior is ceasing to be authentic and is becoming a pathetic,
somewhat forced copy. We Spaniards of today have lost our traditional identity without yet having formed a definite new personality for ourselves.

It is the sense that the old world means killing each other and
the new world means complacent materialism that produces the
contradictory nature of both texts. Goytisolo in particular has been
criticized for contradicting himself, condemning backwardness out
of one side of his mouth and progress out of the other (Schaefer-
Rodríguez 97; Labanyi, *Myth and History* 207ff.). Uneven modernity underlies the contradiction. Both Galdós and Goytisolo are condemned to attack simultaneously the old and the new, since both are
operative in the Spain in which they live.

What does all of this have to do with mass culture? First, we are
dealing with two periods of massive technological, social, and cultural transformation. They bring major changes to the way of life of
large sectors of the population. Both *La desheredada* and *Reivindica-*

*ción* see the lower middle class as the principal beneficiary of the changes, though Galdós also registers the threatening new organization of the working class, which of course could not occur in any overt way in Franco's Spain. One of the major changes appearing with the new modernization, and indeed a principal agent of all the other transformations, was the advent of new, "technologized" discourses. In the nineteenth century, the newly circulated newspaper contributed to the development of the consumer society with its advertising and through the information it provided about new inventions that would soon make life even easier. In the twentieth century, newsreels, billboards, and, later, television fulfilled a similar function. And the mass-produced fictions newly available in serial novels, films, or television shows functioned as industries in themselves (the public would pay to be entertained) and, in addition, had the potential to socialize new sectors of society into the promise of bounty held out by consumer capitalism.

Galdós and Goytisolo are deeply ambivalent about this newly visible, avidly consumerist lower middle class. Its members have thrown themselves headlong into the market which each writer wants unequivocally to reject. Yet the petty bourgeoisie's climb up the ladder of social opportunity is a prerequisite for its ability to read his work. Their rise from uncultured poverty to financial solidity is analogous to the writer's own trajectory from oblivion to literary recognition—and fame seduces him despite his protestations to the contrary. Their consumerism makes him uncomfortable by questioning his progressive political stance; can he condemn their glee at their new, better standard of living and still call himself progressive? Finally, he feels defensive: what if this newly cultured sector *never* reads him, but goes to the movies instead? Perhaps he should condemn their consumption of mass culture to see if they react to pressure.

And the writer is insecure as he confronts the entire social and political scene. What can his role be in the society of modernization without freedom? Given the coexistence of Old Regime structures with modernity, the writer must create a text that includes the whole literary legacy of the past as well as the modern, mass cultural forms in order to survey the entire situation and attempt to find himself a niche. Ultimately, his role is precisely to cry apocalypse, to denounce Golden Age literature as superannuated and mass culture as a threat to individuality (Ramos 204–05), and to do so in a discourse emphasizing style, creativity, and cultural capital—just what civilization threatens to lose in its rush to conformity.

Despite the coincidence of the spread of mass culture with a repressive political system, neither writer reduces the potential political impact of mass cultural fictions to the reactionary alone; this is perhaps why these novels provide suggestive reflections for the mass cultural theorist long after Horkheimer and Adorno have ceased to seem productive. Galdós's narrator is uneasy precisely because Isidora believes so deeply in her rights, is not prepared to accept *a priori* any status but the highest. She is taking democratization at its word in a way that threatens the continued, unequal social structure. The working class, too, is using the print media to spread its ideas. So if mass culture means frivolity and corruption on the part of the dominant bourgeoisie, it can nevertheless provide revolutionary sparks for those on the lower end of the social scale. Goytisolo at first glance seems to condemn mass culture unequivocally, showing it as consolidating approval of Franco. But from his vantage point outside Spain, his narrator also sees a subversive potential for mass culture. It could be the dynamite that could blow apart repressive ideologies which have weighed on the Spaniard since the Golden Age. This is how he uses it in *Reivindicación*. On the level of plot, he attacks the old traditions by imitating James Bond, using high-tech weapons like radio-equipped helicopters, fumigation equipment, and meteorological tables to destroy the landscape of "sacred Spain." Isabel la Católica's devotion is rendered farcical by her greater ecstasy upon hearing the Rolling Stones. On the level of discourse, the narrator juxtaposes the new mass culture to the old values in a way that irreversibly prevents the latter from being taken as authoritative. While mass culture may not in itself represent much the narrator stands for, it does offer the opportunity to shatter a system of values he likes even less.

We can now begin to specify the conditions of possibility of remarkable panoramas of culture like *La desheredada* and *Reivindicación*. We may start with exclusionary criteria, by asking how these novels differ from the avant-garde novel of the 1920s, which took modernization and new technologies, including film, as their *raison d'être*. Several differences are salient. First, the avant-garde novel can be seen as aspiring to render the impact of the new technologies "from within"—that is, to use formal techniques that duplicated the new kinds of perception made possible by the inventions of moder-

nity. Various novels attempted, for example, to duplicate the experience of looking out of the window of a speeding train, unable to slow
down for a beautiful landscape (Salinas, "Mundo cerrado" in *Víspera
del gozo*); to look down on the world from the new vantage point of
the airplane; to exploit the principle of montage by narrating in disconnected scenes and refusing an overarching plot (Espina, *Luna de
copas*).[4] The novelist thus situates himself at the forefront of modernity, showcasing the new kinds of experience it can provide and
creating the "new subject" whose mode of perception will be unre-
cognizable to premodern man.[5] The avant-garde novel thrills to the
*newness* of the technologies it narrates. The novels I am considering,
by contrast, come decades *after* a new wave of technology makes its
appearance, after it has spread to large segments of the population
and is taken for granted as everyday fare. Where avant-garde texts
show the artist at play with the new inventions, novels like *La desheredada* and *Reivindicación* step back to consider first the impact
of these inventions on "the masses," and then the effect of this new
mass consumption on their own readership and possible role. Where
the avant-garde novelist sees in modernity an opportunity to revolu-
tionize narration, the "uneven modernist" rather fears his own marginalization by the ubiquitous fictions of mass culture. Finally, the
avant-garde emphasis on the actual mechanics of the new inventions
precludes a thoroughgoing reflection on their political implications
(Cano Ballesta 16–17, 190–91; Spires, *Transparent Simulacra* 148).
Galdós and Goytisolo take as their starting point the changes in social relations involved in the new way of life of the masses and consider the new inventions and mass-produced fictions primarily for
their role in such changes. In fact, all four novels here considered
focus on the concrete circumstances and aspirations of the lower

4. See Cano Ballesta 165–72. Robert Hughes remarks on the new kinds of perception that developed in the late nineteenth century through the experience of fast travel
in a machine on wheels, and through the view of the ground from the Eiffel Tower. The
first provided "the succession and superimposition of views, the unfolding of landscape in flickering surfaces as one was carried swiftly past it." (12). The second offered
the view of the earth "seen flat, as pattern, from above. . . . [A] new kind of landscape
began to seep into popular awareness. It was based on frontality and pattern, rather
than on perspective recession and depth" (14).

5. Walter Benjamin describes the changes in perception linked to the new technologies in essays such as "The Work of Art in the Age of Mechanical Reproduction"
(1936) and "On Some Motifs in Baudelaire" (1939). See *Illuminations*.

middle class. This in turn entails a consideration of the political system that permits, conditions, or prevents opportunities for that class.

The two "apocalyptic" novels analyzed here (*La desheredada* and *Reivindicación*) survey an impressive array of works from the traditional literary canon. They must engage with such works because their primary emphasis is the impact of modernity and the modern city, and this new reality brings the old canon's role into question. The two novels written later in each decade (*Tormento* and *El cuarto de atrás*) focus, interestingly, on earlier periods than the apocalyptic ones, and their principal field of inquiry is the potential roles mass culture can play within a situation of stifling repression, economic penury, and backwardness. They therefore lack the monstrous, encyclopedic quality of their predecessors in each decade. But they retain the focus on the lower middle class as the sector whose lives might be most significantly influenced by mass cultural forms in periods where consumerism has *not yet* become widespread.

*Tormento* and *El cuarto de atrás* work to balance the apocalyptic view of mass culture and consumerism found in *La desheredada* and *Reivindicación*, as if the body of literature were keeping itself honest. Written after the "apocalyptic" novels, they question the notion that modernity and mass culture have made everything worse. They do this by looking further back in time to the period *before* the advent of consumerism. Where *La desheredada* and *Reivindicación* register the confusion brought on by the new, *Tormento* and *El cuarto* recall the stifling, all-too-predictable uniformity of the old. Where the outside world of the city may be overwhelming and disorienting in *La desheredada* and *Reivindicación*, in *Tormento* and *El cuarto* the outside world is positively dangerous, forcing a retreat to inner spaces. In *La desheredada* and *Reivindicación*, the pressing agenda for the narrators is to claim *superiority*; in *Tormento* and *El cuarto*, the issue is rather to *survive* and wait for freedom.

The superiority vs. survival opposition determines the very different assumptions about, and use of, mass culture in the two pairs of texts. The "apocalyptic" texts postulate an "authentic" reality that has been hidden, adulterated, or obliterated by consumer culture. If mass culture is falsifying everything in sight, art, which is associated with truth, must at all costs keep itself separate from the public sphere in order not to be engulfed or irreversibly contaminated. This

determines both the insistence on the high/low division in *La desheredada* and *Reivindicación* and the use of the family romance
which claims the highest literary parentage for the narrators. A very
different view of the relationship of "reality" to the discourses of
mass culture is present in *Tormento* and *El cuarto*. In these novels, ideology, disseminated through the discourses of mass culture
(newspapers, serial novels, magazines), has created the repressive reality which the novels' characters must suffer. There is no primitive
"reality" pre-existing and independent of ideology. Rather, reality
is made, unmade, and modified as ideologies (and their supporting
mass cultural texts) attain or lose hegemony. For this reason, *Tormento* and *El cuarto* insist more on a *dialogue* between the narrator's
text (not clearly classifiable as either "high" or "mass") and the mass
cultural discourses which have given reality its current shape. Both
novels admit that mass cultural forms (the serial novel, the romance
novel) pre-existed them and even served as their precursors. *Tormento* introduces Don José Ido and his fertile imagining of serial
plots before the narrator can start his own story. Martín Gaite's protagonist explains that her apprenticeship in literature began in childhood with the writing of stories modeled on romance novels. In *La
desheredada* and *Reivindicación*, some plot events are borrowed
from popular texts (serial novels, James Bond), but the narrators' discourse remains as distanced as possible from that of mass culture.
*Tormento* and *El cuarto*, by contrast, feature the overt use of phrases
typical of serial novels or romances. In *El cuarto*, the narrator even
stops the action to point out the borrowing. Though mass cultural
texts play a crucial role in creating and maintaining the current repressive regime (Isabel II, Franco), these novels recognize that mass
cultural texts could also be important in *changing* things. Thus, both
*Tormento* and *El cuarto* represent the double-edged nature of *all*
texts, including mass cultural ones: they may serve to reinforce existing norms, or they may powerfully implant the notion of an alternative.

The governing question of superiority in *La desheredada* and *Reivindicación* entails that mass culture is primarily shown as an instrument for getting or retaining money and power. Isidora wants to
follow the plots of the serial novels all the way into the palace; the
working class mouths socialist slogans, which are spread in its newspapers, and tries to bring down the bourgeoisie. In *Reivindicación*,

Franco makes washers, dryers, cars, and computers available in return for the masses' endorsement of his regime.[6] The intellectual narrators attack all these uses of mass culture and defend a literary canon in an attempt to assert their own importance—at everyone else's expense. Mass culture in these novels becomes primarily a means to an end involving superiority, whether political, economic, or gender-based.

Mass culture may be a means to power in times when it is linked to consumerism, but in *Tormento* and *El cuarto*, mass culture plays a decisive role precisely because it is a *substitute* for consumer goods, for economic betterment, for freedom—even for food. As means of survival, the characters must actively engage with it—use it to feed their resistance, like the child C., or deliberately mimic its strategies in order to gain protection, like Amparo. The specific content of the mass cultural text becomes important, as its particularities will be pressed into service by its readers or listeners on a daily basis.

All four novels represent the fusion of "highbrow" literature with mass cultural genres as being linked to social change. But their attitudes toward this fusion, and toward social change, differ markedly. *La desheredada* and *Reivindicación*, written in reaction to sweeping and disorienting changes accompanying mass culture and consumerism, are suspicious of social change as a probable threat to artistic purity. (This is why *La desheredada*'s narrator locates artistic purity in a palace.) Both are heterogeneous texts that are nostalgic for homogeneity. *Tormento* and *El cuarto*, however, portray a caste system in which separations based on class, occupation, or political creed have created a stifling hierarchy which straitjackets individual initiative, mobility, and freedom. The determination *not to mix* has led to stagnation, to lives devoted to eliminating dust from dark apartments. The novels present themselves as hybrids of "high" and "mass" by way of advocating a society in which such artificial separations are not enforced. They present mixtures as healthy, invigorating to life and art, rather than as the death of culture.

6. Computers were not in fact widely available, even during the final years of the Franco regime. But Goytisolo presents IBM and its computers as a salient feature of the new modernization attacked in *Reivindicación*. Goytisolo may be anticipating social transformations which were more pervasive in Europe, but only incipient in Spain. In this, he again echoes Galdós, whose fears of modernity in *La desheredada* were exacerbated by the filter of Zola.

I have always wondered why novels featuring readers or writers of mass cultural texts appeared more consistently within the Hispanic world than in Europe. A further, unscientific impression I have is that within the Hispanic world, they are most prominent in Spain and Argentina, although numerous and famous novels of this kind have appeared in many other countries as well.[7] Answers to such questions will always be tentative conjectures. But I think we can hypothesize that the combination of new forms of mass culture with political repression of varying degrees provides a basic matrix for the appearance of such novels in the whole Hispanic world.[8] The intense yearnings of the protagonist who consumes mass cultural fictions and who dares to dream about a better life take on political overtones when set against the backdrop of dictatorship or stagnant oligarchy. The protagonists of such texts are invariably politically and socially marginal (women in the nineteenth century or under Franco, a schizophrenic or a homosexual in the 1970s). Their powerlessness is an emblem of the powerlessness of the majority of people under repressive conditions. As to what sets Spain and Argentina apart, I think that the concept of *cursilería*, so well elaborated by Noël Valis, puts us on the right track. Just as the consumers of mass culture in these novels are mainly of the lower middle class and are tortured, like Isidora, by the perpetual, frustrating sensation of "quiero y no puedo," so Spain and Argentina are peculiarly "in-between" nations. As they begin to modernize at various periods, they are acutely aware of their lateness and backwardness with respect to Europe or the United States. (They are "el furgón de cola," to quote the title of a

7. To name but a few, Mario Vargas Llosa's *La tía Julia y el escribidor* (*Aunt Julia and the Scriptwriter*, Perú, 1977), Luis Rafael Sánchez's *La guaracha del Macho Camacho* (*Macho Camacho's Beat*, Puerto Rico, 1976), and Guillermo Cabrera Infante's *Tres tristes tigres* (*Three Trapped Tigers*, Cuba, 1967). Argentina's prolific practice of the "mass cultural novel" is represented by the novels of Roberto Arlt and Manuel Puig; the parody of detective stories by Borges, Sábato, and others; Tomás Eloy Martínez's *La novela de Perón* (*The Peron Novel*, 1985); and Osvaldo Soriano's *Una sombra ya pronto serás* (*You'll Soon Be A Shadow*, 1990).

8. The trend begins, of course, with *Don Quijote* (1605, 1615), which registers the impact of print in a Spain that has come under the sway of both Inquisitorial repression and the grip of a centralizing, absolutist royal bureaucracy. *Don Quijote*, like our "apocalyptic" novels, models sections of text on all the highbrow genres of the day (pastoral, picaresque, hagiographical, etc.), as well as on the bestselling novel of chivalry.

book of essays by Goytisolo.) They are "lower-middle-class countries," neither fully developed nor underdeveloped. Spain has always
been taunted by the saying "Africa begins at the Pyrenees," and its
authors, who have rarely accepted the isolationism of reactionary
Spain, have always wanted to see Spain on an equal footing with
Europe. Argentina traditionally denied its connection with backward
Spain and claimed England and France as its main cultural parents, in
a family romance like that of Isidora. And the male writers dealt with
in this book both felt recognition in Europe to be of paramount importance for their own literary careers. Galdós energetically tried to
have more of his works translated into French and was never satisfied with the limited recognition he did achieve (Berkowitz 174, 280).
Goytisolo escaped the cultural backwater of the Spain of the 1950s
and, to a large extent, made his literary name while residing in
France. Spanish writers, then, are doubly tormented. On the one
hand, their lateness in modernization makes them feel inferior. On
the other, even those Spanish creations that do rank with or above
those of Europe (as is the case with much of Spanish literature) will
never be recognized according to their merits because of the longstanding marginalization of Spain from mainstream Europe. All of
this frustration is projected onto the literary characters who dream of
grandeur through mass culture; Isidora represents the predicament of
Spain and that of Galdós himself in ways the latter might not have
cared to admit.

Finally, it is important to look at the timing of our novels and the
reasons for it. Going on the premise that these novels appear once a
given mass cultural form and the concomitant changes in social and
economic life have become routine, it is logical that La desheredada
appear in the early 1880s, to comment on the vast changes of the
1860s and early 1870s. The lateness of the novels reacting to the impact of film, however, might surprise us. If film arrived on the scene
in the late teens, and by the 1940s was a fixture of middle-class life in
any sizable city, why do we have to wait until the 1970s for the
flowering of our "mass cultural novels"? One reason is that the cinema was not by any means universally available in the 1940s. The
annual statistics of 1944 show only five hundred cinemas in all of
Spain, plus another hundred or so establishments that did double
duty as theaters and cinemas. By 1955, however, there were over five

thousand cinemas in Spain.[9] But economic and political factors also come into play. Since the 1940s and early 1950s saw economic privation and almost no modernization in Spain, the spread of film was not accompanied by the consumerism, changing social relations, and general dynamism that accompanied the spread of the serial novel. The economic boom did not occur until the 1960s. And most crucial, of course, was that the political questions that give these novels their spark could not be addressed fully under Franco. Goytisolo writes from exile, and Carmen Martín Gaite must wait to discuss the significance of the film, radio, and romance novels of the 1940s until after Franco's death.

Martín Gaite's novel is written at the beginning of Spain's transition to democracy. For the first time, intellectuals (not only writers of literature but the remarkable journalists of El País, and many others) could play out to a large extent their Enlightenment role of making sure that full freedom was regained. Whereas Galdós and Goytisolo were obliged to meditate on the complex relationship of mass culture to political repression, Martín Gaite's circumstances were somewhat different. Born in 1925, she was able to remember the flavor of the Republic of 1931–36 in a way that Goytisolo, born in 1932, could not. In 1978, the narrator of El cuarto de atrás could contemplate her fifty years of life as beginning and ending with freedom—an ironic frame to the long middle years of the Franco regime. Martín Gaite is the only one of our writers to be able to see mass culture during dictatorship as a rehearsal for something better which would finally arrive.

It seems that democracy in Spain, despite all its incompleteness and defects, is now here to stay. Spain is again experiencing a period of rapid modernization, and even Europeanization, as it races to meet the standards of the European Community, which it joined in 1986. Symptomatically, Spain's perennial two television stations have given way to a whole panoply of private stations; VCRs are so widespread that many provincial cinemas have closed. As the cultural panorama changes, it is to be expected that another wave of mass cultural novels will react to the sweeping transformations in Spanish life. This time, however, the transformations are occurring under the auspices of a freely elected government. In the cards for the

9. AEE 1945–46, 529–30; AEE 1956, 800.

Spanish cultural critic will be to find out what the new generation of novelistic protagonists dreams about through the filter of mass culture. What changes will occur in the mass cultural novel once the link between mass culture and political repression has been broken? To find out the answers, we can only stay tuned.

# Appendix

## Plot Summaries

*La desheredada (The Disinherited Woman)*

The action of *La desheredada* takes places from 1872 to 1877; the novel appeared in 1881. Isidora Rufete is a strikingly beautiful girl in her late teens whose mad father, Tomás, has convinced her that she and her brother Mariano are the illegitimate children of a now-deceased marchioness. As the novel begins, Isidora arrives from her provincial town in La Mancha to try to claim her inheritance from her ostensible grandmother, the marchioness of Aransis.[1] She goes to live with a doting godfather, Don José Relimpio, and his poor but aspiring family. The young doctor Augusto Miquis courts her briefly; he will provide her with prudent advice throughout the text, but never to any avail. Isidora is aided in her communication with the *marquesa* by the comely Joaquín Pez, himself the widower of another young marchioness, and an irrepressible seducer. His handsome features and distinguished air make Isidora fall in love with him. Her younger brother, meanwhile, has been living in the squalor of Madrid's southern quarter with an aging aunt and has been put to

---

1. The marchioness of Aransis will be referred to throughout as the *marquesa*.

hard labor in a rope factory. In a neighborhood children's fight, he accidentally kills another boy, beginning a career of delinquency.

Meanwhile, the *marquesa* arrives from abroad. We watch her in her funereal palace, opening the room where her daughter Virginia died nine years before. We learn that Virginia, having had a prolonged affair with a commoner in the military, was imprisoned by her puritanical mother and died under this rigor ("She died of imprisonment"), leaving two children. But at the end of part I, the *marquesa* confronts Isidora at the palace with the news that she is not her granddaughter and that any resemblance of Isidora to Virginia is purely coincidental. Isidora's expulsion by the *marquesa* leads to anger and carelessness about her reputation; she spends the night with Joaquín Pez rather than returning to the humble Relimpio abode. The "non-recognition" scene between Isidora and the *marquesa* coincides with the abdication of King Amadeo and the declaration of the Republic; Isidora resolves that, since everyone is now equal, she will gain what she still believes to be her rightful place through the law courts.

Two years have elapsed when the second part begins. The Bourbon dynasty has been restored, but without the capricious power it exercised in the Old Regime. Isidora has had Joaquín's child and lives in her own apartment. But Joaquín's dissolute lifestyle has caused his money to dry up; Isidora will repeatedly liquidate all her possessions and then take up with different "protectors" simply in order to eat and to fulfill her love of high fashion. She remains constant, however, in her love for Joaquín Pez, and often sacrifices much to rescue him from debt. Her lovers gradually descend in social rank. The millionaire politician Botín ruthlessly keeps her shut up in her apartment; Juan Bou, the bourgeois owner of a printing factory, falls in love with her and wants to marry her, but he is physically repulsive to her. Eventually, she is jailed, accused of falsifying the documents that attest to her nobility. The documents turn out to have been falsified by her mad father; Isidora is forced to renounce all claims on the house of Aransis to get out of jail.[2] Her last "protector" is a ruffian and gambler named Gaitica who mistreats her physically, and whose

2. The *marquesa*'s daughter did in fact have two children who were brought up by a plebeian family; the latter lived next to the Rufete family, enabling Tomás to steal and modify their certificate of nobility.

coarse language and manners she now picks up owing to the demise of her noble dreams. Meanwhile, her brother Mariano has worked for a time in Bou's print shop and picked up his socialist ideas. He then enters a brief anarchist phase in which he sets off bombs to scare the rich and damage their property. Convinced that society is corrupt and has deprived him of a luxurious lifestyle, Mariano attempts to assassinate the king, misses, and is jailed and executed. Isidora then leaves her godfather and takes to the streets as an anonymous prostitute.

### Tormento (Torment)

*Tormento* (1884) is the story of a beautiful, shy, hard-working young girl named Amparo Sánchez Emperador. She and her sister Refugio were left penniless orphans upon her father's death, and Amparo spends her days as the glorified servant of distant relatives, the Bringas family, who give her leftover food and a few pennies which do not suffice to cover even the bare necessities of life. Next door to Amparo lives Don José Ido del Sagrario, an eccentric author of serial novels, the main mass cultural fictions of the day. He is writing one inspired by the two sisters, about poor, orphaned women who work their fingers to the bone, sewing, but who live happily and chastely, refusing the many suitors with dishonorable intentions who try to obtain their favors through money. (In fact, however, Refugio will drift into prostitution over the course of the novel.)

Amparo's "protector," Francisco Bringas, is a lowly civil servant, yet he and his pretentious wife Rosalía appear at every play, palace dance, or social gathering where the wealthy are to be found; they often skimp on food in order to afford the necessary finery. They are ardent representatives of establishment values—Church, order, money, and above all monarchy. But the action of the novel is set in late 1867 and early 1868, so the reader knows that their adored queen, Isabel II, is about to be overthrown in the revolution of September 1868. Bringas's rich cousin, Agustín Caballero, has made a fortune in America and, now in his forties, has returned to Spain to lead a comfortable life based on order and conventional morality. But he is shy and uncomfortable with the frivolity and superficial chatter of Spanish society. Soon he falls in love with Amparo, in whose timidity and beauty he sees the prototype of the virtuous woman. What he does not know is that Amparo has had a short-lived affair with a priest, into which she fell out of misguided weakness; she is now thoroughly repentant. The priest, Pedro Polo, is a man dominated by his passions, utterly unsuited to the ecclesiastical state, who feels imprisoned in his clerical garb and longs for far-off lands where he can be free from narrow convention. Still enamored of Amparo, whom he calls Tormento, he threatens to starve to death or to raise a scandal if she will not come to see him; afraid that he will reveal her secret, she visits him twice, trying to convince him to go abroad and forget her.

Meanwhile, Caballero has proposed marriage to Amparo and has begun to give her a monthly allowance to live on while she prepares for the wedding. Afraid to confess to Caballero after having taken his money, Amparo lives in constant fear that her secret will be revealed and thus spoil marriage to the man she loves and respects. And the secret does eventually come out, through the agency of the priest's sister, Marcelina Polo, a fanatical Catholic who spends all day at mass but is utterly vindictive in her conduct. Marcelina reveals to Rosalía Bringas the existence of two letters written by Amparo to her brother; Rosalía, consumed by envy at the riches which the penniless Amparo would enjoy if she married Agustín, is only too glad to make sure that the latter learns of the stain on Amparo's honor. Finally, after a suicide attempt, Amparo makes a full confession to Agustín, and he, having rejected the conventional mores of Spain as pure hypocrisy, makes Amparo his mistress and takes her to France by train.

Throughout the novel, the narrator openly competes with the serial novels written by Don José Ido. He ends chapters at suspenseful moments, uses ample dashes of melodrama in the scenes between Amparo and Polo, and repeatedly contrasts Ido's view of how things will turn out to the "reality" which he himself claims to present to the reader.

### Reivindicación del conde don Julián (Vindication of Count Julian)

The title of Reivindicación del conde don Julián (1970) alludes to the legend surrounding the Moorish invasion of Spain in 711. The story goes that the Visigothic King Rodrigo raped the daughter of

Count Julian, whose name was Cava. Julian retaliated by betraying his country and guiding the Moors in their invasion. The Moorish presence in Spain lasted almost eight hundred years, and periods of mutual tolerance and economic collaboration between Moors and Christians alternated with periods of fanaticism and mutual hatred. By the latter centuries of the "Reconquest," however, a strong ideological line had developed that preached that Spain was "by nature" a Catholic country. Both Moors and Jews were expelled from the country in 1492 by Ferdinand and Isabella, the "Catholic monarchs." Centuries of Inquisitorial intolerance followed, but in the nineteenth century, liberalism began to tamper with the power of the Church and to attempt to bring Spain into line with Europe. The Catholic intransigents never truly lost their strength, and Franco relied upon them to win the Civil War. Franco claimed to have restored Spain to its true role as defender of Catholic, spiritual values—a path from which at various previous periods it had unfortunately veered because of Communism, Judeo-Masonic conspiracies, liberalism, materialism, and other aberrations. One of these aberrations was, of course, the period of Moorish domination. The very title of our novel, then, proclaims its rebel status by praising Count Julian's act of treason in the face of official dogma which regarded him as the supreme villain.

The narrator-protagonist of *Reivindicación* is a nameless Spanish man of about thirty-five who lives in exile in Tangiers, in an apartment from which he can see the coast of Spain. The text represents a day of his life in the city. The narrator's psychological state resembles that of a paranoid schizophrenic. He is internally divided between his Spanish, repressed self (personified in his imagination by the character Alvarito) and his instinctual desires and drives (personified in the "Moorish" character Julián). Alienated from any sense of a unified self, he refers to himself as "tú" throughout the novel. The characters he encounters in the city personify his own obsessions. The text is punctuated by colons rather than periods and uses no capital letters, inverted question marks, or exclamation marks. The discourse is a hodgepodge of quotations, mixing citations from the Spanish literary canon with newspaper ads, passages from the school textbooks of the narrator's childhood, church sermons, segments from a James Bond film, and references to classical mythology.

The novel is divided into four parts, of which parts 1 and 3 are approximately double the length of parts 2 and 4. Part 1 is the most connected to the "outside world" of Tangiers. We watch the narrator get up, take inventory of his very few possessions, and collect a bagful of insects which he has earlier attracted with sugar and crumbs, then sprayed with DDT. Once outside, he endures repeated pleas from beggars, stops for an injection of penicillin, and enters the library, where he profanes the great classics of Spanish literature by squashing the insects between their pages. He then wanders through the chaotic streets of Tangiers, accosted by the sounds of traditional Arab music and the Rolling Stones on the radio. He describes the open-air market and satirizes a group of American tourists buying souvenirs. He stops in a café and reads the paper to avoid a stereotypical Spaniard who wants to make conversation. He finally escapes his interlocutor by seeking out the toilet, only to accidentally urinate on the head of a man sitting in the darkness below. Fleeing the café, he runs into a young Arab boy who offers to guide him through the city; the guide will suddenly disappear, having been a projection of the narrator's childhood self. Encountering the tourists again, the narrator begins to invent stories, imagining that the everyday scene of the tourists with the snake charmer suddenly turns tragic when the fat American woman is bitten and poisoned by the serpent coiled around her body. He watches part of the James Bond film *Thunderball* he has seen advertised in the streets and is then nabbed by the typical mustachioed Spaniard, who buys him Castilian red wine and chick-peas at a bar and lectures him on Francoist austerity and spiritual values. He eventually flees and takes refuge in an Arab sauna. Throughout this chapter, he has invoked the Baroque poet Góngora as his muse and guide; segments of text are often introduced by a quotation from Góngora's poetry.

Part 2 takes place in a Tangiers café where the narrator, accompanied by Arab acquaintances, smokes Kif and watches a Spanish television program on Seneca, whom Francoist ideology wants to portray as incarnating an "eternal Spanish essence" still present today. The narrator hallucinates based on what he sees on the screen. He evokes his school science class, where he was forced to watch a scorpion kill a grasshopper. He remembers the suburban mansion where his grandmother read him "Little Red Riding Hood" while the

neighbors gossiped about sex scandals. The terrifying church sermons of the 1940s about the consequences of sex are reproduced in
detail, juxtaposed with the science class and the tourists. He imagines his childhood self doing penance in church for his sexual urges.
He satirizes the program on Seneca, comically conflating Seneca's
life with the biography of Franco. He watches interviews on the 1966
referendum in which Spaniards voted "yes" or "no" for Franco; predictably, all of the diverse people interviewed sing the dictator's
praises. He concludes by giving himself a pep talk to ready himself
for a new invasion of Spain in which he will destroy the "sacred"
Spanish tradition, violate grammatical convention, and penetrate
the enforced chastity of Francoism with Moorish "serpents."

In part 3, the desired invasion is played out in the narrator's head,
most of it carried out by the narrator's imaginary alter ego, Julián. It
includes episodes such as the following:

(1) The narrator infects the Spanish blood supply with rabies, which
spreads to the entire population.

(2) Julián and his band of Moors invade the austere Castilian landscape
mythified as the "essence of Spain" by the famous writers of the Generation
of 1898 (Miguel de Unamuno, Antonio Machado, "Azorín," and others).
They gather clouds and change the harsh, rocky landscape of their texts into
green valleys and marshes, to "quench the poet's nauseating spiritual thirst"
(147).

(3) Julián attacks the quintessential Spaniard, Don Alvaro Peranzules,
a "perfect Christian gentleman" with a gigantic crustacean mask. As Don
Alvaro picks up Spanish classics to recite them, he is accosted by insects
hidden in the books and gradually self-destructs. His daughter, "Isabel la
Católica," is raped by the Moors.

(4) The narrator, echoing Virgil, manfully precedes a group of tourists into
a huge cavern previously zealously protected but now open to the public
through Spain's "prudent adaptation" to the needs of the tourist industry. It
turns out to be the Vagina, sacred center of concern of the Spain of the 1940s.

(5) The solemn procession of Holy Week is infiltrated by Julián and his
Moors and turned into an orgy.

(6) Julián takes Spain at its word in its desire to be purely Christian, and
eliminates all Arabic words and their corresponding referents. This deprives
the country of such items as pillows, tar, chess, rice, tariffs, algebra, alcohol,

and sewers. And, most crucially, the famous "olé" of the bullring gives way to silence.

In part 4, the narrator goes deep into his own psyche to try to eradicate his own "Spanishness." He reworks the Little Red Riding Hood story as he splits himself into two and imagines the nine-year-old, innocent Alvarito enthralled by Julián, the Moorish caretaker of a construction site in the Spanish suburb. Alvaro goes every day after school to see Julián, who sodomizes him, extorts money from him, and infects him with syphilis. Finally, Julián demands that Alvaro bring his mother to visit as well; Alvaro, under the threat that his previous misdeeds will be exposed if he does not comply, commits suicide. Julián embraces the dead Alvaro, declaring that he has finally achieved unity of self. The Church ("the house of fear") is then infiltrated by Moors disguised as priests, who spike the host with hashish and provoke an orgy among the female congregation. The infant Jesus and the Virgin, referred to as "dolls," fall among the ruins of the church; the scene then shifts to Tangiers, where the Jesus doll, alias Alvaro, reappears amid the garbage from the market and then, in a manger, is reborn as a new Muslim Messiah. The narrator then returns to his apartment, where he kills the insects collected during the day, enumerates his belongings, reads a few lines of Góngora, and goes to bed, ready to start the invasion over again the next day. The text closes with an "Advertencia" which lists for the reader many of the writers who have been quoted or rewritten during the novel.

### El cuarto de atrás (The Back Room)

*El cuarto de atrás* is a memoir-novel. The protagonist is a woman writer in her fifties whose literary production is identical to that of Carmen Martín Gaite herself. As the text begins, C. is trying in vain to get to sleep. She is in a disillusioned state, feeling alienated from her own past, distanced from her friends, unable to write. Finally nodding off, she is awakened around midnight by a call from a stranger who claims she had agreed to interview him at that hour. He arrives, dressed in black and wearing a black hat; we do not know his name. He offers C. a little gold box containing tiny pills which stimulate memories and shuffle their chronology. Under their influence, and spurred by the questions and challenging comments of the man in black, C. recalls in vivid detail aspects of her childhood during the Spanish Republic, the Civil War and the Francoist forties. She has been wanting to write up these memories but has been at a loss for an adequate form for them. Chief among her memories is the back room in her childhood home in Salamanca, where she learned to read and play, and where no rules limited behavior. As she tells her stories, typewritten pages magically appear under the hat of the man in black—they contain the text we are reading. The possibility of romance between the two characters hovers in the air but is never realized. C. last sees the man in black reading the manuscript as she dozes off on the couch. Later, she awakens in bed when her daughter comes home from a party. She is unsure of whether the visit actually took place but finds both the manuscript and a present from the man in black—the gold box of pills.

# Bibliography

Abella, Rafael. *La vida cotidiana en España bajo el régimen de Franco.* Barcelona: Argos Vergara, 1985.

Alas, Leopoldo. *Galdós.* Madrid: Renacimiento, Sociedad Anónima Editorial, 1912.

———. *La Regenta.* Ed. Gonzalo Sobejano. 2 vols. Madrid: Editorial Castalia, 1989.

Aldaraca, Bridget. "El ángel del hogar: The Cult of Domesticity in Nineteenth-Century Spain." *Theory and Practice of Feminist Literary Criticism.* Ed. Gabriela Mora and Karen S. Van Hooft. Ypsilanti, Mich.: Bilingual Press, 1982. 62–87.

———. "*Tormento:* La moral burguesa y la privatización de la virtud." *Texto y sociedad: problemas de historia literaria.* Ed. B. Aldaraca, Edward Baker, and John Beverley. Amsterdam: Editions Rodopi, 1990. 215–29.

Alfieri, J. J. "El arte pictórico en las novelas de Galdós." *Anales galdosianos* 3 (1968): 79–86.

*Almanaque Universal: 1964.* Madrid: Editorial Dossat, 1964.

Alonso, Carlos J. "La tía Julia y el escribidor: The Writing Subject's Fantasy of Empowerment." *PMLA* 106 (1991): 46–59.

Alsina, Jean, Claude Chauchadis, and Michèle Ramond. "Approches d'une autobiographie féminine: *El cuarto de atrás* de Carmen Martín Gaite." *L'Autobiographie en Espagne.* Actes du IIᵉ colloque internationale de la

Baume-les-Aix, 23–25 May 1981. Aix–en-Provence: Université de Provence, 1982.

Alter, Robert. *Partial Magic: The Novel as a Self-Conscious Genre*. Berkeley: University of California Press, 1975.

Andreu, Alicia G. "Arte y consumo: Angela Grassi y 'El Correo de la Moda.' " *Nuevo hispanismo* 1 (1982): 123–36.

——. "El folletín: De Galdós a Manuel Puig." *Revista Iberoamericana* 49 (1983): 541–46.

——. "El folletín como intertexto en *Tormento*." *Anales galdosianos* 17 (1982): 55–61.

——. *Galdós y la literatura popular*. Madrid: Sociedad General Española de Librería, 1982.

*Anuario Estadístico de España: Edición manual*. Madrid: Instituto Nacional de Estadística. Vols. 1945–46; 1956; 1965; 1969.

Armstrong, Nancy. *Desire and Domesticity*. New York: Oxford University Press, 1987.

Armstrong, Nancy, and Leonard Tennenhouse, eds. *The Ideology of Conduct*. New York: Methuen, 1987.

Artola, Miguel. *La burguesía revolucionaria (1808–1874)*. Madrid: Alianza Editorial, 1975.

Austin, Karen. "Madness and Madmen in Galdós' Early Fiction and in *La desheredada*." *Galdós's House of Fiction*. Ed. A. H. Clarke and E. J. Rodgers. Llangrannag, Wales: Dolphin, 1991. 29–40.

Ayto, John. *The Bloomsbury Dictionary of Word Origins*. London: Bloomsbury, 1990.

Bahamonde Magro, Angel. "Crisis de la nobleza de cuna y consolidación burguesa (1840–1880)." *Madrid en la sociedad del siglo XIX*. Ed. Luis E. Otero Carvajal and Angel Bahamonde. 2 vols. Madrid: Consejería de Cultura de la Comunidad de Madrid and Revista Alfoz, 1986. 1:325–75.

Bakhtin, M. M. *Problems of Dostoevsky's Poetics*. Trans. and ed. Caryl Emerson. Theory and History of Literature, vol. 8. Minneapolis: University of Minnesota Press, 1984.

——. *The Dialogic Imagination*. Trans. Caryl Emerson and Michael Holquist. Ed. Michael Holquist. Austin: University of Texas Press, 1981.

Barnes, Julian. "Unlikely Friendship." Review of *Flaubert-Sand: The Correspondence*, trans. Francis Steegmuller and Barbara Bray. *New York Review of Books* 10 June 1993: 5–6, 8, 10, 12.

Barrows, Susanna. *Distorting Mirrors: Visions of the Crowd in Late Nineteenth-Century France*. New Haven: Yale University Press, 1981.

Barthes, Roland. *Sade/Fourier/Loyola*. Trans. Richard Miller. New York: Hill and Wang, 1976.

Begley, Louis. "Who the Novelist Really Is." *New York Times Book Review,* 16 Aug. 1992: 1, 22–23.

Bellver, Catherine G. "War as Rite of Passage in *El cuarto de atrás.*" *Letras femeninas* 12 (1986): 69–77.

Benjamin, Walter. *Charles Baudelaire: A Lyric Poet in the Era Of High Capitalism.* Trans. Harry Zohn. New York: Verso, 1983.

———. *Illuminations.* Trans. Harry Zohn. Ed. Hannah Arendt. New York: Schocken, 1969.

Bennett, Tony. "Marxism and Popular Fiction." *Popular Fictions.* Ed. Peter Humm, Paul Stigant, and Peter Widdowson. London: Methuen, 1986. 237–65.

———, ed. *Popular Fiction: Technology, Ideology, Production, Reading.* London: Routledge, 1990.

Berkowitz, H. Chonon. *Pérez Galdós: Spanish Liberal Crusader.* Madison: University of Wisconsin Press, 1948.

Bianchi, Soledad. "Manuel Puig: la tentación de espiar." *Revista chilena de literatura* 38 (1991): 109–13.

Bly, Peter A. *Galdós's Novel of the Historical Imagination.* Liverpool: Francis Cairns, 1983.

———. *Vision and the Visual Arts in Galdós: A Study of the Novels and Newspaper Articles.* Liverpool: Francis Cairns, 1986.

Boheemen, Christine van. *The Novel as Family Romance.* Ithaca: Cornell University Press, 1987.

Bonet, Laureano, ed. *Benito Pérez Galdós: Ensayos de crítica literaria.* 2d ed. Barcelona: Peninsula, 1990.

Borges, Jorge Luis. *Otras inquisiciones.* Buenos Aires: Alianza-Emecé, 1976.

Botrel, Jean-François. "La novela por entregas: unidad de creación y consumo." *Creación y público en la literatura española.* Ed. Jean-François Botrel and S. Salaün. Madrid: Editorial Castalia, 1974. 111–55.

———. "L'Aptitude à communiquer: Alphabétisation et scholarisation en Espagne de 1860 à 1920." *De l'Alphabétisation aux circuits du livre en Espagne, XVII–XIX siècles.* Paris: Centre National de la Recherche Scientifique, 1987. 105–40.

Botrel, Jean-François, and S. Salaün, eds. *Creación y público en la literatura española.* Madrid: Editorial Castalia, 1974.

Bourdieu, Pierre. *Distinction: A Social Critique of the Judgement of Taste.* Trans. Richard Nice. Cambridge, Mass.: Harvard University Press, 1984.

Bowlby, Rachel. *Just Looking: Consumer Culture in Dreiser, Gissing and Zola.* New York: Methuen, 1985.

Brantlinger, Patrick. *Bread and Circuses: Theories of Mass Culture as Social Decay.* Ithaca: Cornell University Press, 1983.

Braun, Lucille V. "The 'Intertextualization' of Unamuno and Juan Goyti-solo's *Reivindicación del conde don Julián.*" *Hispanófila* 30.2 (1987): 39–56.

Brown, Joan Lipman. "A Fantastic Memoir: Technique and History in *El cuarto de atrás.*" *Anales de la literatura española contemporánea* 6 (1981): 13–20.

———, ed. *Women Writers of Contemporary Spain: Exiles in the Homeland.* Newark, Del.: University of Delaware Press; London: Association of University Presses, 1991.

Calinescu, Matei. *Five Faces of Modernity.* Durham, N.C.: Duke University Press, 1987.

Cano Ballesta, Juan. *Literatura y tecnología: (Las letras españolas ante la revolución industrial: 1900–1933).* Colección Tratados de Crítica Literaria. Madrid: Editorial Orígenes, 1981.

Carr, Raymond. *Spain: 1808–1975.* 2d ed. Oxford: Clarendon, 1982.

Casalduero, Joaquín. *Vida y obra de Galdós.* 3a. edición ampliada. Madrid: Gredós, 1970.

Castillo, Debra. "*La desheredada:* The Institution and the Machine." *Modern Language Studies* 18. 2 (1988): 60–72.

———. "Never-Ending Story: Carmen Martín Gaite's *The Back Room.*" *PMLA* 102 (1984): 814–28.

Castro, Américo. "An Introduction to the *Quijote.*" *An Idea of History: Selected Essays of Américo Castro.* Trans. and ed. Stephen Gilman and Edmund King. Columbus: Ohio State University Press, 1977. 77–139.

Cawelti, John C. "Notes toward an Aesthetic of Popular Culture." *Journal of Popular Culture* 5 (1971): 255–68.

———. "The Concept of Formula in the Study of Popular Literature." *Journal of Popular Culture* 3 (1969): 371–90.

Cervantes, Miguel de. *Don Quijote de la Mancha.* Ed. L. A. Murillo. 2 vols. Madrid: Editorial Castalia, 1982.

Chamberlin, Vernon. *Galdós and Beethoven.* London: Tamesis, 1977.

Chambers, Ross. *Story and Situation: Narrative Seduction and the Power of Fiction.* Theory and History of Literature, vol. 12. Minneapolis: University of Minnesota Press, 1984.

Charnon-Deutsch, Lou. "On Desire and Domesticity in Spanish Nineteenth-Century Women's Novels." *Revista canadiense de estudios hispánicos* 14 (1990): 395–414.

———. *Gender and Representation.* Amsterdam: John Benjamins, 1990.

———. "Inhabited Space in Galdós' *Tormento.*" *Anales galdosianos* 10 (1975): 35–43.

Clark, T. J. *The Painting of Modern Life.* Princeton: Princeton University Press, 1984.

Cluff, David. "The Structure and Meaning of Galdós' *Tormento.*" *Reflexión* 3–4 (1974–75): 159–67.

Compagnon, Antoine. *La seconde main ou le travail de la citation.* Paris: Editions du Seuil, 1979.

Corbin, Alain. "Commercial Sexuality in Nineteenth-Century France: A System of Images and Regulations." *The Making of the Modern Body.* Ed. Catherine Gallagher and Thomas Laqueur. Berkeley: University of California Press, 1987. 209–19.

——. *Women for Hire.* Trans. Alan Sheridan. Cambridge, Mass.: Harvard University Press, 1990.

Correa, Gustavo. *Realidad, ficción y símbolo en las novelas de Pérez Galdós.* Madrid: Gredós, 1977.

Cuevas, Matilde. "Aproximación a la consideración social de la prostitución madrileña." *Madrid en la sociedad del siglo XIX.* Ed. Luis E. Otero Carvajal and Angel Bahamonde. 2 vols. Madrid: Consejería de Cultura de la Comunidad de Madrid and Revista Alfoz, 1986. 2:165–73.

Dällenbach, Lucien. *The Mirror in the Text.* Trans. Jeremy Whiteley with Emma Hughes. Chicago: University of Chicago Press, 1989.

Darío, Rubén. *Poesía.* Introducción y selección de Pere Gimferrer. Barcelona: Planeta, 1987.

Debord, Guy. *The Society of the Spectacle.* Trans. of *La societé du spectacle.* 1967. 3d ed. Detroit: Black and Red, 1983.

Dendle, Brian J. "Isidora, the *Mantillas Blancas,* and the Attempted Assassination of Alfonso XII." *Anales galdosianos* 17 (1982): 51–54.

Díaz, José Simón. "Bibliografía madrileña del siglo XIX." *Madrid en la sociedad del siglo XIX.* Ed. Luis E. Otero Carvajal and Angel Bahamonde. 2 vols. Madrid: Consejería de Cultura de la Comunidad de Madrid and Revista Alfoz, 1986. 2:343–73.

*Diccionario de Autoridades.* 1726. Madrid: Real Academia Española. Edición facsimilar. Madrid: Gredos, 1964.

*Diccionario de la lengua castellana.* 2d ed. Madrid: Real Academia Española, 1783.

*Diccionario de la lengua castellana.* 10th ed. Madrid: Real Academia Española, 1852.

*Diccionario de la lengua castellana, con correspondencia catalana.* Dirigido por Delfín Donadíu y Puignau. Barcelona: Espasa y Compañía, 1890–95.

*Diccionario de la lengua española.* 21st ed. Madrid: Real Academia Española, 1992.

*Diccionario enciclopédico de la lengua castellana.* Madrid: Imprenta y Librería de Gaspar, 1872.

*Diccionario filológico comparado de la lengua castellana.* By M. Calandrell. Buenos Aires: Imprenta de Biedma, 1882.

*Diccionario general de la lengua castellana.* Dirección de D. José Caballero. Sexta edición, corregida y aumentada. Madrid: Librería de D. Leocadio López, 1882.

*Diccionario general etimológico de la lengua española.* Dirección Roque Barcia. Madrid: J. M. Faquineto, 1887–89.

Díez de Baldeón, Clementina. "Barrios obreros en el Madrid del siglo XIX: ¿Solución o amenaza para el orden burgués?" *Madrid en la sociedad del siglo XIX.* Ed. Luis E. Otero Carvajal and Angel Bahamonde. 2 vols. Madrid: Consejería de Cultura de la Comunidad de Madrid and Revista Alfoz, 1986. 1:117–34.

DiMaggio, Paul. "Cultural Entrepreneurship in Nineteenth-Century Boston: The Creation of an Organizational Base for High Culture in America." *Rethinking Popular Culture.* Ed. Chandra Mukerji and Michael Schudson. Berkeley and Los Angeles: University of California Press, 1991. 374–97.

Donato, Eugenio. "The Museum's Furnace: Notes Towards a Contextual Reading of *Bouvard et Pécuchet.*" *Textual Strategies: Perspectives in Post-Structuralist Criticism.* Ed. Josué V. Harari. Ithaca: Cornell University Press, 1979. 213–38.

Dorfman, Ariel. *The Empire's Old Clothes.* New York: Pantheon, 1983.

Dorfman, Ariel, and Armand Mattelart. *Para leer al Pato Donald: Comunicación de masa y colonialismo.* 26th ed. Mexico City: Siglo XXI, 1985.

Durán, Manuel. "*El cuarto de atrás:* Imaginación, fantasía, misterio: Todorov y algo más." *From Fiction to Metafiction: Essays in Honor of Carmen Martín Gaite.* Lincoln, Neb.: Society of Spanish and Spanish-American Studies, 1983. 129–37.

Durand, Frank. "The Reality of Illusion: *La desheredada.*" *Modern Language Notes* 89 (1974): 191–201.

———. "Two Problems in Galdós' *Tormento.*" *Modern Language Notes* 79 (1964): 513–25.

Eco, Umberto. *Apocalípticos e integrados.* Barcelona: Editorial Lumen, 1965.

———. *The Role of the Reader: Explorations in the Semiotics of Texts.* Bloomington: Indiana University Press, 1979.

El Saffar, Ruth. "Liberation and the Labyrinth: A Study of the Works of Carmen Martín Gaite." *From Fiction to Metafiction: Essays in Honor of Carmen Martín Gaite.* Lincoln, Neb.: Society of Spanish and Spanish-American Studies, 1983. 185–96.

———. "Redeeming Loss: Reflections on Carmen Martín Gaite's *The Back Room.*" *Revista de estudios hispánicos* 20 (1986): 1–14.

Epps, Brad. "The Politics of Ventriloquism: Cava, Revolution and Sexual Discourse in *Conde Julián.*" *Modern Language Notes* 107 (1992): 274–97.

———. "The Space of Sexual History: Reading Positions in *El cuarto de atrás* and *Reivindicación del conde don Julián.*" *Critical Essays on the Literatures of Spain and Spanish America.* Ed. Luis T. González-del-Valle and Julio Baena. Supplement to *ALEC.* Boulder, Colo.: Society of Spanish and Spanish-American Studies, 1991. 75–87.

Espina, Antonio. *El cuarto poder.* Madrid: Aguilar, 1960.

———. *Luna de copas.* Madrid: Revista de Occidente, 1929.

Fedorchek, Robert M. "Social Reprehension in *La desheredada.*" *Revista de estudios hispánicos* 8 (1974): 43–59.

Fernández, Celia. "Entrevista con Carmen Martín Gaite." *Anales de la narrativa española contemporánea* 4 (1979): 165–72.

Fernández Cifuentes, Luis. "Signs for Sale in the City of Galdós." *Modern Language Notes* 103 (1988): 289–311.

Ferreras, Juan Ignacio. *La novela por entregas, 1840–1900: Concentración obrera y economía editorial.* Madrid: Taurus, 1972.

Fontanella, Lee. *La imprenta y las letras en la España romántica.* Utah Studies in Literature and Linguistics. Frankfurt: Peter Lang, 1982. 137–63.

Forcione, Alban K. *Cervantes, Aristotle and the Persiles.* Princeton: Princeton University Press, 1970.

Forgacs, David, ed. *An Antonio Gramsci Reader.* New York: Schocken, 1988.

Foucault, Michel. *Discipline and Punish.* Trans. Alan Sheridan. New York: Vintage-Random House, 1977.

———. *Madness and Civilization.* Trans. Richard Howard. New York: Vintage-Random House, 1965.

Franco, Jean. "What's in a Name?: Popular Culture Theories and Their Limitations." *Studies in Latin American Popular Culture* 1 (1982): 5–14.

Frank, Anne. *The Diary of a Young Girl.* Trans. B. M. Mooyaart. New York: Doubleday, 1967.

Freud, Sigmund. "Family Romances." *The Standard Edition of the Complete Psychological Works of Sigmund Freud.* Trans. James Strachey. 24 vols. London: Hogarth and the Institute for Psycho-Analysis, 1959. Vol. 9 (1906–8), 237–41.

Frye, Northrop. *The Secular Scripture.* Cambridge, Mass.: Harvard University Press, 1976.

Fuentes, Víctor. *Galdós demócrata y republicano.* Santa Cruz de Tenerife: Universidad de la Laguna, 1982.

Furustad, Mauritz, ed. *España y sus provincias: Datos estadísticos.* Stockholm: Almqvist and Wiksell, 1965.

Fusi, Juan Pablo. *Franco: Autoritarismo y poder personal.* Madrid: Ediciones El País, 1985.

Galerstein, Carolyn, ed. *Women Writers of Spain: An Annotated Bio-Bibliographical Guide.* New York: Greenwood, 1986.

Gil Novales, Alberto, ed. *La revolución burguesa en España.* Madrid: Universidad Complutense, 1985.

Gilman, Stephen. *Galdós and the Art of the European Novel: 1867–1887.* Princeton: Princeton University Press, 1981.

Glenn, Kathleen M. "Communication in the Works of Carmen Martín Gaite." *Romance Notes* 19 (1979): 277–83.

——. "*El cuarto de atrás:* Literature as Juego and the Self-Reflexive Text." *From Fiction to Metafiction: Essays in Honor of Carmen Martín Gaite.* Lincoln, Neb.: Society of Spanish and Spanish-American Studies, 1983. 149–60.

——. "From Social Realism to Self-Reflection: Carmen Martín Gaite and the Postwar Novel." *Letras femeninas* 10 (1984): 18–26.

——. "Martín Gaite, Todorov, and the Fantastic." *The Scope of the Fantastic: Theory, Technique, Major Authors.* Ed. Robert A. Collins and Howard D. Pearce. Westport, Conn.: Greenwood, 1985.

Godzich, Wlad, and Nicholas Spadaccini, eds. *Literature Among Discourses: The Spanish Golden Age.* Minneapolis: University of Minnesota Press, 1986.

Gold, Hazel. "A Tomb with a View: The Museum in Galdós' *Novelas contemporáneas.*" *Modern Language Notes* 103 (1988): 312–34.

——. "Show and Tell: From Museum to Novel in Clarín's *La Regenta.*" *España contemporánea* 3 (1990): 47–70.

——. "*Tormento:* Vivir un dramón, dramatizar una novela." *Anales galdosianos* 20.1 (1985): 35–46.

Goldberg, Harriet. "Sexual Humor in Misogynist Medieval Exempla." *Women in Hispanic Literature.* Ed. Beth Miller. Berkeley and Los Angeles: University of California Press, 1983. 67–83.

Goldman, Peter B. "Toward a Sociology of the Modern Spanish Novel: The Early Years." *Modern Language Notes* 89 (1974): 173–211.

Gordon, M. " 'Lo que le falta a un enfermo le sobra a otro': Conception of Humanity in *La desheredada.*" *Anales galdosianos* 12 (1977): 29–37.

——. "The Medical Background to Galdós' *La desheredada.*" *Anales galdosianos* 7 (1972): 67–77.

Goytisolo, Juan. *Coto vedado.* Barcelona: Editorial Seix Barral, 1985.

——. *Count Julian.* Trans. Helen Lane. New York: Viking, 1974.

——. *Disidencias.* Barcelona: Editorial Seix Barral, 1977.

——. *España y los españoles.* Barcelona: Editorial Lumen, 1979.

——. *Libertad, libertad, libertad.* Barcelona: Editorial Anagrama, 1978.

——. *Reivindicación del conde don Julián.* Barcelona: Editorial Seix Barral, 1976.

——. *Reivindicación del conde don Julián.* Ed. Linda Gould Levine. Madrid: Ediciones Cátedra, 1985.

Gramsci, Antonio. *Selections from Cultural Writings.* Trans. William Boelhower. Ed. David Forgacs and Geoffrey Nowell-Smith. Cambridge, Mass.: Harvard University Press, 1985.

———. *Selections from the Prison Notebooks.* Trans. and ed. Quintin Hoare and Geoffrey Nowell-Smith. New York: International, 1971.

Gullón, Germán. *El narrador en la novela del siglo XIX.* Madrid: Taurus, 1976.

———. *La novela como acto imaginativo.* Madrid: Taurus, 1983.

———. "Originalidad y sentido de *La desheredada.*" *Anales galdosianos* 17 (1982): 39–50.

Gullón, Ricardo. "Desdoblamiento interior en *La desheredada.*" *Insula* 26. 300–301: 9–10.

———. *Galdós, novelista moderno.* New edition. Madrid: Gredós, 1966.

———. *Técnicas de Galdós.* Madrid: Taurus, 1970.

Gutiérrez Sánchez, María de las Mercedes. "Anarquistas en el Madrid de la Restauración." *Madrid en la sociedad del siglo XIX.* Ed. Luis E. Otero Carvajal and Angel Bahamonde. 2 vols. Madrid: Consejería de Cultura de la Comunidad de Madrid and Revista Alfoz, 1986. 2:97–116.

Habermas, Jürgen. *The Structural Transformation of the Public Sphere.* Trans. Thomas Burger. Cambridge, Mass.: MIT Press, 1989.

Hamburger, Käte. *The Logic of Literature.* 2d. rev. ed. Trans. Marilynn J. Rose. Bloomington: Indiana University Press, 1973.

Harari, Josué V., ed. *Textual Strategies: Perspectives in Post-Structuralist Criticism.* Ithaca: Cornell University Press, 1979.

Harding, D. W. "The Notion of 'Escape' in Fiction and Entertainment." *Oxford Review* 4 (1967): 23–32.

Hauser, Arnold. *The Social History of Art.* Trans. Stanley Godman. 4 vols. New York: Vintage, 1957.

Hebdige, Dick. *Subculture: The Meaning of Style.* London: Methuen, 1979.

Hennessy, C. A. M. *The Federal Republic in Spain: Pi y Margall and the Federal Republican Movement 1868–74.* Oxford: Clarendon, 1962.

Hernández Sandoica, Elena. "La Universidad de Madrid en el siglo XIX. Una aproximación histórica." *Madrid en la sociedad del siglo XIX.* Ed. Luis E. Otero Carvajal and Angel Bahamonde. 2 vols. Madrid: Consejería de Cultura de la Comunidad de Madrid and Revista Alfoz, 1986. 2:375–93.

Herrnstein Smith, Barbara. "Contingencies of Value." *Critical Inquiry* 10 (1983): 1–35.

Horkheimer, Max, and Theodor W. Adorno. *Dialectic of Enlightenment.* Trans. John Cumming. New York: Continuum, 1988.

Hughes, Robert. *The Shock of the New.* London: British Broadcasting Corporation, 1980.

Humm, Peter, Paul Stigant, and Peter Widdowson, eds. *Popular Fictions: Essays in Literature and History.* New York: Methuen, 1986.

Huyssen, Andreas. *After the Great Divide.* Bloomington: Indiana University Press, 1986.

Jaffe, Catherine. "El motivo del espejo en *La desheredada.*" *Selected Proceedings of the Mid-America Conference on Hispanic Literature.* Lincoln, Neb.: Society of Spanish and Spanish-American Studies, 1986. 33–39.

———. "Mothers and Orphans in *La desheredada.*" *Confluencia* 5 (1990): 27–38.

Jagoe, Catherine. "Disinheriting the Feminine: Galdós and the Rise of the Realist Novel in Spain." *Revista de estudios hispánicos* 27 (1993): 225–48.

———. *Gender in the Novels of Galdós, 1870–1915.* Berkeley and Los Angeles: University of California Press, forthcoming.

Jameson, Fredric. "Magical Narratives: Romance as Genre." *New Literary History* 7. 1 (1975): 135–63.

———. "Reification and Utopia in Mass Culture." *Social Text* 1 (1979): 130–48.

———. *The Political Unconscious: Narrative as a Socially Symbolic Act.* Ithaca: Cornell University Press, 1981.

Jardine, Alice. *Gynesis.* Ithaca: Cornell University Press, 1985.

Jenny, Laurent. "La stratégie de la forme." *Poétique* 27 (1976): 257–81.

Kerr, Lucille. *Suspended Fictions: Reading Novels by Manuel Puig.* Urbana: University of Illinois Press, 1987.

Kipnis, Laura. "'Refunctioning' Reconsidered: Towards a Left Popular Culture." *High Theory/Low Culture.* Ed. Colin MacCabe. Manchester: Manchester University Press, 1986. 11–36.

Kirkpatrick, Susan. *Las Románticas: Women Writers and Subjectivity in Spain, 1835–1850.* Berkeley and Los Angeles: University of California Press, 1989.

Kraus, Henry. "Eve and Mary: Conflicting Images of Medieval Woman." *Feminism and Art History.* Ed. Norma Broude and Mary D. Garrard. New York: Harper and Row, 1982. 79–99.

Kronik, John W. "Narraciones interiores en *Fortunata y Jacinta.*" *Homenaje a Juan López-Morillas.* Ed. José Amor y Vázquez and A. David Kossoff. Madrid: Castalia, 1982. 275–91.

Krow-Lucal, Martha G. "The Marquesa de Aransis: A Galdosian Reprise." *Essays in Honor of Jorge Guillén on the Occasion of his Eighty-fifth Year.* Cambridge, Mass.: Abedul, 1977. 20–31.

Labanyi, J. M. *Myth and History in the Contemporary Spanish Novel.* Cambridge: Cambridge University Press, 1989.

———. "The Political Significance of *La desheredada.*" *Anales galdosianos* 14 (1979): 51–58.

Laqueur, Thomas. *Making Sex: Body and Gender From the Greeks to Freud.* Cambridge, Mass.: Harvard University Press, 1990.

Lázaro, Jesús. *La novelística de Juan Goytisolo.* Madrid: Editorial Alhambra, 1984.

LeBon, Gustave. *The Crowd.* London: Ernest Benn, 1952.

Ledford-Miller, Linda. "History as Myth, Myth as History: Juan Goytisolo's *Count Julian.*" *Revista canadiense de estudios hispánicos* 8 (1983): 21–30.

Levine, Lawrence. *Highbrow/Lowbrow: The Emergence of Cultural Hierarchy in America.* Cambridge, Mass.: Harvard University Press, 1988.

Levine, Linda Gould. "Carmen Martín Gaite's *El cuarto de atrás:* A Portrait of the Artist as Woman." *From Fiction to Metafiction: Essays in Honor of Carmen Martín Gaite.* Lincoln, Neb.: Society of Spanish and Spanish-American Studies, 1983. 161–72.

———. *Juan Goytisolo: La destrucción creadora.* Mexico City: J. Mortiz, 1976.

Lewis, Thomas E. "*Fortunata y Jacinta:* Galdós and the Production of the Literary Referent." *Modern Language Notes* 96 (1981): 316–39.

Lindstrom, Naomi. "The Problem of Pop Culture in the Novels of Manuel Puig." *The American Hispanist* 4 (1978): 28–31.

Lipsitz, George. *Time Passages: Collective Memory and American Popular Culture.* Minneapolis: University of Minnesota Press, 1990.

Litvak, Lily. *A Dream of Arcadia.* Austin: University of Texas Press, 1975.

Lloret Carbó, Caterina. *La lucha de los trabajadores y la transformación de la escuela (1872–1936).* Barcelona: Miguel Barroso, 1977.

Lotman, Jurij. *The Structure of the Artistic Text.* Trans. Gail Lenhoff and Ronald Vroon. Ann Arbor: Michigan Slavic Contributions, 1977.

Lovell, Terry. *Consuming Fiction.* London: Verso, 1987.

Ludmer, Josefina. "Tretas del débil." *La sartén por el mango.* Ed. Patricia Elena González and Eliana Ortega. Río Piedras, Puerto Rico: Ediciones Huracán, 1984. 47–54.

MacCabe, Colin, ed. *High Theory/Low Culture.* Manchester: Manchester University Press, 1986.

Marco, Joaquín. *Literatura popular en España en los siglos XVIII y XIX.* 2 vols. Madrid: Taurus, 1977.

Marcus, Greil. *Lipstick Traces: A Secret History of the Twentieth Century.* Cambridge, Mass.: Harvard University Press, 1989.

Marcuse, Herbert. *Negations: Essays in Critical Thinking.* Trans. Jeremy Shapiro. Boston: Beacon, 1968.

Martín Gaite, Carmen. *The Back Room.* Trans. Helen Lane. New York: Columbia University Press, 1983.

———. La búsqueda de interlocutor y otras búsquedas. Barcelona: Destino, 1982.

———. El cuarto de atrás. Barcelona: Destino, 1978.

———. Usos amorosos de la postguerra española. Barcelona: Editorial Anagrama, 1987.

Martinell Gifre, Emma. "El cuarto de atrás: Un mundo de objetos." Revista de literatura 45 (1983): 143–53.

Matamoro, Blas. "Carmen Martín Gaite: El viaje al cuarto de atrás." Cuadernos hispánicos: Revista mensual de cultura hispánica 117 (1979): 581–605.

Michie, Helena. The Flesh Made Word: Female Figures and Women's Bodies. New York: Oxford University Press, 1987.

Minc, Rose S., ed. Literature and Popular Culture in the Hispanic World. Gaithersburg, Md: Hispamérica and Montclair State College, 1981.

Monsiváis, Carlos. "De las relaciones literarias entre 'alta cultura' y 'cultura popular.'" Texto crítico 11 (1985): 46–61.

Montesinos, José F. Galdós. 3 vols. Madrid: Editorial Castalia, 1969.

Moscovici, Serge. The Age of the Crowd: A Historical Treatise on Mass Psychology. Trans. J. C. Whitehouse. Cambridge: Cambridge University Press; Paris: Editions de la Maison des Sciences de l'Homme, 1985.

Mukerji, Chandra, and Michael Schudson, eds. Rethinking Popular Culture. Berkeley and Los Angeles: University of California Press, 1991.

Naremore, James, and Patrick Brantlinger, eds. Modernity and Mass Culture. Bloomington: University of Indiana Press, 1991.

Ordóñez, Elizabeth J. "Reading, Telling and the Text of Carmen Martín Gaite's El cuarto de atrás." From Fiction to Metafiction: Essays in Honor of Carmen Martín Gaite. Lincoln, Neb.: Society of Spanish and Spanish-American Studies, 1983. 173–84.

Ortega, José. "Aproximación estructural a Reivindicación del conde don Julián." Explicación de textos literarios 3 (1974): 45–50.

Ortega y Gasset, José. La rebelión de las masas. Madrid: Revista de Occidente en Alianza Editorial, 1980.

———. Meditaciones del Quijote: Ideas sobre la novela. Madrid: Espasa-Calpe, 1964.

Ouimette, Victor. "'Monstrous Fecundity': The Popular Novel in Nineteenth-Century Spain." Canadian Review of Comparative Literature 9 (1982): 383–405.

Paolini, Gilbert. "Polivalente rebeldía en La desheredada de Benito Pérez Galdós." Lingua e letteratura 5 (1985): 115–22.

Paterson, Janet M. "L'Autoreprésentation: Formes et Discours." Texte 1 (1982): 177–94.

Payne, Stanley G. *The Franco Regime: 1936–1975.* Madison: University of Wisconsin Press, 1987.

Percival, Anthony. "Melodramatic Metafiction in *Tormento.*" *Kentucky Romance Quarterly* 31 (1984): 153–60.

Pérez, Genaro J. "Some Leitmotifs and Bridges in the Sonata Form Structure of Juan Goytisolo's *Reivindicación del conde don Julián.*" *Hispanófila* 22.3 (1979): 41–52.

Pérez, Janet. *Contemporary Women Writers of Spain.* Boston: Twayne, 1988.

———, ed. *Novelistas femeninas de la postguerra española.* Madrid: Ediciones José Porrúa Turanzas, 1983.

Pérez, José-Carlos. *La trayectoria novelística de Juan Goytisolo: El autor y sus obsesiones.* Boston: Twayne, 1984.

Pérez-Firmat, Gustavo. "Apuntes para un modelo de la intertextualidad en la literatura." *Romanic Review* 69 (1978): 1–14.

———. *Idle Fictions: The Hispanic Vanguard Novel, 1926–1934.* Durham, N.C.: Duke University Press, 1982.

———. *Literature and Liminality.* Durham, N.C.: Duke University Press, 1986.

———. "Metafiction Again." *Taller Literario* 1 (1980): 30–38.

———. "Propiedad y palabra en un trébol de Jorge Guillén." *Modern Language Notes* 101 (1986): 392–94.

Pérez Galdós, Benito. *Novelas.* 3 vols. Madrid: Aguilar, 1970 (vols. 1–2) and 1973 (vol. 3).

Petit, Mme. J-P. "La folie et la mort dans *La desheredada.*" *Cahiers du monde hispanique et Luso-Brésilien* (Caravelle) 11 (1968): 193–204.

Piedrahita Rook, Carmen. "La 'toma' de la palabra por Juan Goytisolo en *Reivindicación del conde don Julián.*" *Hispanófila* 28. 3 (1985): 43–50.

Plà, Carlos, et al. *El Madrid de Galdós.* Madrid: Editorial El Avapiés, 1987.

Plaza, Julio. *Tradução Intersemiótica.* São Paulo: Perspectiva, 1987.

Porrúa, María del Carmen. "La función de la ambigüedad en la protagonista de *La desheredada* de Galdós." *Filología* 20 (1985): 139–51.

Postman, Neil, and Camille Paglia. "She Wants Her TV! He Wants His Book!" *Harper's* Mar. 1991: 44–55.

Radway, Janice. *Reading the Romance.* Chapel Hill: University of North Carolina Press, 1984.

Ramos, Julio. *Desencuentros de la modernidad en América Latina.* Mexico City: Fondo de Cultura Económica, 1989.

Reisz de Rivarola, Susana. "Ficcionalidad, referencia, tipos de ficción literaria." *Lexis* 3 (1979): 99–170.

Ribbans, Geoffrey. "*La desheredada,* novela por entregas: Apostillas sobre su primera publicación." Unpublished essay.

Rice, Mary. "La novela femenina del siglo XX: Bombal, Laforet y Martín Gaite." *Mester* 15.2 (1986): 7–12.

Rignall, John. *Realist Fiction and the Strolling Spectator.* New York: Routledge, 1992.

Risley, William. "Galdós, 'Poet of Space': On the Interrelationship of Character and Milieu, and Physical Symbols of Mental Process, in the Early *Novelas Españolas Contemporáneas.*" *Selected Proceedings of the Mid-American Conference on Hispanic Literature.* Lincoln, Neb.: Society of Spanish and Spanish-American Studies, 1986. 113–27.

——. " 'Narrative Overture' in Galdós' Early *Novelas españolas contemporáneas.*" *Kentucky Romance Quarterly* 31.2 (1984): 135–46.

Robert, Marthe. *The Old and the New: From "Don Quixote" to Kafka.* Trans. Carol Cosman. Berkeley: University of California Press, 1977.

——. *Origins of the Novel.* Trans. Sacha Rabinotiz. Bloomington: Indiana University Press, 1980.

Robin, Claire-Nicolle. *Le naturalisme dans "La desheredada" de Pérez Galdós.* Paris: Annales Littéraires de l'Université de Besançon, no. 185, 1976.

Rodgers, Eamonn. *From Enlightenment to Realism: The Novels of Galdós 1870–1887.* Dublin: Jack Hade, 1987.

——. "Galdós' *La desheredada* and Naturalism." *Bulletin of Hispanic Studies* 45 (1968): 285–98.

Rodríguez, Alfred. *Aspectos de la novela de Galdós.* Almería: Estudios literarios Almería, 1967.

Rodríguez, Alfred, and Linda Hidalgo. "Las posibles resonancias de un título galdosiano: *La desheredada.*" *Anales galdosianos* 20.2 (1985): 19–23.

Roger, Isabel M. "Recreación crítica de la novela rosa en *El cuarto de atrás.*" *Romance Notes* 27 (1986): 121–26.

Rogers, Douglass. "Amparo, o la metamorfosis de la heroína galdosiana." *Selected Proceedings of the Mid-America Conference on Hispanic Literature.* Ed. Luis T. González-del-Valle and Catherine Nickel. Lincoln, Neb.: Society of Spanish and Spanish-American Studies, 1986. 137–46.

Romero Tobar, Leonardo. *La novela popular española del siglo XIX.* Madrid: Fundación Juan March, 1976.

Rose, Jonathan. "Rereading the English Common Reader: A Preface to a History of Audiences." *Journal of the History of Ideas* 52 (1992): 47–70.

Ruíz-Avilés, Miguel R. "*El cuarto de atrás:* Diferentes vistas según diferentes 'horizontes de experiencias' y 'horizontes de expectativas.'" *Selected Proceedings of the Mid-America Conference on Hispanic Literature.* Ed. Luis T. González-del-Valle and Catherine Nickel. Lincoln, Neb.: Society of Spanish and Spanish-American Studies, 1986. 147–58.

Ruiz Salvador, Antonio. "La función del trasfondo histórico en *La desheredada.*" *Anales galdosianos* 1 (1966): 53–62.

Russell, Robert. "The Structure of *La desheredada.*" *Modern Language Notes* 76 (1961): 794–800.

Salinas, Pedro. *La realidad y el poeta.* 1940. Trans. and ed. Soledad Salinas de Marichal. Barcelona: Editorial Seix Barral, 1976.

———. *Víspera del gozo.* Madrid: Revista de Occidente, 1926.

Scanlon, Geraldine. *La polémica feminista en la España contemporánea: 1868–1974.* Trans. Rafael Mazarrasa. 2d ed. Madrid: Ediciones Akal, 1986.

Schaefer-Rodríguez, Claudia. *Juan Goytisolo: Del "realismo crítico" a la utopía.* Madrid: Ediciones José Porrúa Turanzas, 1984.

Schnepf, Michael A. "Galdos's *La desheredada* Manuscript: Isidora in the Prado Museum." *Romance Quarterly* 37 (1990): 321–30.

———. "Mirror, Mirror, on the Wall: Narcissism in Galdós's *La desheredada.*" *Revista canadiense de estudios hispánicos* 13 (1989): 231–40.

Schor, Naomi. *Reading in Detail: Aesthetics and the Feminine.* New York: Routledge, 1987.

Seoane, María Cruz. *Historia del periodismo en España: II: El siglo XIX.* Madrid: Alianza, 1983.

Servodidio, Mirella d'Ambrosio, and Marcia L. Welles. *From Fiction to Metafiction: Essays in Honor of Carmen Martín Gaite.* Lincoln, Neb.: Society of Spanish and Spanish-American Studies, 1983.

Shiach, Morag. *Discourse on Popular Culture.* Stanford: Stanford University Press, 1989.

Sieburth, Stephanie. "Enlightenment, Mass Culture and Madness: The Dialectic of Modernity in *La desheredada.*" *A Sesquicentennial Tribute to Galdós.* Ed. Linda Willem. Newark, Del.: Juan de la Cuesta, 1993.

———. "Reading and Alienation in *Reivindicación del conde don Julián.*" *Anales de la literatura española contemporánea* 8 (1983): 83–93.

Simmel, Georg. *On Individuality and Social Forms.* Chicago: University of Chicago Press, 1971.

———. *Philosophy of Money.* 2d ed. London: Routledge, 1990.

Simón Palmer, María del Carmen. *Escritoras españolas del siglo XIX: Manual bio-bibliográfico.* Madrid: Editorial Castalia, 1991.

Sinnigen, John H. "Galdós' *Tormento:* Political Partisanship/Literary Structures." *Ideologies and Literature* 3 (1981): 19–32.

Six, Abigail Lee. *Juan Goytisolo: The Case for Chaos.* New Haven: Yale University Press, 1990.

Sobejano, Gonzalo. "Enlaces y desenlaces en las novelas de Carmen Martín Gaite." *From Fiction to Metafiction: Essays in Honor of Carmen Martín Gaite.* Lincoln, Neb.: Society of Spanish and Spanish-American Studies, 1983. 209–23.

Solotorevsky, Mirna. *Literatura/Paraliteratura.* Gaithersburg, Md.: Ediciones Hispamérica, 1988.

Sommer, Doris. *Foundational Fictions.* Berkeley and Los Angeles: University of California Press, 1991.

Spender, Dale. "Women and Literary History." *The Feminist Reader.* Ed. Catherine Belsey and Jane Moore. New York: Basil Blackwell, 1989. 21–33.

Spires, Robert C. *Beyond the Metafictional Mode: Directions in the Modern Spanish Novel.* Lexington, Ky.: University Press of Kentucky, 1984.

——. "Intertextuality in *El cuarto de atrás.*" *From Fiction to Metafiction: Essays in Honor of Carmen Martín Gaite.* Lincoln, Neb.: Society of Spanish and Spanish-American Studies, 1983. 139–48.

——. "The Metafictional Codes of *Don Julián* vs. the Metafictional Mode of *El cuarto de atrás.*" *Revista canadiense de estudios hispánicos* 7 (1983): 306–09.

——. *Transparent Simulacra: Spanish Fiction, 1902–1926.* Columbia, Mo.: University of Missouri Press, 1988.

Stallybrass, Peter, and Allon White. *The Politics and Poetics of Transgression.* Ithaca: Cornell University Press, 1986.

Suleiman, Susan Rubin. "Reading Robbe-Grillet: Sadism and Text in *Projet pour une révolution à New York.*" *Romanic Review* 68 (1977): 43–62.

——. *Subversive Intent: Gender, Politics, and the Avant-Garde.* Cambridge, Mass.: Harvard University Press, 1990.

Swartz, Jacqueline. "You Tarzan, Me Jane." *Saturday Night* Oct. 1991: 36–40, 95–100.

Timoteo Alvarez, Jesús. "Estructura subterránea de la prensa en la Restauración." *Madrid en la sociedad del siglo XIX.* Ed. Luis E. Otero Carvajal and Angel Bahamonde. 2 vols. Madrid: Consejería de Cultura de la Comunidad de Madrid and Revista Alfoz, 1986. 1:229–48.

Torres, David. "La fantasía y sus consecuencias en *La desheredada.*" *Boletín de la Biblioteca de Menéndez y Pelayo* 52 (1976): 301–07.

Turner, Harriet. *Benito Pérez Galdós, Fortunata and Jacinta.* Cambridge: Cambridge University Press, 1992.

Ugarte, Michael. "Juan Goytisolo's Mirrors: Intertextuality and Self-Reflection in *Reivindicación del conde don Julián* and 'Juan sin tierra.' " *Modern Fiction Studies* 26 (1980–81): 613–23.

——. *Trilogy of Treason: An Intertextual Study of Juan Goytisolo.* Columbia, Mo.: University of Missouri Press, 1982.

Unamuno, Miguel de. *En torno al casticismo.* Madrid: Espasa-Calpe, 1972.

——. *Vida de Don Quijote y Sancho.* Vol. 3 of *Obras completas.* 9 vols. Madrid: Escelicer, 1968.

Urey, Diane. *Galdós and the Irony of Language.* Cambridge: Cambridge University Press, 1982.

———. "Repetition, Discontinuity and Silence in Galdós' *Tormento.*" *Anales galdosianos* 20.1 (1985): 47–63.

Valis, Noël. "Adorning Women: The Feminine as *Cursi.*" Paper presented at Modern Language Association Convention. Washington, D.C., 29 Dec. 1989.

———. "Novel into Painting: Transition in Spanish Realism." *Anales galdosianos* 20.1 (1985): 9–22.

———. "On Monstrous Birth: Leopoldo Alas and the Inchoate." *Naturalism in the European Novel: Modern Essays in Criticism.* Ed. Brian Nelson. Oxford and New York: Berg, 1992. 191–209.

Valle-Inclán, Ramón del. *Luces de bohemia.* Madrid: Espasa-Calpe, 1974.

Valls, Josep Francesc. *Prensa y burguesía en el siglo XIX español.* Barcelona: Anthropos, 1988.

Vázquez Montalbán, Manuel. *Crónica sentimental de España.* Madrid: Espasa-Calpe, 1986.

Walkowitz, Judith R. *Prostitution and Victorian Society: Women, Class, and the State.* Cambridge: Cambridge University Press, 1980.

Welles, Marcia L. "Carmen Martín Gaite: Fiction as Desire." *From Fiction to Metafiction: Essays in Honor of Carmen Martín Gaite.* Lincoln, Neb.: Society of Spanish and Spanish-American Studies, 1983. 197–207.

White, Allon. "Pigs and Pierrots: The Politics of Transgression in Modern Fiction." *Raritan* 2.2 (Fall 1982): 51–70.

Williams, Raymond. *Culture and Society: 1780–1950.* New York: Columbia University Press, 1983.

———. "The Idea of Culture." 1953. *Literary Taste, Culture, and Mass Communication.* Ed. Peter Davison, Rolf Meyersohn, Edward Shils. 2 vols. Cambridge: Chadwyck-Healey; Teaneck, N.J.: Somerset House, 1978. 1:29–56.

———. *The Politics of Modernism.* London: Verso, 1989.

Williams, Rosalind H. *Dream Worlds: Mass Consumption in Late Nineteenth-Century France.* Berkeley: University of California Press, 1982.

Wright, Chad. " 'La eterna mascarada hispanomatritense': Clothing and Society in *Tormento.*" *Anales galdosianos* 20.2 (1985): 25–37.

———. "The Representational Qualities of Isidora Rufete's House and Her Son Riquín in Benito Pérez Galdós' Novel *La desheredada.*" *Romanische Forschungen* 83 (1971): 230–45.

# Index

## About the Author

Stephanie Sieburth is Associate Professor
of Spanish at Duke University. She is the
author of *Reading La Regenta:
Duplicitous Discourse and the Entropy of
Structure* (1990).

Library of Congress Cataloging-in-Publication Data

Sieburth, Stephanie Anne.
Inventing high and low : literature, mass culture, and uneven
modernity in Spain / Stephanie Sieburth.
p.   cm.
Includes bibliographical references (p.     ) and index.
ISBN 0-8223-1444-4 (alk. paper). — ISBN 0-8223-1441-X (pbk.)
1. Spanish fiction—19th century—History and criticism.
2. Spanish fiction—20th century—History and criticism.
3. Literature and society—Spain.   4. Popular culture—Spain.
I. Title.
PQ6144.S54   1994
863.009'355—dc20        93-38920        CIP